Race, Politics, and
Governance in the
United States

Race, Politics, and Governance in the United States

Edited by
Huey L. Perry

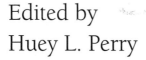

University Press of Florida
Gainesville/Tallahassee/Tampa/Boca Raton
Pensacola/Orlando/Miami/Jacksonville

Copyright 1996 by the Board of Regents of the State of Florida
Printed in the United States of America on acid-free paper ∞
All rights reserved

01 00 99 98 97 96 C 6 5 4 3 2 1
01 00 99 98 97 96 P 6 5 4 3 2 1

Library of Congress Cataloging-in-Publication Data
Race, governance, and politics in the United States / edited by Huey
   L. Perry
p.   cm.
Includes bibliographical references (p.) and index.
ISBN 0-8130-1456-5 (cloth: alk. paper). — ISBN 0-8130-1481-6
   (paper: alk. paper)
1. Afro-Americans—Politics and government.   2. Racism—Political
   aspects—United States.   I. Perry, Huey.
E185.615.R2123   1996
324′.089′96073—dc20   96-19925

The University Press of Florida is the scholarly publishing agency for the State
University System of Florida, comprised of Florida A & M University, Florida Atlantic University, Florida International University, Florida State University, Uni-
versity of Central Florida, University of Florida, University of North Florida, Uni-
versity of South Florida, and University of West Florida.

University Press of Florida
15 Northwest 15th Street
Gainesville, FL 32611

Contents

Tables

Figures

Foreword

I f there is still so much latent and manifest, covert and overt evidence of racism in American society, why is it seemingly still necessary to talk about the "politics of deracialization"? Is this politics yet another way to avoid confronting racial reality? Is it a denial of the obvious, that African Americans, as a minority, continue to face obstacles based *purely* on their identity? Does a "deracialization" strategy—that is, minimizing the existence and impact of racism and emphasizing cross-racial interests—suggest that, by doing so, such a pernicious factor of social life will erode and slowly disappear?

In the four centuries blacks have been in this country, there has never been a time when critical questions of how to negotiate their existence here have *not* been debated and dissected. Other groups, to be sure, have faced similar problems, but no honest discussion of race in the United States would deny that Americans of African descent present a most exceptional case. Compounding the problems are the blatant realities of historical, constitutionally sanctioned subjugation, minority numerical status, a complex, multilayered, check-and-balance political system characterized by separation of powers and a federalist structure, and a society that has a long tradition of skepticism toward activist governmental action, especially when aimed at helping those in least-favored socioeconomic status. And yet, African Americans must engage in that system, must seek to maximize benefits from it and to do so without succumbing to the illusion of a "color-blind" society, so prominently championed by those who are (and have always been) in preferred positions of power and privilege.

This has never been an easy row to hoe. Therefore, it is not surprising that "political deracilization" is such an important (and at times, contentious) topic in today's society. Keeping history in mind, and in the face of enormous positive and negative changes in all spheres, it is crucial to study this political phenomenon. This book provides that opportunity. It is not burdened by the naiveté that, frankly and understandably, accompanied some earlier civil rights struggles. It focuses on an area—electoral politics—that has opened up considerably for blacks in the last three decades. But as with all changes of such magnitude, new problems come in the wake. The electoral arena has great possibilities, but it also has many built-in limits. The struggle for racial justice is a continuing one; it is not one that rewards loss of memory, or permits unwarranted assumptions about irreversible gains.

This study offers a needed corrective to the unfortunate social-science scholarship of an earlier time, which assumed that the path of blacks in America would largely mirror that of other groups, especially the European immigrants. That scholarship, while well-intended, was far too simplistic and perhaps prematurely optimistic in its predictions. From the liberal left, the emphasis was on class rather than race. From the conservative right, the preferred explanatory variable was the market. Both theoretical positions tended to deemphasize race and racism. The actual situation, however, is far more complex than either of these formulations suggests.

To pursue "deracialized" political strategies—when, where, how—is a much more perplexing matter, as this book documents. The book will add to our knowledge and insights. And if we are sincere about the issues it raises, it could also contribute to solutions, however difficult those might be in the short and long terms.

Charles V. Hamilton
Wallace S. Sayre Professor of Government
Columbia University

Preface

T his book examines major themes in the concept of deracialization and analyzes the campaigns of African American candidates to determine if race is becoming less of a cleavage in American politics, as some scholars have suggested. The 1989 elections were characterized by an unusually large number of black electoral victories. Several of those African Americans elected to office conducted a campaign strategy characterized by the soft-pedaling of black issues and a rigorous appeal for white voter support—a campaign strategy that has become known as deracialization. Other blacks used this same strategy and were elected to office in 1990 and 1992.

Some analysts argue that, given the small number of black majority districts and jurisdictions that have not elected black representation, any continuing increase in the number of African American elected officials will have to come primarily from black electoral victories in majority white districts and jurisdictions. This book examines the deracialization concept to determine its usefulness for explaining such black electoral victories. The book also explores the administration of several black elected officials who conducted a deracialization campaign, in order to determine whether deracialization as a campaign strategy leads to deracialization as a governance strategy.

Deracialization is a useful concept for explaining African American electoral victories in the 1990s as well as the election of several black candidates to public office in the 1970s and 1980s. While deracialization as a campaign strategy is especially useful to African American candidates running in majority white districts and jurisdictions, it does not automatically lead to deracialized governance. Thus, black elected officials who conduct deracialized campaigns often pursue themes of racial justice in their governance.

While deracialization is an important ingredient in the fabric of successful African American electoral politics, the importance of traditional black politics has not diminished. For the foreseeable future, deracialization and traditional black politics will exist as twin pillars in black electoral politics, with the former being more successfully deployed in majority white districts and jurisdictions and the latter being more successfully deployed in majority black districts and jurisdictions. A consequence of this dual structure in African American politics may be the emergence of ideological and class divisions in the structure of black politics, which may compromise the ability of African American politicians to produce benefits for black constituents.

This book has undergone an interesting gestation period. Substantially abridged versions of three of its thirteen chapters were published as a symposium in *PS: Political Science and Politics* in 1990. Additionally, abridged versions of two of these five chapters were published as a minisymposium in *Urban Affairs Quarterly* in 1991. The chapters in this book are both substantially longer and considerably more complex than their predecessors in the earlier publications. The book chapters, as contrasted to the two earlier publications, incorporate more empirical data and focus more on assessing the governance style of black elected officials who ran deracialized campaigns.

I am very grateful to the book's contributors for their fine contributions to scholarship on the deracialization concept. I am also very grateful to Robert Huckshorn of Florida Atlantic University for his careful review of the manuscript; his insightful suggestions immeasurably improved its quality. I am also grateful to Walda Metcalf of the University Press of Florida for her support of the book. I especially want to thank Deidre Bryan, my editor at the Press for this and my first UPF book; her outstanding work and cheerful professionalism were invaluable.

I also thank Marvin L. Yates, chancellor, and William E. Moore, vice chancellor for academic affairs, at Southern University at Baton Rouge, for their support. Three former support staff members—Elenora C. Anderson, Veronica L. Howard and Lorita N. Ford—and seven former and current graduate research assistants—Aegeda Davis, Bernita Frazier, Tamisha Green, Adrian Lewis, Katherine Penn, Marva Spencer, and Stacy Williams—worked on the book at various stages, and I thank them all for their contributions. I especially thank Katherine, my former senior research assistant, and Tamisha for their extraordinary assistance.

Finally, I would like to thank my family for their support. My wife, Emma, and our two sons, David and Jeffrey, never complained about the long hours that I was unable to spend with them because of my work. Their encouragement, in words and actions, sustained me throughout the period that I worked on this book.

Huey L. Perry

Introduction: An Analysis of Major Themes in the Concept of Deracialization

Huey L. Perry

Current scholarship on black politics in the United States is characterized by a very lively debate on the importance of deracialization as a development in American politics. Deracialization, as applied to American electoral politics, is the conduction of an electoral campaign in which racial issues and themes are minimized, if not avoided, in order to attract increased white electoral support. Although deracialization has existed in American politics for a much longer time, the concept of deracialization is most prominently associated with the 1989 elections in which nine African American candidates were elected or reelected to public office.[1] The 1989 elections are important in this regard because of the large number of blacks who won election to public office and the fact that some were the first blacks elected to the positions.[2] Four of the nine successful black candidates ran deracialized campaigns. The successful application of the deracialization concept in the 1989 elections was followed by two major unsuccessful attempts to deploy the concept in the 1990 elections. In their attempts to use deracialization, both Andrew Young in the Georgia gubernatorial election and Harvey Gantt in the North Carolina senate race were unsuccessful.

The 1989 and 1990 elections provide an important empirical basis for analyzing the deracialization concept and the interplay of race and politics in the United States. This book examines these elections within the context of the deracialization concept to determine the extent to which the concept elucidates patterns of campaign behavior and activities and electoral behavior. The book provides insight on the changing role of local politicians, the role of race in multiethnic politics, and the impact of internal class differences within racial and ethnic groups on political outcomes. In this chapter, I examine the major themes of deracialization as a strategy for black electoral politics in the United States and in doing so provide an organizational framework for the remaining chapters.

The lively ongoing debate on deracialization in the scholarly literature centers on two principal components. First, does deracialization increase the number of black elected officials? Second, and perhaps a more important question, what is the quality of representation that black constituents receive from public officials who conduct deracialized campaigns? The concern is that these public officials may not vigorously serve black interests. Both of these components are substantively and theoretically important and should be subjected to additional empirical and theoretical inquiry to determine the most apposite conclusions. To conclude merely on the basis of ideological speculation that deracialization is anathema to the interest of blacks, based on the untested assumption that public officials who use deracialization to win elections will not effectively serve black interests, does not promote scholarly inquiry on this important issue.

While deracialization increases the number of African American elected officials, it does not threaten traditional black politics. The election of black public officials from majority black districts and jurisdictions is the foundation of black political life in the United States. Although the distinct historic tendency of black public officials to be elected from majority black districts and jurisdictions is approaching a mathematical limitation because there are few remaining majority black districts and jurisdictions that have not elected black public officials, it is possible for blacks to use litigation to create more majority black districts, as was the case in 1992 when blacks persuaded the U.S. Department of Justice to create several new majority black congressional districts. A similar development occurred in Alabama in 1988 when a court ordered the state to discontinue the use of at-large elections in favor of district elections for 180 municipal and county jurisdictions. The change resulted in the election of 252 additional black public officials in one year.[3]

This is precisely the kind of development that Abigail Thernstrom criticizes in her analysis of voting rights applications in the 1980s.[4] Thernstrom's admonishment notwithstanding, the creation of new majority black districts and jurisdictions to increase the number of black elected officials is a limited strategy that will produce only a small number of additional black districts and jurisdictions. The limitation of this strategy is somewhat attributable to political considerations but more largely due to the demographics of the black population in the United States.

Deracialized political campaigns require black candidates to run campaigns different from traditional black candidates, in that they must appeal to whites, ethnic groups, and other racial minorities.[5] This new requirement is relevant for addressing a developing criticism of deracialization in regard to black politics, that is, that deracialization forces the victims of racial prejudice to bear the brunt of racism in American society.

Deracialization results in African American candidates having to restrain their natural political-cultural impulses to openly advocate black causes in order to attract white electoral support, rather than white voters having to make some political attitudinal adjustments that would lead them to support black candidates who make traditional calls for the full inclusion of blacks into the American political and economic systems. While there is some merit in this formulation, it is not entirely accurate. At the theoretical level, deracialization challenges white voters to be less race-bound in their voting preferences. Martin Kilson specifically delineates the need for an increasing number of whites to vote for black candidates if deracialization is to be a successful strategy for increasing the number of black elected officials.[6]

At the practical level, the need to appeal to white voters is not always as confining to African American candidates as is popularly thought, in terms of black candidates being able to advocate black issues. U.S. Representative Ronald Dellums (D-CA), who has consistently advocated black issues, has been reelected several times in a white majority district. While Dellums's success in this regard may in part be explained by the fact that his district is liberal, the same argument does not hold for Representative Alan Wheat (D-MO), who represents a conservative district. Reelected to a fifth term in 1990, Wheat, whose district was 20 percent black in 1980, says that he has few problems in advocating black causes despite differences between his black and white constituents on certain issues. Wheat says the fact that those differences exist "usually does not reflect itself in a limiting way in how I am able to respond to an issue."[7]

Deracialization and Divisions among African Americans

The black politics of the 1990s possesses two central tendencies: traditional black politics in majority black districts and jurisdictions, and deracialized politics in majority white districts and jurisdictions. Black electoral support is central in both cases, particularly to traditional black politics. Its importance to deracialized politics, while not as apparent, is nonetheless discernible. Even under the most successful applications of the deracialization strategy, black candidates will seldom be able to win an election without an appreciable percentage, if not the majority, of the black vote. For example, the overwhelming majority support received by L. Douglas Wilder from black voters was critical to his gubernatorial election in Virginia in 1989. Thus, deracialization in no way suggests a devaluation of black electoral support to continued black success in electoral politics. In the Georgia gubernatorial election in 1990, Andrew Young's unsuccessful deracialized campaign, which ignored and alienated black electoral support, dramatically substantiated this observation.

The negative consequence of the emergence of deracialization in American politics, stemming from the dual structure of black politics, is likely to be the accentuation of ideological and class divisions among African American political leaders and their followers. This would be a significant departure from the group cohesion that has been a major, long-standing characteristic of black politics over the last sixty years.[8]

There are three types of successful black electoral activity in contemporary African American politics.[9] The first type involves black candidates running against white opponents, usually in majority white districts and jurisdictions. The campaigns are characterized by black candidates emphasizing black issues. In these elections, black candidates generally can expect to receive no more than 20 percent of the white vote. Black electoral victories in these situations were dominant in the first two decades following the passage of the Voting Rights Act of 1965. This type of successful black electoral activity constitutes the essence of traditional black politics. The hallmark of these elections was the intensity of race as a basis for electoral choice and a subpattern of middle-and upper-income white support for black candidates. While middle- and upper-income white support for black candidates was limited, it was enough to provide the critical margin of difference for electing them.

More recently, a second type of black electoral success has been characterized by blacks running for office against other black candidates in majority black districts and jurisdictions and quietly appealing for white voter support. This type of black electoral activity emerged on the political landscape with some success within the last ten years. In this case, white voters usually determine the winner of the election, and successful black candidates generally receive strong majority support from whites. This type of election has the greatest potential to result in ideological divisions among African Americans. Often the ideological rift takes the form of the defeated candidate accusing the successful candidate of being too beholden to whites and not accountable to blacks. The foundation of this accusation often emerges during the campaign.

This second type of black electoral success is illustrated by two campaigns. In his first campaign for mayor of New Orleans in 1986, Sidney Barthelemy sought and received white voter support, winning 85 percent of the white vote.[10] Similarly, in the race in Georgia's Fifth Congressional District (centered in Atlanta) in 1988, John Lewis defeated Julian Bond by attracting a significant minority of the black vote and successfully appealing to the white electorate.[11] Lewis's victory surprised many informed observers given the widespread feeling that Bond was a much more attractive candidate than Lewis. Lewis received 40 percent of the black vote and 80 percent of the white vote. The Fifth Congressional District in 1988 had a black population of 65 percent and a black voting-age population of 60 percent. Lewis won the election with 52 percent of the vote. Lewis's winning coalition was apparently composed of low-income blacks and middle- and upper-income whites.[12] His appeal to low-income blacks was based on his low-income origin, his personal style, and issue stances that reflected concern for low-income blacks. Both Barthelemy's and Lewis's elections resulted in an ideological rift between the black candidates and their black supporters.

Lewis's winning coalition has additional significance in its implication that class divisions within the black electorate may come to be politically relevant in African American politics. Low-income blacks voted for Lewis, and middle- and upper-income blacks voted for Bond. Since the personas of the two men mirror those class distinctions, we could conclude that the votes were based on class interests. This issue of class distinctions within the African American population has recently emerged, with powerful implications for the future of black politics. The same is true of ideological divisions among blacks. The issue of class coincides with the ideological division issue in that both usually reinforce rather than challenge ideological currents.

The third and most recent type of successful black electoral activity consists of African American candidates running in majority white districts and jurisdictions, usually against white opponents, and strongly appealing for white voter support. In the effort to attract white electoral support, these candidates usually do not make strong racial appeals in their campaign. This type constitutes the essence of a deracialized campaign. This strategy, in varying degrees, was successfully employed in the 1989 elections by Norman Rice to win the mayoral election in Seattle, Washington, by David Dinkins to win the mayoral election in New York City, by Chester Jenkins to win the mayoral election in Durham, North Carolina, and by Douglas Wilder to win the gubernatorial election in Virginia. As the 1989 elections indicate, white support for black candidates in this type ranges from strong minority support to majority support. This type of successful black electoral strategy has been developing for almost two decades. For example, Tom Bradley used this strategy as early as 1973 to win his first election as mayor of Los Angeles.[13]

This third type of black electoral activity gives rise to two important questions about black political life in the United States. Will the need to win majority white districts and jurisdictions produce black candidates different from those of the first and second type? Will black elected officials who successfully employ the deracialized campaign approach govern differently from the black elected officials of the first and second type who generally seek to provide benefits for blacks? Both questions constitute fertile ground for scholarly research, and both are relevant for explaining the development of ideological and class divisions among African Americans as a result of the increased use of deracialization. Black candidates who win with strong white electoral support will increasingly be viewed with some dissonance by more traditional black candidates and their supporters.

Deracialization and Governance

The most important component of the deracialization discussion is whether deracialization as a campaign style leads to a deracialized governance strategy, and here, the potential to produce ideological divisions among blacks is abundant. This concern is at the heart of the issue of whether deracialization is good or bad for black politics in the United States.[14] In other words, deracialization is adverse to black interests if as a campaign style it leads to deracialization as a governance strategy.

Manning Marable believes that deracialization as a campaign strategy has a good deal of carryover value for governance. He asserts that black candidates who run deracialized candidacies favor programs that have little in common with the traditional agendas of the civil rights movement. According to Marable, "Their election can be viewed as a psychological triumph for African Americans, but they represent no qualitative resolution to the crises of black poverty, educational inequality, crime, and unemployment."[15] Marable's argument is less than persuasive. It is possible for successful African American candidates to favor nontraditional civil rights issues and still govern in a manner inclusive of black interests, thus diminishing the chance for the emergence of ideological divisions among blacks. Candidate and Mayor Harvey Gantt of Charlotte, North Carolina, is an example of such a combination. Although traditional black public officials have prevailed in providing certain benefits to their black constituents,[16] these officials have not been successful in solving the intractable problems of the black underclass.

A deracialized campaign style will not necessarily lead to a deracialized governance strategy. Despite Bradley's deracialized mayoral campaigns, his policies as mayor of Los Angeles were similar to those pursued by other black mayors: "appointment of minorities to city commissions, affirmative action in city hiring, the use of federal aid instead of tax funds to fight poverty, and downtown economic development."[17] Similarly, Barthelemy's deracialized campaign in 1986 did not preclude him from implementing the most vigorous affirmative action plan for allocating municipal contracts in the city's history. The early policy objectives and actions of the black officials elected in

1989 suggest that deracialization as a campaign style may well have little relevance for governance. David Dinkins's deracialized campaign to become the first black mayor of New York City did not prevent him from appointing Lee Brown as the first black commissioner of the 2,600-member New York Police Department and Grigsby Brandford Powell, a black municipal finance firm, as the senior book manager for New York City's new $250 million equipment leasing program.[18]

Another concern regarding deracialization is whether it will lead to a full reemergence of race baiting in American politics. A casualty of increased black voting in the South due to the 1965 Voting Rights Act, race baiting for all intents and purposes disappeared from the American political landscape in the 1970s and 1980s. The elimination of race baiting from southern politics has generally been regarded as one benefit that had accrued to southern blacks as a result of their increased political participation. Race baiting first reappeared in American politics in the presidential campaign of 1988 with the Willie Horton television advertisement used by George Bush's campaign. The Willie Horton advertisement was followed by the use of race baiting by Senator Jesse Helms of North Carolina and Governor Guy Hunt of Alabama in their successful reelection campaigns in 1990. Helms's opponent in the race was Harvey Gantt, an African American and the former mayor of Charlotte, North Carolina. The U.S. Senate race in North Carolina suggests that an increased use of race baiting may well accompany the efforts to employ deracialization in the South.

Overview

The objective of this introductory chapter has been to frame the discussion of the major themes associated with the deracialization concept as a means of providing an organizational framework for the remaining chapters. The two major themes of deracialization are whether it increases the number of black elected officials and whether it impacts negatively on the quality of representation received by black constituents. Both of these themes are examined in this book.

Part I focuses on deracialization in statewide politics. Alvin J. Schexnider analyzes the governance of L. Douglas Wilder as governor of Virginia in chapter 1. Schexnider's analysis provides a favorable assessment of Governor Wilder's gubernatorial administration. In chapter 2, Charles L. Prysby analyzes the unsuccessful attempt by Harvey Gantt to utilize the deracialization strategy in his 1990 U.S. Senate election campaign against Jesse Helms in North Carolina. This race suggests that it is difficult for a black candidate to successfully employ the deracialization strategy against a conservative white incumbent in the South. In the third chapter, Roger K. Oden analyzes Carol Moseley-Braun's historic election as a U.S. senator from Illinois.

Part II focuses on deracialization in city politics. In the fourth chapter, J. Phillip Thompson analyzes the election and governance of David Dinkins as mayor of New York City. Thompson adds a useful contribution to the scholarly literature on New York City politics, which after years of scholarly inattention following Wallace S. Sayre and Herbert Kaufman's *Governing New York City*,[19] has increased significantly in recent years.[20] The fifth chapter is Mylon Winn and Errol G. Palmer's analysis of Norman Rice's election and governance as mayor of Seattle, Washington. Among other reasons, Winn and Palmer's analysis is significant because not much research has been done on Seattle or on cities with as small a black population proportion as Seattle. Blacks comprise only 8 percent of Seattle's population.

In chapter 6, Carol A. Pierannunzi and John D. Hutcheson examine Andrew Young's unsuccessful attempt to employ the deracialization strategy in his campaign for the Democratic party's nomination for governor in Georgia. Pierannunzi and Hutcheson's chapter is particularly useful in that it demonstrates the disastrous effects that can ensue when a candidate attempts to employ deracialization to the point of ignoring and alienating the black electorate. Young was unsuccessful in his attempt to employ the deracialization strategy because he was not able to strike a balance between appealing to white voters and keeping his potential black support base intact. An often overlooked fact is that strong black support is usually critical to the successful application of the strategy. Young did not receive the massive black support characteristic of viable black political candidacies, especially for important political offices, because he ignored the black vote in the intensity of his appeal for the white vote. Another important consideration of Young's failure to win the Democratic party nomination for governor is that his principal opponent and the person who won the nomination and governorship, Zell Miller, has a strong civil rights record. Thus, the 1990 Georgia gubernatorial election suggests it is difficult for a black candidate to employ the deracialization strategy against a white candidate who has a strong civil rights record.

Part III, which consists of a single chapter, focuses on deracialization in a state legislative campaign. Written by James L. Llorens, Sharon K. Parsons, and Huey L. Perry, chapter 7 analyzes the election of Troy Carter to the Louisiana House of Representatives and is a solid blend of theoretical and empirical analysis of the deracialization concept. The chapter advances the literature on deracialization in two important ways: (1) it is the first published analysis of a deracialized campaign and election for a seat in a state legislature, and (2) its empirical analysis is the most quantitatively sophisticated examination of deracialization in the published literature.

Part IV provides a critical analysis of the deracialization concept and strategy. The chapters in this section make an important contribution to the literature because they provide a contextual assessment of the limitations of deracialization. In chapter 8, Mary Summers and Philip A. Klinkner analyze John Daniels's election as the first black mayor of New Haven, Connecticut, and the first year of his administration. Significantly, Summers and Klinkner reject the deracialization concept as an explaination of Daniels's election and governance. They argue that Daniels did not subdue racial issues in his campaign but rather ensconced them in a progressive campaign strategy. Summers and Klinkner argue that Daniels did not adopt the deracialization concept either in his campaign or in his mayoral administration. Summers and Klinkner's findings clearly indicate that the deracialization model is not applicable to all components of African American urban politics.

In chapter 9, Sharon D. Wright analyzes the failure of the deracialization strategy for the African American mayoral candidates in Memphis, Tennessee. Wright's chapter makes an important contribution to the deracialization literature because her analysis focuses on both the inability of the deracialization concept to explain the election of W. W. Herenton as mayor of Memphis and the inability of the concept to explain the electoral performance of an entire generation of black mayoral candidates in Memphis. The election of Kurt Schmoke in Baltimore, Maryland, is discussed by Lenneal J. Henderson, Jr., in chapter 10. Henderson points out some inapplicabilities of the deracialization concept to Schmoke's victory.

Part V of the book, which consists of chapter 11, provides a comprehensive assessment of deracialization within the context of the new black politics. Although it has been asserted rather than clearly defined, the concept of the new black politics is most useful in describing a black politics of the 1970s and 1980s characterized by blacks winning election to public office and directly participating in the governing process rather than simply attempting to influence the election of sympathetic white candidates, which constituted the black politics of the pre-1970s.[21] In chapter 11, Robert B. Albritton, George Amedee, Keenan Grenell, and Don-Terry Veal offer a comprehensive assessment of deracialization and the new black politics.

The conclusion of the book is an assessment of the deracialization concept. My objective in this chapter is to produce a synthesis of the literature on deracialization, which is likely to be a central issue of discussion in the African American politics literature of the foreseeable future.

Notes

1. These victories include the reelections of Coleman Young as mayor of Detroit and Carrie Perry as mayor of Hartford, Connecticut, the election of Maynard Jackson as mayor of Atlanta after having been out of the office for eight years, the first-time election to the mayor's office of Norman Rice in Seattle, John

Daniels in New Haven, Connecticut, David Dinkins in New York City, Chester Jenkins in Durham, North Carolina, and Michael White in Cleveland, and the election of L. Douglas Wilder as governor of Virginia.

2. These include the elections of Rice, Daniels, Dinkins, Jenkins, and Wilder.

3. James A. Barnes, "Into the Mainstream," *National Journal,* Feb. 1960, 263.

4. Abigail M. Thernstrom, *Whose Votes Count? Affirmative Action and Minority Voting Rights* (Cambridge, Mass.: Harvard University Press, 1987).

5. See Martin Kilson, "Problems of Black Politics: Some Progress, Many Difficulties," *Dissent* 36 (1989): 529–30; Manning Marable, "A New Black Politics," *Progressive,* Aug. 1990, 23; Huey L. Perry, "Deracialization as an Analytical Construct in American Urban Politics," *Urban Affairs Quarterly* 27 (Dec. 1991): 181–91.

6. Kilson, "Problems of Black Politics."

7. Barnes, "Into the Mainstream," 264.

8. Angus Campbell, Phillip E. Converse, Warren E. Miller, and Donald E. Stokes, *The American Voter* (New York: John Wiley and Sons, 1960), 316.

9. See Perry, "Deracialization as an Analytical Construct," for a full discussion of these three types.

10. Stan J. Makielski, Jr., "The New Orleans Mayoral Election," *Urban Politics and Urban Policy Section Newsletter* 4 (1990): 11.

11. Mack H. Jones, "Black Mayoral Leadership in Atlanta: A Comment," paper presented at the annual meeting of the National Conference of Black Political Scientists, 1988, 7.

12. Marilyn Davis and Alex Willingham, "Taking the Fifth," *Southern Changes* 8 (1986): 9.

13. Raphael J. Sonenshein, "The Dynamics of Biracial Coalitions: Crossover Politics in Los Angeles," *Western Political Quarterly* 42 (1989): 342–43.

14. For some insight into this question, see Robert C. Smith, "Recent Elections and Black Politics: The Maturation or Death of Black Politics?" *PS: Political Science and Politics* 23 (June 1990): 160–62.

15. Marable, "New Black Politics," 20–21.

16. See for example, Paul K. Eisinger, "Black Employment in Municipal Jobs: The Impact of Black Political Power," *American Political Science Review* 76 (1982): 380–92; Rufus P. Browning, Dale R. Marshall, and David H. Tabb, *Protest Is Not Enough: The Struggle of Blacks and Hispanics for Equality in Urban Politics* (Berkeley: University of California Press, 1984); James W. Button, *Blacks and Social Change: Impact of the Civil Rights Movement in Southern Communities* (Princeton, N.J.: Princeton University Press, 1989); Kenneth R. Mladenka, "Blacks and Hispanics in Urban Politics," *American Political Science Review* 83 (1989): 165–91; Huey L. Perry, "The Evolution and Impact of Biracial Coalitions and Black Mayors in Birmingham and New Orleans," in *Racial Politics in American Cities,* edited by Rufus Browning, Dale R. Marshall, and David H. Tabb (New York: Longman, 1990), 140–52.

17. Sonenshein, "Dynamics of Biracial Coalitions," 343–44.

18. Frank McCoy, "Black Power in City Hall," *Black Enterprise,* Aug. 1990, 152.

19. Wallace S. Sayre and Herbert Kaufman, *Governing New York City* (New York: Russell Sage Foundation, 1960).

20. See for example John Hull Mollenkopf, *A Phoenix in the Ashes: The Rise and Fall of the Koch Coalition in New York City Politics* (Princeton, N.J.: Princeton University Press, 1992).

21. The first use of the term "new black politics" appears in Michael B. Preston, Lenneal J. Henderson, Jr., and Paul L. Puryear, *The New Black Politics: The Search for Political Power* (New York: Longman, 1982).

I

Deracialization in
Statewide Politics

1

Analyzing the Wilder Administration through the Construct of Deracialization Politics

Alvin J. Schexnider

The election of L. Douglas Wilder as governor of Virginia in 1989 was both historic and precedent-setting: historic because Wilder was the first African American elected to the position of governor, and precedent-setting because it occurred in a conservative southern state where blacks comprise 19 percent of the population. Wilder's political career has been characterized by several "firsts." In 1969, he was the first black elected to the Virginia Senate since Reconstruction; he was the first black to win statewide office in Virginia (lieutenant governor in 1985); and he was the first black elected governor in the United States. Wilder's twenty-year rise in Virginia politics has been gradual but steady. In the campaign for governor, he ran against Republican Marshall Coleman, a former state's attorney general. In order to win, Wilder raised $6.86 million compared to Coleman who raised almost a third more, $9.27 million. The main factors contributing to Wilder's election were as follows:

- strong support in the state's most populous areas (e.g., Tidewater and northern Virginia);
- strong support among black voters;
- substantial support among white voters;
- substantial support among women voters; and
- strong support among younger voters.

The election of Wilder as governor of Virginia will be viewed as one of the most extraordinary political events of the twentieth century. On the day of Wilder's election, African Americans were also elected mayors of New York City, New Haven, Connecticut, Durham, North Carolina, and Seattle, Washington. These political victories raise interesting speculation about the significance of race in electoral politics. Black political leaders such as Ronald H. Brown, former chairman of the Democratic National Committee and secretary of the Department of Commerce in the Clinton administration, argue that "race continues to be a factor in American Politics as it is in American life . . . [but] the situation is improving."[1]

The fact that L. Douglas Wilder in Virginia and David Dinkins in New York distanced themselves from racial issues in their successful bids for elective office has caused some observers to hypothesize about "deracialization" (i.e., the minimizing of explicitly racial concerns) as a construct for understanding urban politics. In a rather lively minisymposium devoted to this subject, scholars made an effort to determine the applicability of deracialization in describing and explaining the political behavior of African American candidates. According to one of the proponents of deracialization as an analytical construct, "The 1989 elections stand out because of the large number of blacks who won public election to public office, the fact that some of these blacks were the first black elected to the positions, and the fact that several of the successful black candidates ran deracialized campaigns in which racial issues were subdued in the effort to attract white voter support."[2]

During his campaign for governor, Wilder distanced himself from Jesse Jackson. He did not, however, distance himself from black voters who overwhelmingly supported him. In fact, he courted them assiduously, just as he courted the votes of whites, women, and organized labor. If anything, Wilder waged a strongly conventional and highly pragmatic campaign that reached out to every segment of Virginia's electorate. On the basis of his election, one could suggest that deracialization may be viewed as novel political theory, but in fact it may offer little help in understanding Wilder's victory.

Another way of looking at deracialization is to turn the construct on its head and ask whether, in a state where African Americans comprise 19 percent of the population, Wilder could have been elected without broad-based support. Yet another point of view is that rather than call the phenomenon deracialization, we might conclude that "it is possible [for an African American] to win the top office in a majority white constituency if the [candidate] is willing to run a moderate, mainstream, non-threatening campaign."[3] In a major address to African American and Hispanic elected officials, Wilder summarized the issue of campaign style: "When all is said and done, each candidate has to find a style and a message with which he or she is most comfortable while on the campaign trail."[4] While the issue of race was modulated in the campaign, realistically, Wilder could not, nor did he attempt to, deny its existence. In this sense, deracialization may well be an oxymoron. In American politics and society, race is omnipresent.[5]

Huey L. Perry's discussion of deracialization as an analytical construct draws a useful distinction in that it differentiates between campaign strategy and governance: "The most important component of the deracialization discussion is whether deracialization as a campaign style leads to a deracialized governance strategy. . . . This concern is at the heart of the issue of whether deracialization is good or bad for black politics in the United States. In other words, deracialization is adverse to black interests if as a campaign style it leads to deracialization as a governance strategy."

Deracialization has little or no explanatory power regarding L. Douglas Wilder's gubernatorial election. Wilder ran a pragmatic campaign calculated to garner the majority electoral support. Notwithstanding the type of campaign he waged, Wilder's governance bears little or no resemblance to those who Manning Marable labels "post-black politicians who favor programs with little kinship to the traditional agendas of the civil rights movement."[6] In this chapter, I will show that the Wilder administration was sensitive to the concerns of black voters, just as it was sensitive to the concerns of the electorate in general. A serious and protracted set of fiscal problems made it impossible for Governor Wilder to pursue an aggressive agenda. Given his mainstream instincts, it is doubtful that he would have set out on a radical course at any rate. The number of blacks Wilder appointed to his administration and the types of policymaking roles they enjoyed appear in the long-term to have been calculated to benefit Virginia's black citizens beyond Wilder's four-year term. These singular acts of intentionality do not comport with a governance style that is inimical to the interests of black voters.

The Wilder Administration

Many have speculated that Governor Wilder's agenda was more personal than public-oriented. Much of this conjecture is based on an assumption that being elected governor was a mere stepping-stone to higher elective office. One observer, for example, "surmised" that Wilder's many out-of-state trips during his first year in office suggested that he was more interested in having "a place on the national Democratic ticket in 1992 than in developing a coherent vision of his agenda for the next four years."[7] Most would agree that the Wilder administration began under a cloud of fiscal uncertainty more ominous than any in Virginia since the end of World War II. Consequently, the single dominant concern of Governor Wilder's first year in office was "the budget." The budget continued to be a concern to Governor Wilder during his entire administration.

A month after the 1989 election, the outgoing Governor Gerald L. Baliles confirmed widespread speculation that agency budgets would have to be reduced in order to balance the state budget. The $1.4 billion shortfall in state revenues resulting from an economic slump across the Commonwealth, but especially in northern Virginia (a key factor in the state's economic base), reduced national defense spending (a major factor in the state's economy), and a slowdown in the nation's economy contributed to a substantially weakened state treasury.

Virginia's dire fiscal problems denied Wilder an opportunity to pursue new initiatives consistent with his "New Mainstream" campaign theme. In effect, the state's worsening economy curtailed his options. Given the projected shortfall at the onset of his administration, Wilder had little choice but to downscale his predecessor's recommended budget in order to balance it. Consequently, in his first address to the Virginia General Assembly, Governor Wilder affirmed three principles of prudent fiscal discipline: resistance to a tax increase, reduction in his predecessor's proposed budget, and creation of a reserve fund.[8]

In keeping with his theme of fiscal responsibility, Wilder announced a plan to offer budget amendments designed to create a $200 million reserve fund. He argued that the reserve fund was necessary "to fund anticipated salary increases for the second year of the biennium."[9] He also revealed plans to secure the legislature's approval of separating the Transportation and Public Safety Secretariat into two new cabinets (one for transportation and the other for public safety), a move largely in deference to the state's increasing transportation problems, especially in northern Virginia and in rural areas.

The bill to decouple transportation and public safety occasioned some mild resistance, but ultimately the General Assembly approved it. The governor's proposal to establish a $200 million "rainy day" fund received mixed reviews, however. The first and by far most severe test of executive-legislative relations during the Wilder administration was the reserve fund.

Balancing the state's budget was Wilder's highest priority during the onset of his administration. In his first speech to the legislature just two days after his inauguration, Wilder put the General Assembly on notice that he intended to create an emergency reserve fund to ensure that the state would live within its means. Conservatism aside, many legislators were perplexed at the prospect of less pork to deliver to their constituents—in other words, setting aside millions of dollars meant less money to fund various pet projects. Similarly, lobbyists found it hard to believe there would be less money to mollify the interest groups they represented. Traditionally influential business groups in Virginia politics were, however, relatively pleased with the governor's plan. They also liked the governor's promise of no new taxes, which was a profound relief to Democrats and Republicans alike who were convinced that Wilder was a closet liberal.

In a major legislative victory, Wilder succeeded in getting the General Assembly to approve the creation of a $200 million unobligated reserve fund. In his second year in office, as the state's economy worsened, Wilder was forced to tap into the reserve fund. This notwithstanding, Wilder's determination to practice fiscal prudence was established, and it later enabled the state to weather some serious financial storms.

Even with his slim margin of victory (less than 1 percent), Governor Wilder perceived his election as a mandate for vigorous leadership. His attitude was encouraged by a political tradition in Virginia that also supports an ethos of strong gubernatorial leadership. The governor of Virginia is one of the most powerful governors in the United States. According to Matthew Holden, "this is partly because of the governor's official authority over budget preparation and personnel choices, and doubtless because it developed at a time when one consolidated machine controlled both state government and the local governments."[10] Among the state's elected officials exists the perception that there is no higher office to aspire to than the governorship, with the possible exception of president of the United States. This is, of course, a peculiarly provincial point of view more identified with the state's political culture than anything else. It surely does not imply that being governor is more important than being president. Rather, it speaks volumes about the importance Virginians attach to the governorship of an enormously proud state.[11]

Inherent in the governor's legal authority are his appointive powers. This includes the power to appoint eight members of his cabinet as well as over three thousand members of boards and commissions that have purview over a broad array of the state's activities. Another inherent power is the line item veto, which forty-two of the nation's governors enjoy and which more often than not is used to discipline the legislature.[12] Governor Wilder's first appointment was that of a longtime confidant, Jay T. Shropshire, as his chief of staff. Shropshire previously had served as clerk of the Virginia Senate. The governor's chief of staff functions as his political/administrative liaison. The chief of staff also coordinates the work of the cabinet secretaries who administer over sixty departments and agencies. Consequently, the position possesses more actual authority than that of the lieutenant governor and is more akin to a position of deputy governor.

Governor Wilder appointed more African Americans to key positions in his administration than any other governor in Virginia's history. In addition to naming two blacks to his cabinet, he also appointed two blacks as deputy secretaries of cabinet agencies. Seventeen blacks were appointed heads of state agencies and over six hundred blacks were appointed or reappointed to various state boards and commissions.

Most of Wilder's public policy initiatives were designed to address the needs of all citizens (e.g., redressing educational disparity, preparing the state's workforce for the next century, and rural economic development). Some initiatives, however, specifically targeted black and low-income citizens (e.g., an increase of $15 million to Aid to Families with Dependent

Children, increased eligibility for Medicaid coverage for pregnant women and children, and increased funds to expedite the delivery of food stamps).

Wilder's most enduring legacy will probably be his successful management of Virginia's budget crisis, which, over a twenty-seven-month period, resulted in a loss of $2.5 billion in revenues. In order to manage Virginia's fiscal crisis, Wilder established several budget reduction policies:

1. Virginia would not enact any general tax increases or defer any planned tax relief.
2. The state would protect programs that provide direct aid to individuals and other essential public services.
3. The state would protect local government programs.
4. The state would emphasize permanent, ongoing reductions in the state budget while minimizing reliance on one-time budget actions.
5. Reductions would be targeted rather than across the board, in order to protect high-priority programs.
6. Maximum flexibility would be provided to state agencies to determine where cuts would be made.

For the Wilder administration's skillful handling of the state's budget crisis, Virginia was recognized by *Financial World* magazine as the best managed state in the nation (May 12, 1992).

Executive and Legislative Relations

State government, like the federal government, operates within a system of checks and balances. Accordingly, the governor as chief executive must enjoy some measure of support in the legislature if he is to succeed in office. In the Commonwealth of Virginia where the role of governor is inherently strong, the chief executive's power "is shared with the legislature, which is still regarded as one of the more traditional and quietly managed legislatures in the country."[13]

Any effort to assess Governor Wilder's performance must be examined within the context of his relations with the legislature. By most accounts, his first legislative session was successful. Some have argued that this was due to his having forwarded a limited agenda for members of the general assembly to tackle.[14] A conservative newspaper, the *Richmond Times-Dispatch,* editorialized, "Governor L. Douglas Wilder acquitted himself well in his first session. He inherited a situation in which revenues were falling some $1 billion short of original projections through 1992 and yet the state government's spending machine was in high gear" (Mar. 12, 1990).

The adoption of a $26 billion budget for 1990–92 (later downsized to $24 billion due to the state's lagging economy) was the dominant activity of the session. Consistent with his calls for fiscal prudence, Wilder directed all state agencies and institutions to reduce spending. Perhaps most importantly from a performance standpoint, he succeeding in securing, as previously indicated, legislative approval of a $200 million reserve fund. The purpose of this fund was to pay for unfunded commitments in the second year of the biennium.

Governor Wilder also achieved a major legislative victory by getting the general assembly to repeal the sales tax on nonprescription drugs, a measure for which he had previously fought and that he initially indicated a desire to delay until the state's fiscal outlook improved. Even though the effective date of this legislation was delayed and it amounted to an average tax break of only one dollar per month per family, Wilder's adroit handling of this measure is further testimony of his ability to exert influence over the budgeteers in the general assembly.

In addition to the budget crisis, four other issues deeply affected Wilder's relationship with the legislature. Three of these issues had direct implications for the general assembly (i.e., the railroads and retirement system, divestment of South African-linked stocks, and admissions policy of the Virginia Military Institute); the fourth, the governor's out-of-state travel, was indirectly a matter of concern for some legislators. These four issues resulted in a more strained relationship between Wilder and the legislature.

Out-of-State Travel and the National Scene

Wilder's election conferred instant celebrity status upon him. His campaign had attracted national, even international attention, and immediately following his inauguration, his media exposure expanded appreciably through appearances on three major television networks and several syndicated television talk shows. Wilder spent an estimated one-third of his first year in office out of the state attending meetings, campaigning on behalf of other Democrats, as the guest of organizations honoring him, and, as he said, returning favors to people who had supported his election.

Some members of the legislature and the media criticized his travel, suggesting that he was ignoring the state's economic problems. What angered his colleagues in the general assembly was the perception that in "three rounds of budget cuts, Wilder has either locked the legislature out of his decision-making or informed them after the fact" (*Richmond Times-Dispatch,* Jan. 1, 1991). During his rather frequent travels, Wilder administered the duties of his office through his chief and the deputy chief of staff. Wilder's administrative style in this regard was consistent with the standard practice of chief executives at both the local and state levels to delegate responsibility for the day-to-day governmental operations to chief administrative or operating officers.[15] Nonetheless, Wilder's high national visibility, his use of a state helicopter for what some alleged to be private use,[16] and some of his governmental decisions (e.g., eliminating purportedly useless state agencies) earned him scorn among some legislators and other persons active in Virginia politics.

Wilder was correctly perceived by many to have national political ambitions. In November 1990, shortly after the national elections, Wilder's aides formed the Committee for Fiscal Responsibilities in 1992, which Wilder used as a platform to launch his short-lived run for president. Wilder's foray into presidential politics lasted from September 1991 to January 1992. He campaigned on a theme of fiscal responsibility but was unable to generate enthusiasm among blacks or whites. Moreover, his run for president worsened relations with the general assembly. Similarly, Wilder's statewide popularity ratings, never high during the first year of his administration, fell to an all-time low of 23 percent during his second year in office, an unmistakable indicator of voter resentment of his presidential bid. Following his decision to withdraw from the presidential race, Wilder's approval rating rose to 30 percent.

On balance, Wilder's relations with the Virginia General Assembly were strained. His first year witnessed moderate success with the legislature, but his second and third years, during part of which time he sought the Democratic nomination for president, strained his relationship with the general assembly. The state's budget woes were also a major factor in this strained relationship: Wilder did not have the resources to fund various pet projects of key legislative members. The governor's policy regarding disinvestment of South Africa–linked stocks also contributed to his difficulties with the general assembly.

Five months after he took office, Governor Wilder ordered all state agencies, including Virginia's colleges and universities, to divest their financial interests in firms with ties to South Africa. He indicated that divestiture would "be carried out with full adherence to Virginia's fiduciary principles and fiscal responsibilities" (*Richmond Times-Dispatch,* May 13, 1990). Over half of the South Africa–linked investments were held by the Virginia State Retirement System. The state's colleges and universities also had substantial holdings in firms with ties to South Africa. The University of Virginia, for example, had nearly $16 billion in assets tied to South Africa. The governor's ability to appoint members of boards and directors of state agencies clearly enabled him to exact compliance with his wishes. He also invoked moral suasion to achieve his objectives in this regard: "I'm sending a message not just to schools and institutions in Virginia but also around the country and world

about how we feel about freedom-loving people [throughout] the world"
(*Richmond Times-Dispatch,* May 13, 1990).

The governor's announcement of the disinvestment policy was made at
the commencement exercises of Norfolk State University, one of the state's
two historically black institutions. His comments were well received by the
ten thousand people in the audience. The new policy was also favorably received by Wilder's supporters inside and outside of Virginia who viewed investment in South Africa as supportive of that country's oppression of blacks
through apartheid. Randall Robinson, executive director of Trans-Africa,
stated that the governor's policy raised the profile on the issue of South Africa
at a time when the public's attention to it appeared to have been waning.

Wilder's disinvestment directive was met with skepticism by members
of the general assembly and others who feared that its implementation could
jeopardize the state's investments. Former Governor Gerald Baliles, who pre-
ceded Wilder in office and whose administration had not considered divestment, commented that the new policy was mere symbolism. Virginia Senator
Hunter Andrews, chairman of the Senate Finance Committee and an outspoken critic of the governor, stated that divestment could prove to be costly
and potentially harmful to the state's economic interests.

The Virginia State Retirement System, where the bulk of the state's half
billion dollars in investments was held, was the agency most directly affected
by Wilder's orders. Realizing this, Wilder deflected anticipated criticism by
letting the public know that the disinvestment policy would be implemented
so as not to harm the state's economic interests. Later, the governor's press secretary announced that the governor hoped that divestiture would be com-
pleted by 1994 when he left office, even though Wilder realized that it may
not be. Having announced his policy, he provided ample room for agencies to
comply in a manner that would not harm the state's financial holdings.
Wilder's flexibility in this regard served to deflect major opposition from the
legislature.

Another factor that contributed to the issue of Wilder's strained relations with the general assembly was the admission of women to the Virginia
Military Institute (VMI), a publicly supported institution of higher education
with unusually strong alumni ties to Virginia's business and political estab-
lishments. During the 1990 legislative session, a bill was introduced to alter
the policy that excludes women from admission to VMI, one of two state-
supported officer training programs in the country. The bill was quashed in
committee by the then chairman of the Senate Education Committee, an
alumnus of VMI. This matter rapidly became a women's rights issue, partly
because the bill was introduced by a female legislator, but also because the
policy had previously been challenged in court by a female high school student in northern Virginia.

The bill's rejection in the Senate Education Committee ostensibly hinged on the view that the matter should be adjudicated in court, although it was actually rejected because of substantial political opposition from powerful VMI alumni. Governor Wilder's predecessor, Gerald Baliles, had tried to persuade VMI's Board of Visitors to change the admission policy before he left office, but it had declined to do so. Upon his election, Wilder was immediately confronted with this issue; he initially adopted a laissez-faire approach, which greatly disappointed many of his supporters. Wilder argued that the matter was in court and should be resolved there: "I've asked the court to dismiss those of us who feel we are not involved in the decision. And that the decision should be made by the board. And if the court determines that's wrong, then the court should say that. That has been, that is my position" (*Richmond Times-Dispatch,* Apr. 9, 1990).

Wilder's stance regarding the issue of the admission of women to VMI put the state's attorney general, Mary Sue Terry, in an extremely awkward position. As attorney general, she had a constitutional responsibility to defend the VMI board's position. As a woman who wished to preserve her options to run for governor in 1993, she did not want to act in a way that would alienate potential voters and political supporters, among them Senator Elmon Gray, chairman of the Senate Education Committee that defeated a bill to admit women to VMI. Given that it was widely known that the attorney general was interested in the Democratic party's nomination for governor, Wilder's position placed Terry in a no-win situation.

Later, when the court ruled that he could not be dismissed from the suit, Governor Wilder endorsed the admission of women to VMI, ending more than a year of silence on the matter. In doing so, he skillfully avoided criticism of meddling in the internal affairs of VMI while leaving the attorney general to grapple with a thorny political problem on her own. The defeat of the bill in the Senate Education Committee precluded the governor's having to engage the legislature on this issue. Wilder's endorsement of the objective of the lawsuit did not endear him to some members of the general assembly, but it mollified persons who felt the court should resolve the matter. In a ruling handed down in October 1992 by the U.S. Fourth Circuit Court of Appeals, the judges decided that VMI could remain all male if Virginia agreed to provide "parallel institutions or parallel programs."[17]

Wilder and Deracialization

The election of Wilder as governor affords an opportunity to examine the extent to which race remains an enduring fixture on the American political landscape. Observations by some students of American politics suggest that Wilder's victory derived from a deliberate campaign strategy of deracialization politics.[18] Another point of view distinguishes campaign strategy from actual governance, however, and in the final analysis, it may be more important to comprehend how candidates campaign for office and what they do upon election.

Wilder is, and always has been, a pragmatic politician. Jesse Jackson, portrayed as Wilder's nemesis by the national media in recent years, acknowledged the necessity of Wilder's pragmatism borne of the "political burden of race": "By the time Doug became a legislator, developing within the context of the black base, he also showed a sense of outreach, of coalition building beyond the black base. . . . You do the best you can to allay people's fears. You do that by being fair, being non-racist."[19]

A careful analysis of Wilder's political career attests to the fact that he was always predisposed to exact practical results from the body politic. For example, when Congress passed and President Ronald Reagan signed a Martin Luther King holiday bill in 1983, Wilder as a state senator succeeded in convincing the Virginia General Assembly to "reluctantly follow suit and make King's birthday a state holiday."[20]

Simply put, Wilder's campaign strategy and his governance are two different matters. To characterize the Wilder administration as pro-black would be inaccurate, but neither would it be accurate to label it pro-white or antithetical to the interests of African Americans. Virginia is a conservative state with a long history of disdain for its African American citizens. Wilder fully understands this history and was reasonably successful in a political culture that resisted the civil rights movement in the 1950s and whose electorate has not supported a Democratic presidential candidate since Lyndon B. Johnson in 1964. As governor, Wilder appointed record numbers of blacks and women to key policymaking positions in his administration. He also appointed hundreds of blacks and women to important boards and commissions. Equally important, Wilder attempted to bring some modernity to Virginia's public policy approach on issues like divestment in South Africa, the admission of women to the Virginia Military Institute, health care delivery, and equity in state spending for rural and urban school districts. He appointed blacks who are serving in roles where they can influence policy making and actions for years to come: as commissioner of agriculture, state treasurer, commissioner of mental health and mental retardation, director of personnel and training, and chairman of the Virginia State Retirement System, for example.

Wilder's legislative track record will likely be regarded as less distinguished than his administrative accomplishments, especially his achievements as a prudent fiscal manager. Elected governor during a period of economic decline and fiscal austerity, he was forced to deal with a budgetary crisis. His relations with the Virginia General Assembly were difficult almost from the start of his administration, and those relations were exacerbated by the state's worsening fiscal situation. Besides the state's money woes, tension between the Wilder administration and the legislature resulted from the inherent strength of the executive branch and the legislature's "keen sense of institutional boundaries."[21] Put another way, both branches of government in Virginia are about equally balanced: since neither can easily dominate the other, relations between the two can be difficult. State budgetary conditions denied Wilder an opportunity to dispense funds with which to satisfy legislators and required that he reduce the state's operating budget. Virginia's colleges and universities during the first two years of the Wilder administration sustained budget reductions ranging from 10.5 to 12 percent, for example. Moreover, faculty and administrators experienced a 2 percent salary reduction and went for nearly three years without a salary increase.

In addition, Wilder's failed bid for the Democratic presidential nomination strained his relations with the state legislature, and it resulted in a decline in popular support among Virginia's citizens. His 23 percent approval rating in late 1991 during the height of his presidential campaign is the lowest rating ever for a Virginia governor. He was successful in his redistricting efforts, however, which required legislative approval. Consequently, two majority black state senatorial districts and a majority black congressional district were created. Bobby Scott, a former state senator, was elected in November 1992 to become the first black U.S. congressman from Virginia in over one hundred years. History will determine Wilder's ultimate standing as the nation's first black elected governor since Reconstruction, although in the short term it is doubtful that Virginians will view him as a popular governor.

Attempts to assess the election of Wilder within the context of deracialization politics should be viewed with caution. Excessive attention to deracialization runs the risk of reducing consideration of other salient factors such as political skills, experience, charisma, issues orientation, fund-raising ability, and organization ability. Deemphasizing race as a campaign strategy does not mean ipso facto that the successful candidate will disavow issues pertinent to race once elected. Governor Wilder is an excellent case in point. Although he was criticized for having run a deracialized campaign, he showed a willingness to play the race card when it suited his political ends. In a continuing feud with Attorney General Mary Sue Terry and members of the legislature over the Virginia State Retirement System and its economic development arm, Wilder alleged that he was the victim of a double standard based on his race. Arguing that criticism from the media and legislators had little to do with his performance in office but was instead based on his race, Governor Wilder asserted, "The problem is not the job I've done. . . . I'm proud of it, and there's very few things I would change, and there are very few people who would be in a position to do any better" (*Washington Post,* Nov. 11, 1992).

Race remains an enduring part of the nation's social fabric. It is also a constant on the political landscape. Any black candidate who tries to minimize the relevance of race simply calls greater attention to its existence. This is what makes "deracialization" intriguing as an analytical construct. There is ample reason to consider it too simplistic to explain and predict black electoral behavioral except in limited contexts. It is even more limited in explaining and predicting the governing style of successful African American candidates who run deracialized campaigns.

Notes

I am grateful to Huey L. Perry for helpful suggestions that strengthened this manuscript.

1. Quoted in *Washington Post National Weekly Edition,* Nov. 13–19, 1989, 6.
2. Huey L. Perry, "Deracialization as an Analytical Construct in American Urban Politics," *Urban Affairs Quarterly* 27 (Dec. 1991): 181.
3. Larry J. Sabato, *Virginia Votes, 1987–1990* (Charlottesville: Center for Public Service, University of Virginia, 1991), 100.
4. L. Douglas Wilder, keynote address in *1990 Symposium on the State of the States: Women, Black and Hispanic Elected Leaders* (Charlottesville: Center for Public Service, University of Virginia/Eagleton Institute of Politics, Rutgers University, 1991), 12.
5. One eminent legal scholar argues that "racism is an integral, permanent, and indestructible component of this society." See Derrick Bell, *Faces at the Bottom of the Well: The Permanence of Racism* (New York: Basic, 1992), ix.
6. Manning Marable, "A New Black Politics," *The Progressive* 54 (Aug. 1990): 21.
7. Robert D. Holsworth, "Is Wilder's Agenda Personal or Public?" *Roanoke Times,* May 20, 1990.
8. Wilder, "State of the Commonwealth," unpublished speech, Jan. 15, 1990, 3.
9. Ibid., 4.
10. Matthew Holden, Jr., "The Rewards of Daring and the Ambiguity of Power: Perspectives on the Wilder Election of 1989," in *The State of Black America, 1990,* ed. Janet Dewart (New York: National Urban League, 1990), 117. According to Alan Rosenthal, Virginia's governors are powerful due to the state's political culture, which is deferential "with considerable respect accorded to the chief executive." See his *Governors and Legislatures: Contending Powers* (Washington, D.C.: Congressional Quarterly Press, 1990), 197–98.
11. Alvin J. Schexnider, "Pragmatic Politics in Virginia: Understanding the 1989 Gubernatorial Election," paper presented at the annual meeting of the National Conference of Black Political Scientists, 1990, esp. 11–12.
12. Glenn Abney and Thomas R. Lauth, "The Line Item Veto in the United States: An Instrument for Fiscal Restraint or an Instrument for Partnership?" *Public Administration Review* 45 (1985): 372–77.
13. Holden, "Rewards of Daring," 117.
14. *Norfolk Journal and Guide,* Mar. 9, 1990.

15. There is a vast literature on this subject. See, for example, Harlan Cleveland, *The Future Executive* (New York: Harper and Row, 1972); Richard J. Stillman II, *The Rise of the City Manager* (Albuquerque: University of New Mexico Press, 1974); and particularly, Norton Long's insightful "Politicians for Hire," *Public Administration Review* 25 (1965): 115–20.

16. Much of the criticism about the governor's use of the state police helicopter centered around transporting Patricia Kluge, a divorcée and campaign contributor. The governor reimbursed the state for personal travel.

17. See *Chronicle of Higher Education,* Oct. 14, 1992, A22.

18. In addition to the *Urban Affairs Quarterly* minisymposium referenced earlier, several others have discussed this subject. See Joseph P. McCormick II and Charles E. Jones, "Deracialization Revisited: Thinking through the Dilemma," in *Dilemmas of Black Politics: Leadership, Strategy, and Issues,* edited by Georgia A. Persons (New York: HarperCollins, 1993); McCormick, "The November Elections and the Politics of Deracialization," *New Directions,* Jan. 1990, 23–27.

19. Jesse Jackson, "Introduction," in Donald P. Baker, *Wilder: Hold Fast to Dreams* (Washington, D.C.: Seven Locks Press, 1989), xi.

20. Dwayne Yancey, *When Hell Froze Over: The Untold Story of Doug Wilder* (Roanoke, Va.: Taylor Publishing, 1988), 48.

21. Rosenthal, *Governors and Legislatures,* 187.

2

The 1990 U.S. Senate Election in North Carolina

Charles L. Prysby

On the eve of the 1990 U.S. Senate election in North Carolina, observers predicted a very close election. Preelection polls showed conflicting results: one major poll reported Democratic challenger Harvey Gantt ahead of incumbent Republican Jesse Helms, while another major poll showed Helms with a slim lead over Gantt.[1] The widespread consensus was that the election was too close to call. National media attention was focused on the state in anticipation of the remarkable possibility that a liberal black candidate would win a U.S. Senate seat in a southern state. To do so by defeating such a prominent conservative and formidable campaigner as Helms would surely indicate the political arrival of the "New South."

Helms won the election by a surprisingly comfortable margin, 53 to Gantt's 47 percent. Some analysts suggest that Gantt's race affected the inaccuracies of the preelection polls. This possibility was suggested by the results of other elections involving black candidates in which the final outcome differed significantly from polls taken just prior to the election. In the 1989 Virginia gubernatorial election, for example, L. Douglas Wilder won by less than 1 percent of the vote even though he had been projected to triumph by a comfortable margin.[2] Scholars have suggested that in races involving a black candidate some whites are less than completely candid about their voting intentions with pollsters. If in these situations polls overstate support for black candidates by about four points—a figure suggested by some analysts—then the U.S. Senate race in North Carolina may not really have been too close to call on election eve.

Although Gantt lost, his performance was impressive in some ways. Senator Helms beat Jim Hunt by a 52 to 48 percent margin in 1984, and Hunt was a popular two-term white incumbent governor. Gantt, by contrast, was a liberal black who had never run in a statewide election (his political experience consisted of having served as a council member and mayor of the city of Charlotte). Helms not only had the campaign experience and name recognition of a three-term incumbent U.S. senator but also the ability to raise substantial campaign funds as the bête noire of American liberals. That Gantt came almost as close to defeating Helms as did Hunt might suggest that Gantt's race was little, if any, disadvantage.

The widespread interest in this election indicates that it is worthwhile to carefully explore what actually happened in the campaign and election. In the course of discussing the campaign context and election results, several questions about the Gantt-Helms contest are critical. First, why did Gantt almost match Hunt's 1984 performance despite the obvious advantages possessed by Hunt? Second, what factors account for the 1990 election outcome? Third, within these broader questions, what specific effect did Gantt's race have? Finally, what lessons does this election hold for black candidates seeking election to higher office in the South through a deracialization strategy? Answers to these questions will improve our understanding of the future prospects for both black and southern politics.

The Gantt Nomination and Campaign

Gantt's campaign strategy rested in large part on the belief that 1990 would be a better year than 1984 for challenging Helms. Hunt's attempt to defeat Helms occurred during a presidential election year that was extremely favorable to Republicans, both nationally and in North Carolina. But as an off-year election following a Republican presidential victory, 1990 was expected to be a propitious year for Democratic candidates. In fact, 1990 was the first time that Helms would have to run for election in a year considered less than favorable for Republicans. Helms was first elected to the senate in 1972, a presidential election year that was very advantageous for Republicans, especially in the South. In 1978 he was reelected in an off-year election that was moderately beneficial for Republicans, in which he faced a very weak Democratic opponent. Helms's third election coincided with President Ronald Reagan's landslide reelection in 1984 and with a strong showing by Republicans in North Carolina, including a rare gubernatorial victory.

While the political climate in 1990 gave Gantt good reason to believe that he could improve upon Hunt's 1984 performance, such hopes should have been tempered by fears that it would probably not be an outstanding year for Democrats. Off-year gains in congressional elections by the party not in the White House are related to presidential popularity. The less popular the president, the more his party suffers in off-year congressional elections. Bush's job approval rating, although it had declined prior to the election as a result of his handling of the budget negotiations with Congress, still stood at a respectable 54 percent nationally just prior to the election.[3] An October poll of likely voters in North Carolina found 75 percent expressing a favorable assessment of Bush's presidential performance.[4] This would suggest that 1990, while surely better than 1984, would be only a marginally advantageous year for a Democratic challenger.

Gantt also hoped to improve upon Hunt's campaign strategy. The 1984 U.S. Senate election had been extraordinarily expensive—a total of $25 million was spent by the two candidates—and much of the spending went toward the heavily negative advertising campaigns waged by both camps.[5] Many observers felt that Hunt lost in large part because he did not devise an effective response to the negative campaign waged by Helms.[6] Indeed, it is fair to say that Helms won in 1984 primarily by increasing negative views of Hunt, rather than by improving on his own image, which had unusually large negative components for a two-term U.S. senator with a large national following.

Gantt clearly knew what type of campaign Helms would be likely to run, and by 1990 there were more ideas on how to cope with such tactics. While the Gantt strategists may have been confident of their ability to run an effective campaign, they were relative novices compared to the Helms staff, which consisted of a seasoned group of professionals experienced in running a tough statewide race. By contrast, the Gantt team was comprised largely of individuals who had worked with him in his local elections in Charlotte.[7] This difference in campaign experience ultimately may have played a decisive role in the campaign.

Another promising development for Gantt was his ability to secure the nomination without creating deep party rifts. Several candidates opposed Gantt for the nomination, the most serious being Mike Easley, a young prosecuting attorney from the eastern part of the state, R. P. "Bo" Thomas, a former state senator, and John Ingram, a controversial former state insurance commissioner. While no clear leader existed at the start of the primary contest, attacks on opponents were relatively muted, despite the competitive situation. The candidates concentrated their campaigns more on criticism of Helms and arguments about who would be the most likely to defeat Helms in November. The party mood emphasized the need for unity, perhaps because of a feeling that primary divisions had contributed to defeats in some previous general elections, such as the 1984 gubernatorial contest. Thomas, the one candidate to engage in harsh criticism of his opponents, was publicly rebuked by party leaders, who reminded him of the need to concentrate on the real opponent, Helms.[8]

Gantt emerged as the clear leader in the May primary, with 38 percent of the vote. Easley followed with 30 percent, and Ingram and Thomas trailed with 17 percent and 12 percent, respectively. While Gantt's showing was impressive, it was less than what was needed for outright victory under the state's runoff primary provisions. North Carolina's runoff primary, like that of other southern states, was seen by some as a significant barrier to black candidates capturing the nomination for high offices. Black leaders pressed for its elimination. As a compromise, the North Carolina legislature in 1989 lowered the margin required for a first-round victory from 50 percent to 40 percent of the vote. Since Gantt failed to reach even this lowered threshold, he was faced with a runoff in June against Easley. Gantt argued that in the interest of party unity Easley should accept the first round as decisive and not call for a runoff, but Easley was unreceptive to this view.[9]

The fear among Gantt supporters was that the white vote would unite behind Easley in the runoff primary. This was the argument generally made against the runoff primary in the South, and it was in fact what happened in 1982 in the Second Congressional District in North Carolina, when a black candidate led the Democratic field with 42 percent of the vote but lost in the runoff.[10] This case was cited repeatedly by Jesse Jackson in his quest to eliminate runoff primaries in the South. Fears of a divisive runoff campaign marked by racial polarization were quickly dispelled. Both candidates avoided vitriolic attacks. Even in a debate televised statewide, Gantt and Easley were remarkably polite, engaging in only mild criticism of each other's positions. When Gantt emerged from the runoff with 57 percent of the vote and with Easley's warm endorsement, it was clear that he had not only the nomination but also a united party behind him.

Gantt's ability to forge a biracial coalition for the nomination was an early indication of his ability to pursue a deracialized campaign. Even though Gantt could expect to win most black votes, this would not be nearly sufficient for victory in a state where 70 percent of the registered Democrats were white. Gantt's ability to appeal to a significant share of white Democrats allowed him to win the runoff primary—an appeal that was accomplished in part by projecting a reassuring personal style and by avoiding divisive issues.

To run a competitive general election campaign, it was crucial for Gantt to accumulate sufficient campaign funds. Helms was renowned for his ability to raise money, especially through direct mail appeals. Without comparable resources, Gantt would have been unable to run the media campaign that most observers felt would be necessary for victory. Concerns that this could be a serious problem for Gantt were based on his lack of name recognition and inexperience in raising large sums of campaign funds. Surprisingly, money turned out not to be a problem for Gantt; he raised and spent about $7.8 million.[11] This was less than the $13.4 million that Helms reported spending in 1990 (Helms also raised and spent $4.4 million between 1985 and 1989, the majority of which was used to retire debts from the 1984 campaign), but the difference in candidate resources was more perception than reality. Helms's heavy use of direct mailings required that considerable sums of money be spent soliciting funds from a nationwide list of potential contributors. While Helms's campaign finance reports are unclear about the amount spent in soliciting donations, a fair estimate is that Helms had only a small advantage in funds available for actual campaigning. Gantt clearly had sufficient financial resources to run a competitive campaign.

Gantt's success in fund-raising was due in part to opposition to Helms from across the country. Over 60 percent of Gantt's contributions came from outside North Carolina.[12] Much of this probably came from sources who would have contributed to any liberal candidate perceived to have a good chance of defeating Helms. Helms also received about 60 percent of his funds from outside the state, primarily from individuals who enthusiastically support his conservative positions. Not only did Helms polarize the North Carolina electorate, he polarized political contributors around the country, so that fund-raising became a question of symbolically supporting good against evil. For Gantt to tap into this reservoir of funds he had to convince potential contributors that he had a realistic chance of winning. Gantt demonstrated his potential electability both by impressive showings in early polls, such as respected independent statewide polls in June and early August that had him ahead, and by poll results displaying potential vulnerability for Helms because of his high "negatives."[13] The considerable national media attention focused on the race and the fact that the Democratic party was solidly united behind Gantt undoubtedly helped his fund-raising efforts as well. Clearly, Gantt's race was not an impediment to his securing campaign funds. Those wishing to contribute to Helms's defeat displayed little if any reluctance to make a contribution to a black challenger, another sign of Gantt's ability to pursue a deracialization strategy.

Simply having the resources to run does not guarantee an effective campaign, as Hunt discovered in 1984. Gantt's strategy involved several related themes. First, he would not disavow being a liberal, as Hunt did in 1984, but rather would emphasize his difference with Helms on a set of economic issues, including education and environmental protection. Second, he would attempt to portray Helms as a senator who cared little about the concerns of ordinary citizens. And third, he would avoid becoming entangled in the kind of tit-for-tat negative campaigning that characterized the 1984 contest. By focusing the campaign on economic issues and on Helms's performance, Gantt hoped to put Helms on the defensive and make the election into a referendum on whether Helms was the kind of U.S. Senator that North Carolina needed in the 1990s.

Gantt's campaign themes noticeably lacked racial overtones. Not only did he avoid focusing on civil rights issues, he also did not emphasize issues with strong indirect racial ties, such as welfare reform. Gantt's televised commercials in early September repeatedly criticized Helms for opposing federal spending for education. One sound bite stated that Helms "voted against President Bush's plan for educational excellence."[14] Gantt also attacked his opponent for favoring oil companies and for failing to criticize them for price-gouging and environmental damage. Helms responded with commercials defending his positions and charging that Gantt's attacks distorted the truth, but Helms was clearly on the defensive, a new and uncomfortable position for Helms in a campaign.

Gantt proved to be an effective campaigner. At the same time, Helms had difficulties in balancing his time between meeting his Senate obligations and campaigning for reelection. As expected, the Helms strategy aimed at painting Gantt as an extreme liberal, especially on social issues, but the Helms commercials during the early stages did not seem particularly damaging to Gantt. One series of commercials charged that Gantt favored allowing abortions to be conducted in the final weeks of pregnancy, on the basis of the gender of the unborn child.[15] These ads may have backfired, however; such extreme accusations may not have seemed credible, and raising the abortion issue drew attention to the fact that Helms opposed allowing abortion even in cases of rape and incest, which the Gantt campaign highlighted in its response. The net result was that neither candidate had an advantage on this issue.

As the campaign continued, Helms's organization developed a more forceful negative media campaign. Commercials released in late October accused Gantt of backing mandatory gay rights laws, claiming also that he was raising money through advertisements in gay newspapers and visits to gay bars.[16] Commercials also criticized Gantt for opposing the death penalty, favoring tax increases, and supporting massive defense cuts. Repeatedly, Helms's commercials emphasized that Gantt was "extremely liberal" or had "extremely liberal values." Racial issues were also visibly interjected into the campaign in the final weeks. Helms charged that Gantt and other business partners had used their minority status to acquire a television station license from the federal government in 1985, which was then sold to a white-owned company for a substantial profit. The implication was that Gantt had unfairly used his race to make a quick financial gain.

In most observers' view, the most damaging commercial focused on the recent civil rights bill that Bush had vetoed on the grounds that it would lead to quotas—a bill that had been opposed by Helms and favored by Gantt. Broadcast just days before the election, the commercial showed the hands of a white man opening a letter and then crumpling it up. The voice-over stated, "You needed that job. And you were the best qualified. But they had to give it to a minority because of a racial quota."[17]

The emphasis on racial issues in the later stages of the campaign coincided with a more aggressive overall approach by Helms. Eight days before the campaign, he returned from Washington to campaign full-time. Once again North Carolina was treated to vintage Helms. Stumping across the state, Helms stressed conservative values, attacked Gantt for being extremely liberal and a liar, and raised many so-called "hot-button" issues, such as federal funding for obscene art and job quotas for minorities.[18] Gantt seemed on the defensive at this point, unprepared for the Helms campaign blitz and unable to mount an effective counterattack to the assault. Perhaps the greater experience of the Helms campaign staff was a decisive factor in the end game. Exit poll results suggest that the final week of the campaign had a significant impact. About one-seventh of voters reported that they made their decisions during the last week of the campaign, and 60 percent of these voted for Helms.[19]

Election Results

An analysis of both exit poll data and aggregate election statistics provides insight into the election. The exit poll conducted by Voter Research and Surveys (VRS) reveals an interesting demographic portrait of the Helms and Gantt vote. As anticipated, black and white voters divided sharply, with over 90 percent of blacks voting for Gantt but only around 35 percent of whites doing so. The rule of thumb in North Carolina is that a Democratic candidate needs about 40 percent of the white vote to win; had Gantt attained that figure, he would have received 51 percent of the total vote.

The crucial analytical question is why Gantt was unable to attract sufficient white voters to win the election. A separate analysis of the white vote will highlight the relationships that exist within the white electorate, which can be distorted when looking at all voters due to enormous racial differences on many factors. Drawing on the VRS exit poll results, a number of demographic and attitudinal variables can be examined. The VRS North Carolina sample contained about twelve hundred white respondents, about 37 percent of whom voted for Gantt (the discrepancy between this figure and the 35 percent reported above is due to the fact that VRS interviewed additional North Carolina residents as part of a national sample, but a shorter questionnaire was used for this group, so they are not included in the analysis results reported below).

Table 2–1 presents a breakdown of white voters by several social and demographic characteristics. Two notable relationships stand out. First, the usual association between socioeconomic status and partisanship does not appear in this election. Income is relatively unrelated to the reported vote among whites, and while there is a clear connection between education and candidate preference, it is the reverse of what normally exists between

Democrats and Republicans. Second, younger voters were much more likely than older to report having voted for Gantt. Helms was apparently quite successful in capturing the votes of older white voters of lower socioeconomic status, a group that traditionally has been more aligned with the Democratic party but that is also likely to be conservative on a variety of issues. This group of voters is sometimes called "Jessecrats," and their support distinguishes the Helms base of support from that of most other Republicans in the state.[20] This pattern would be expected if white voters cast their ballots on the basis of racial issues. Older and less educated whites would be more likely to hold conservative views on race-related issues and more likely to be personally opposed to having a black individual hold high elected office.

Extending this argument, "Jessecrat" support should be more prevalent in rural areas where conservative, older, low-income whites are disproportionately concentrated. Unfortunately, the VRS data do not permit a geographical breakdown of respondents, so aggregated election statistics are used to help identify the geographic base of "Jessecrat" support. To facilitate

TABLE 2–1

Social and Demographic Characteristics of Whites Voting for Gantt, 1990

Characteristic	Gantt %	Number
Gender		
Female	40	613
Male	35	379
Age		
18–29	46	227
30–49	37	611
50 and over	33	375
Education		
High school only	25	355
Some college	33	321
College graduate	48	485
Income		
Less than $30,000	37	400
$30,000–50,000	36	662
$50,000 and up	39	361
State residency		
Less than 10 years	54	170
More than 10 years	42	326
Native of state	32	710

Source: North Carolina exit poll data, 1990, supplied by Voter Research and Surveys.

the analysis in this regard, North Carolina's counties are categorized as (1) metropolitan (the counties containing the five major cities in the state—Charlotte, Raleigh, Greensboro, Winston-Salem, and Durham), (2) urban (the counties containing the cities of Asheville and Wilmington plus four urbanized counties adjacent to the metropolitan counties), (3) eastern rural counties, (4) western rural counties, and (5) piedmont rural counties (located in the center of the state, where the five metropolitan counties are also located).

Table 2–2 provides election results for the 1984, 1986, and 1990 U.S. Senate elections by county type. This is the total vote, not just the white vote (the 1990 data on blacks are included in the table to aid the interpretation). Two conclusions are clear from the table. First, Gantt did well in the metropolitan and urban counties that collectively accounted for 42 percent of the total vote, although this performance obviously was not strong enough to make up for his poorer performance in the rural counties. Second, the Gantt vote was not solely a function of the proportion of African Americans. Gantt did much better in the urban counties than in the piedmont rural counties, even though both areas have a similar racial composition. These data, combined with the data in Table 2–1, confirm the conclusion that the rural, older, less-educated white vote went heavily to Helms.

The strength of the Helms electoral base can also be ascertained by comparing the 1990 data with the 1984 and 1986 data in Table 2–2. The two elections involving Helms, 1984 and 1990, have similar patterns. In those two elections, the Democratic opponent ran strongest in the metropolitan counties and weakest in the western and piedmont rural counties. The 1986 U.S. Senate election in North Carolina between Democrat Terry Sanford and Republican Jim Broyhill was quite different. Sanford ran best in the eastern

TABLE 2–2

Election Results by County Type, 1984, 1986, and 1990

County Type[1] (N)	Black[2] % 1990	Gantt % 1990	Hunt % 1984	Sanford % 1986
Metropolitan (5)	22.6	55.7	52.8	52.7
Urban (6)	16.0	49.2	49.1	51.2
Eastern rural (39)	28.3	46.7	50.9	61.4
Western rural (23)	3.3	41.7	42.8	44.6
Piedmont rural (27)	15.3	40.0	42.4	47.0
Entire state (100)	19.0	47.4	48.1	51.9

Source: Calculated from aggregate election results and registration data supplied by the North Carolina Board of Elections.

1. See text for an explanation of county classifications.

2. Refers to percentage of registered voters who are black.

rural counties, and he did better in the western and piedmont rural counties than Hunt in 1984 and Gantt in 1990.

Additional insight into the appeal of Gantt to white voters may be obtained by a deeper analysis of these geographical patterns, specifically with respect to the relationship between the Helms vote and the racial composition of the electorate (Table 2–3). The key calculation is the ratio of the Helms percentage of the vote to the white percentage of the electorate. If it is assumed that the Helms vote came entirely from whites and that the racial composition of those who voted was identical to that of registered voters, then the ratio would be a measure of the proportion of white registered voters who voted for Helms. Although not completely accurate, these assumptions permit some meaningful comparisons. For example, the ratio for the entire state indicates that Helms received the vote of 66 percent of whites, which is close to the 65 percent reported by the VRS exit poll.

The highest ratio occurs in the eastern rural counties that have the highest concentration of blacks. The next highest ratio is in the piedmont rural counties that have a smaller but significant black population. But in the western rural counties, which are almost entirely white, Helms received 61 percent of the white vote, not much different from what he received in the metropolitan and urban counties. The appeal of Helms to white voters in rural areas is directly related to the presence of blacks, suggesting that the "Jessecrat" appeal is based in part on race-related issues. The relationship between the size of the black population and the political conservatism of whites on racial issues is a familiar one in southern politics,[21] and it is not sur-

TABLE 2–3

White Component of Helms Vote by County Type, 1990

County Type[1] (No.)	Helms %	White %[2]	Helms/White Ratio[3]
Metropolitan (5)	44.3	76.8	.58
Urban (6)	50.8	83.3	.61
Eastern rural (39)	53.3	68.8	.77
Western rural (23)	58.3	96.1	.61
Piedmont rural (27)	60.0	84.1	.71
Entire state (100)	52.6	80.0	.66

Source: Calculated from aggregate election results and registration data supplied by the North Carolina Board of Elections.

1. See text for an explanation of county classifications.

2. Refers to percentage of registered voters who are white.

3. This column represents the ratio of the percentage in the first column to the percentage in the second column (i.e., the ratio of the Helms percentage to the white percentage).

prising to find it pronounced in this election.[22] These findings reinforce the earlier conclusion about the significance of race-related issues in the election.

These demographic patterns fit with the results of an analysis of the attitudinal sources of the votes cast in the 1990 U.S. Senate election in North Carolina. Drawing on the VRS exit poll data, and focusing only on whites, Table 2–4 shows that Gantt received votes from only 62 percent of self-identified Democrats. Many of the defecting Democrats undoubtedly fit the "Jessecrat" profile. Although Gantt had trouble with this group, he did reasonably well among white independents and even attracted a modest number of votes from Republicans. Had Gantt been able to win the vote of 70 percent of white Democrats, he would have received about 40 percent of the total white vote, enough to have won the election.

Several factors hampered Gantt's ability to attract more white voters. The attitudinal sources of voting behavior are usually divided into three basic categories: (1) evaluations of government performance, (2) orientations on issues of public policy, and (3) assessments of candidate characteristics. Each of

TABLE 2–4

The Gantt Vote by Selected Attitudes of Whites, 1990

	Gantt (%)	(No.)
Party identity		
Democrat	62	(423)
Independent	41	(213)
Republican	14	(504)
Ideology		
Liberal	80	(145)
Moderate	50	(528)
Conservative	10	(484)
Bush job performance		
Approve	25	(619)
Disapprove	67	(338)
Evaluation of national economy		
Excellent/good	21	(308)
Fair/poor	43	(858)
Evaluation of state economy		
Excellent/good	24	(535)
Fair/poor	48	(654)

Source: North Carolina exit poll data, supplied by Voter Research and Surveys.

these can be briefly examined with the VRS exit poll data. Table 2–4 provides some information on the relationship between performance evaluations and the vote for whites. As expected, Gantt did much better among those who disapproved of Bush's presidential performance and who had a more pessimistic view of the national and state economy. While these relationships are strong, the distributions on the variables are fairly favorable for Helms (last column in Table 2–4). A large number of white voters thought that Bush was doing a good job as president, and, while a large number of white voters had an unfavorable assessment of the national economy, the evaluation of the North Carolina economy was not nearly so negative.

Since the election pitted a well-known conservative against an avowed liberal, there is little surprise in finding that candidate choice was strongly related to the voter's ideological placement, with Gantt receiving 80 percent of the white liberal vote but only 10 percent of the white conservative vote (Table 2–4). What may be surprising, however, is the fact that Gantt was not hurt by his stand on several key policy issues. While the exit poll data contain only limited information about issues, respondents were asked to indicate which one or two issues (out of a list of five) were most important in deciding their vote (Table 2–5). Abortion was the most frequently cited issue, reflecting the considerable attention it received in the campaign. But among whites, abortion was cited only slightly more by Gantt voters than by Helms voters as a crucial factor in their electoral decision. A preelection poll by the National Abortion Rights Action League suggested much the same finding—there were as many votes to be won on one side of the abortion issue as on the other. Similar conclusions can be reached for other important policy issues, such as defense spending and the budget deficit reduction plan. The death penalty, which Helms supported and Gantt opposed, was one issue where Helms had a big advantage among white voters, but it was cited as important by only one out of five Helms voters.

The VRS exit poll data did not include affirmative action as one of the issues on the list given to respondents, and there were no other items about affirmative action or civil rights on the questionnaire. This omission is unfortunate, because there is reason to believe that these issues played an important role. As discussed earlier, the Helms campaign concentrated on race-related issues during the final days of the campaign. The "white hands" commercial was credited by numerous analysts as pulling many whites over to Helms. Although the effect of affirmative action or civil rights issues on white voters cannot be directly measured with the available data, strong indirect evidence suggests that the effect was considerable. The movement toward Helms during the final week of the campaign, when these issues were being stressed by Helms, is consistent with this interpretation. The stronger support for Helms among whites in rural areas with high black concentrations also

TABLE 2-5

The Most Important Gantt-Helms Issues for Whites by Vote, 1990

Issue	Gantt %	Helms %
Abortion	36	33
Federal budget deficit plan	26	27
National economy	30	22
Defense spending	20	20
Death penalty	7	19
(No.)	(455)	(763)

Source: North Carolina exit poll data, 1990, supplied by Voter Research and Surveys.

Note: This table indicates the percentage of Gantt and Helms voters who cited a particular issue as one of the two most important issues that decided their vote (e.g., 36 percent of the Gantt voters said that abortion was a key issue in their voting decision). Issues that were cited by less than 10 percent of both sets of voters are not included. Percentages total to more than 100 percent because respondents were allowed to select up to two important issues.

supports this conclusion. Finally, the fact that other key issues did not give Helms a particular advantage suggests that it was this set of issues that played an important role in the Helms victory.

Voters are influenced by the personal characteristics of the candidates as well as by issues. The VRS exit poll also asked respondents to indicate which one or two candidate characteristics (out of a list of seven) were most influential in deciding their vote (Table 2-6). Helms voters cited "experience," "hardworking," and "able to get things done"—all of which are tied to incumbency—considerably more than did Gantt voters. Of course, such results are expected in an election in which a three-term incumbent faces a challenger who has never won a statewide office. More interestingly, the Gantt voters generally cited characteristics that had to do with his opponent (e.g., "too extreme," "too negative") as being crucial factors in their voting decisions. Even the 31 percent of the Gantt voters who said that they wanted a "new face" could be classified as reacting more to Helms's characteristics. The same is true about the 26 percent of Gantt voters who said they wanted a candidate who "cares more about North Carolina."

Thus, Helms polarized the electorate not only on racial issues but also in terms of his personal characteristics. Some voters felt that he was a dedicated man of principle who fought hard to defend basic American values.

TABLE 2–6

The Most Important Gantt-Helms Candidate
Characteristics for Whites by Vote, 1990

Characteristic	Gantt %	Helms %
Experience	5	51
Able to get things done	9	15
Hardworking	10	18
Cares more about North Carolina	26	19
Opponent too extreme	31	20
Opponent too negative	25	5
New face	31	1
(No.)	(455)	(763)

Source: North Carolina exit poll data, 1990, supplied by Voter
Research and Surveys.

Note: This table indicates the percentage of Gantt and Helms
voters who cited a particular candidate characteristic as one of the
two most important factors that decided their vote (e.g., 5 percent
of the Gantt voters said that his experience was a key factor in their
voting decision). Characteristics that were cited by less than 10
percent of both sets of voters are not included. Percentages total to
more than 100 percent because respondents were allowed to select
up to two important characteristics.

Others saw him as a nasty, divisive demagogue. Many of these perceptions
undoubtedly were present well before the election, and the campaign apparently reinforced both views. It does appear, however, that Gantt was unable
during the campaign to create a sufficiently positive image among the white
electorate of his own abilities, such as being capable and hardworking. Negative assessments of Gantt's personal characteristics were not particularly
prevalent, although some did exist, but strong positive attitudes were absent.

Thus, Gantt lost the election because he was unable to win about 40
percent of the white vote, and he was unable to do so because of the conservatism of white voters, especially on race-related issues, the strongly positive
evaluations whites had of Bush's job performance, and the somewhat tepid assessment whites had of Gantt's personal characteristics. However, Gantt did
as well as he did because he was as close as Helms to the midpoint of public
opinion on several key issues, most notably abortion and dissatisfaction with
the performance of the national economy, and because in personal terms he
evoked little negative reaction, unlike his opponent.

Elections are won not only by winning the allegiance of those who in-
tend to vote but also by mobilizing potential supporters to go to the polls. In

TABLE 2–7

Registration and Turnout Data, 1986 and 1990

	1986 %	1990 %
Registered people who voted	51.3	61.3
Total registration increase, Apr. to Oct.	2.0	6.3
White registration increase, Apr. to Oct.	2.0	5.3
Black registration increase, Apr. to Oct.	2.0	10.6
Democratic regist. increase, Apr. to Oct.	1.3	5.6
Republican regist. increase, Apr. to Oct.	3.6	6.2

Source: Calculated from aggregate election results and registration figures supplied by the North Carolina Board of Elections.

Note: Registration increases are calculated from April to October because
registration closes thirty days prior to the May primary and the November
general election.

this regard, the Helms-Gantt contest was an election that both motivated
people to register and stimulated registered voters to cast a ballot. Over 61 percent of those registered voted in the 1990 U.S. Senate election in North Carolina, a figure that is close to the turnout rate of a presidential year and is ten
points higher than the turnout rate in 1986, the previous off-year U.S. Senate
election in North Carolina (Table 2–7). Moreover, it was 61 percent of an en-
larged base of registered voters. Registration surged during the months prior
to the election; over 6 percent more voters registered between April and October, more than three times the increase in 1986 for the same period. Gantt
probably benefited slightly from the large black registration increase in 1990.

Conclusion

What effect did Gantt's race have on the election outcome? To answer this
question, this analysis has distinguished between the race of the candidate
and race-related issues. The latter probably played a pivotal role in this election, as the analysis indicates, but that is different from claiming that Gantt's
race had a major impact. The proper question is whether a white candidate
who was otherwise identical to Gantt would have fared better.

A case can be made that Gantt's race had only a small impact on the
election outcome. First, Gantt does not appear to have experienced rejection
by racially antagonistic white voters; if anything, the analysis indicates that
Gantt benefited slightly from the unusually large registration increases and
turnout in 1990. Moreover, if a significant number of people voted against
Gantt solely because he is black, then the geographical and demographic

correlates of the vote in 1990 would differ from those observed in 1984, when Helms faced a white Democrat. Such is not the case. Very little difference in the geographical patterns between the two elections is evident (Table 2–2), and the 1984 polling data reveal very similar social and demographic sources of the vote.[23]

Yet there is evidence that Gantt's race was not irrelevant. Eleven percent of the white Helms voters interviewed in the VRS exit poll responded that the race of the candidate was the single most important factor in deciding how they would vote. On the other hand, only 3 percent of the same respondents selected race from a list of nine candidate characteristics as one of the two most important factors affecting their vote. Why is there such a discrepancy in responses to these two items? Further complicating the interpretation is the likelihood that of the respondents who indicated in one or both items that race was an important factor, some may have been conservative Republicans who would have voted for Helms over a white liberal in any case.

One other factor suggests that Gantt's race had at least a small effect: preelection polls overestimated Gantt's support. The reason for this lies in the undecided respondents. In recent elections where a black candidate has faced a white candidate, the undecided voters in the preelection polls have been almost entirely white, and they have voted very heavily for the white candidate on election day.[24] No doubt some of these undecided respondents would have voted for Helms even if Gantt had been white, but some may represent truly ambivalent voters who in the end were swayed partly by the race of the candidates. Thus, both the preelection and exit poll data suggest that race had a small effect. The number of voters who altered their ballot decision because of this factor is probably very small—perhaps 1–2 percent—but even a small fraction of the electorate could be decisive in a close race. Unfortunately, these data are not sufficiently precise to allow specification of the exact magnitude of the effect.

While Gantt's race appears to have had only a very small effect, race-related issues appear to have been quite important. These issues also could have been used by Helms in a campaign against a white liberal, but it is likely that a black candidate is somewhat more vulnerable in this area. Even when a black candidate pursues a deracialization strategy and avoids emphasizing racial issues, voters may still assume that the candidate holds liberal views on these issues. In the case of a white candidate, voters may be less willing to impute liberal views in the absence of much information about the candidate's issue positions.

The results of this study suggest an ambivalent conclusion. There is a "New South." Black candidates can win the nomination of a united Democratic party for a major statewide office, and they can run just as well as white candidates in the general election, winning or losing for much the same reasons that whites win or lose. In this regard, Gantt's campaign surely was an encouragement to other black candidates. But there is still an "Old South." Race-related issues, such as affirmative action, remain salient, and they would have been important even if a white liberal Democrat had faced Helms. In this sense, race is still a wedge that Republicans can use to split the black-white coalition necessary for Democratic success. But the existence of this wedge does not prevent a successful deracialized campaign for a major office in the South. Gantt's loss was not inevitable. Quite plausibly, a different strategy during the final few weeks of the campaign could have blunted the Helms attack and changed the election outcome. Gantt's success in obtaining the nomination of a united party, raising sufficient campaign funds, and avoiding strong negative personal assessments among voters provides a strong foundation for a successful deracialized campaign in southern politics.

Notes

A number of individuals and organizations contributed to this study. Warren Mitofsky and Lee C. Shapiro, of Voter Research and Surveys, kindly supplied me with exit poll data for North Carolina. Seth Effron, of the *Greensboro News and Record,* provided important data and shared his insights into the campaign. Bob Flaherty, Jim Clotfelter, and Dave Olson made valuable suggestions that contributed to this project. Support for this research was provided by a Research Council grant from University of North Carolina at Greensboro. I appreciate the assistance of the above individuals and organizations.

1. Robert Christensen, "Helms Holds Slim Lead over Gantt New Poll Shows," *Raleign News and Observer,* Nov. 2, 1990, 1A; Jim Morrill, "Gantt Retains Lead Going into Final Days," *Charlotte Observer,* Nov. 3, 1990, 1A.

2. Richard Morin, "The Outcome Is There in Black and White," *Washington Post National Weekly Edition,* Feb. 25, 1991, 37.

3. *Gallup Poll Monthly: October 1990* (Princeton, N.J.: Gallup Poll Organization, 1990).

4. Kate Michelman and Ruth Zieglar, *Recent North Carolina Poll Reports on Choice,* pamphlet (Durham, N.C.: National Abortion Rights Action League, North Carolina PAC, October 17, 1990).

5. William O. Snider, *Helms and Hunt: The North Carolina Senate Race, 1984* (Chapel Hill: University of North Carolina Press, 1985), 209.

6. Snider, *Helms and Hunt,* 209; Paul Luebke, *Tar Heel Politics: Myths and Realities* (Chapel Hill: University of North Carolina Press, 1990), 140–42.

7. Elizabeth Leland, "Campaign Teams Help Call Shots," *Charlotte Observer,* Oct. 7, 1990, 1A.

8. Steve Riley, "Party Criticizes Thomas," *Raleigh News and Observer,* May 6, 1990, 1A.

9. Paul Taylor, "Runoff Issue Pits Minorities, Parties," *Raleigh News and Observer,* May 14, 1990, 2A.

10. Luebke, *Tar Heel Politics,* 118.

11. Seth Effron, "Helms' Pockets Deeper," *Greensboro News and Record,* Feb. 26, 1991.

12. Ted Mellnick and Jim Morrill, "Both Camps Bank on Helms' Image," *Charlotte Observer,* Oct. 21, 1990, 1A.

13. *North Carolina Poll: Survey Report (August),* pamphlet (Baltimore, Md.: Mason-Dixon Opinion Research, 1990).

14. Effron, "Gantt versus Helms: The Air Waves," *Greensboro News and Record,* Sept. 7, 1990a, B2.

15. Effron, "Gantt versus Helms: The Air Waves," *Greensboro News and Record,* Sept. 8, 1990b, B2.

16. Effron, "Helms TV Ad Accuses Gantt of Running Secret Campaign,'" *Greensboro News and Record,* Oct. 24, 1990c, B2.

17. Effron, "Gantt vs. Helms: The Air Waves," *Greensboro News and Record,* Nov. 3, 1990d, B2.

18. John Drescher, "Helms Got Home, Heat Came On," *Charlotte Observer,* Nov. 9, 1990, 1A.

19. Voter Research and Surveys, "Results of the VRS North Carolina 1990 Exit Poll" (New York: Voter Research and Surveys, 1991).

20. Jack D. Fleer, Roger C. Lowery, and Charles L. Prysby, "Political Change in North Carolina," in *The South's New Politics: Realignment and Dealignment,* edited by Robert H. Swansbrough and David M. Brodsky (Columbia: University of South Carolina Press, 1988), 94–111.

21. Charles L. Prysby, "Attitudes of Southern Democratic Party Activists toward Jesse Jackson: The Effects of the Local Context," *Journal of Politics* 51 (1989): 305–18; Gerald C. Wright, Jr., "Contextual Models of Electoral Behavior: The Southern Wallace Vote," *American Political Science Review* 71 (1977): 497–508; William R. Keech, *The Impact of Negro Voting: The Role of the Vote in the Quest for Equality* (Chicago: Rand McNally, 1968).

22. Prysby, "Attitudes of Southern Democratic Party Activists," 305–18; Wright, "Contextual Models," 497–508.

23. Fleer et al., "Political Change," 94–111.

24. Morin, "Outcome Is There."

3

The Election of Carol Moseley-Braun in the U.S. Senate Race in Illinois

Roger K. Oden

This chapter focuses on Carol Moseley-Braun's election as the first African American woman to the U.S. Senate and how it relates to the concept of deracialization. Deracialization is a recent concept whose central tenet is built around a set of assumptions that holds that African American electoral candidates in majority white districts and jurisdictions must deemphasize racial themes in their campaigns in order to maximize their chances of attracting enough white votes to win elections.

The concept has its foundation in the literatures of post–World War II southern politics and black and urban politics, as well as in the political experiences of the 1960s and 1970s. A selected literature review in the next section establishes a theoretical framework for understanding these origins.

Deracialization and Contemporary African American Politics

In its current context, deracialization was advanced with the elections of 1989, in which nine African American candidates were elected or reelected to public office. Huey L. Perry notes in the introduction to this volume that the 1989 elections are important in this regard because of the large number of blacks who won election to public office and the fact that some of these positions had never before been filled by blacks. Four of the nine successful black candidates ran deracialized campaigns.

The theoretical and practical significance of deracialization as a concept relates to its ability to explain the increase in the number of black elected officials in districts and jurisdictions that are not predominantly black and in which campaign strategies and rhetoric are not racially centered. Studies examining the validity of the concept have focused on elections that cover municipal as well as statewide jurisdictions. Elections in which black candidates have won with a combination of majority white and minority black support from a congressional district are also addressed with the concept of deracialization. In his introduction Perry provides a typology that facilitates an understanding of the emergence of black elected officials who have successfully employed the deracialization concept:

> The first type involves black candidates running against white opponents, usually in majority white districts and jurisdictions. The campaigns in this type are characterized by black candidates emphasizing black issues. . . . A second type of black electoral success has been characterized by blacks running for office against other black candidates in majority black districts and jurisdictions and quietly appealing for white voter support. This type of black electoral activity emerged on the political landscape within the last five to ten years. In this case, white voters usually determine the winner of the election, and successful black candidates generally receive strong majority support from whites. . . . The third and most recent type of successful black electoral activity consists of African American candidates running in majority white districts and jurisdictions, usually against white opponents, and strongly appealing for white voter support. In the effort to attract white electoral support, these candidates usually do not make strong racial appeals in their campaign. This type of election constitutes the essence of a deracialized election.

The third type of black electoral activity holds the greatest potential for increasing the number of black elected officials. It also prompts two important questions about political life in the United States: Will the need to win majority white districts and jurisdictions produce black candidates different from those of the first and second type? Will black elected officials who successfully employ the deracialized campaign approach govern differently from the black elected officials of the first and second type who based their campaign on issues of relevance for blacks? These are two important questions that constitute fertile ground for scholarly research.

Addressing the deracialization phenomenon and using the 1989 elections as the basis for their analysis of the deracialization concept, Joseph McCormick II and Charles E. Jones offer a reformulation of the concept of deracialization. Central to their reformulation is an emphasis on the distinction between deracialization as an agenda-setting strategy and its use as an electoral strategy. In McCormick and Jones's definition, the agenda-setting strategy component of deracialization is "connected with governance after elections have been won" and the electoral strategy component of deracialization is "connected with attempts to capture office in majority white jurisdictions."[1]

Having distinguished between agenda-setting and electoral strategies, McCormick and Jones restrict their analysis to the "electoral variant" of deracialization. They divide the electoral variant of deracialization into three components:

> (1) The "saturation thesis/counterthesis" argues that limits have been reached in terms of the number of African Americans who have been elected in predominantly black districts and jurisdictions. Therefore, African Americans who aspire to be elected to public office are most likely to do so in majority white districts and jurisdictions. The "counter-argument to the saturation thesis maintains that a saturation point of majority black political jurisdictions having reached their limits in terms of their potential yield of black elected officials (BEOs) has yet to be reached" (73).
>
> (2) The "ambition factor" refers to the "fundamental recognition on the [African American] candidate's part that a vital part of the means to the desired electoral end, in a predominantly white political jurisdiction, is the need not only to appeal to black voters—the 'natural' constituent base—but to also generate sufficient white support" (74).
>
> (3) The "subtle racism factor" indicates that in order to maximize one's vote potential, African American candidates running in predominantly white districts or jurisdictions must deemphasize racially explicit policy options during the course of the campaign. This strategy of deemphasis is based on the reality of racism prevalent in white communities (75).

McCormick and Jones's discussion of the three factors in their reformulation of deracialization leads to a particular definition of deracialization as an electoral strategy: "Conducting a campaign in a stylistic fashion that defuses the polarizing effects of race by avoiding explicit reference to race-specific issues, while at the same time emphasizing those issues that are perceived as racially transcendent, thus mobilizing a broad segment of the electorate for the purpose of capturing or maintaining public office" (76).

McCormick and Jones divide deracialization as an electoral strategy into three components: political style, mobilization tactics, and issues (76). Political style indicates that black candidates believe that the way to achieve success in predominantly white districts and jurisdictions is to project a nonthreatening image. The mobilization component means "that African-American candidates in majority white political jurisdictions . . . should avoid employing direct racial appeals in organizing the black community" (76). The issue component of the deracialized electoral strategy indicates that "black candidates should avoid emphasis of a racially specific issues agenda" (76)

McCormick and Jones qualify their reformulation with the observation that the degree to which an African American candidate attempts to deracialize a campaign is dictated by the political context of the interracial contest, in other words, the type and level of elected office being sought, as well as the time and context, geographical region, and political culture in the electoral district or jurisdiction. Their reformulated concept provides a tentative response to Huey L. Perry's question in the introduction: "Will the need to win majority white districts and jurisdictions produce black candidates different than those whose campaigns emphasize black issues?"

McCormick and Jones's deracialized electoral strategy calls for accommodationist political behavior by African Americans seeking to win elections in predominantly white districts and jurisdictions. Their position is akin conceptually to an earlier body of literature on black political leadership, represented by James Q. Wilson. This literature, published in the 1960s, often concentrated on components of black political life—for example, African American votes and leadership—and conclusions were often touted as universal truths about the nature of black politics. The deficiency of this body of literature is that it did not provide a critical analysis of the institutions, structures, and system that limited choices for blacks in their efforts to become fully incorporated into the mainstream of American political life.

While McCormick and Jones's study postdates the Wilson era literature by more than a generation, their reasoning and conclusions do not sufficiently address local and state issues and factors that constrain black candidates from seeking election in majority white districts and jurisdictions. Historical, structural, and institutional constraints on blacks' efforts to seek election to office in majority white districts and jurisdictions are acknowledged by McCormick and Jones, but such acknowledgment appears to be an afterthought (77). An examination of these structures as a primary component of their analysis undoubtedly would have strengthened their redefinition of deracialization. Political culture, liberal and conservative ideological tendencies, community and institutional linkages, black and minority coalitions, cross-community and cross-racial linkages, and the nature of intra- and interpolitical party arrangements should have been integrated into McCormick and Jones's reformulation of deracialization.

The U.S. Senate Primary and Election in Illinois, 1992

Types one and three from Perry's typology of black electoral campaigns can be used in analyzing Carol Moseley-Braun's senatorial primary and general elec-

tion. The first type involves black candidates running against white opponents, usually in majority white districts and jurisdictions. These campaigns
characteristically emphasize black issues. The third type consists of African
American candidates running against white opponents, strongly appealing
for white voter support. Perry identifies type three as the ideal deracialized
campaign.

Illinois statewide demographics and voting patterns provide an analytical and comparative background of how race, gender, city and suburban,
and socioeconomic characteristics played a part in Moseley-Braun's election
to the U.S. senate.

The Primary

Many women responded with anger to the treatment of Anita Hill by the all-
white male Senate Judiciary Committee on the issue of sexual harassment.
After having been encouraged to run for the U.S. Senate by a cross-section of
women who were offended by Hill's treatment at the Clarence Thomas hear-
ings, Moseley-Braun announced her candidacy for the U.S. Senate seat occu-
pied by Alan Dixon. From the outset of her candidacy, Moseley-Braun, a vet-
eran Illinois legislator and the then-incumbent Cook County Registrar of
Deeds, was ideal for the "long-shot" opportunity to challenge Dixon.
Moseley-Braun's performance as a public official had earned her the respect of
Chicago's black voting population, and she had gained access to key segments
of the county and state political apparatus. In addition, her position on
women's issues placed her squarely between moderate and radical feminists.
As such, she entered the primary with the competitive advantage of substantial support from women voters in addition to her very strong support from
black voters in the Chicago metropolitan area. Even though Chicago voters
comprise 80 percent of the votes for the Democratic primary—which helped
her to win it—her victory in the general election was not certain.

Throughout the primary campaign, Moseley-Braun was portrayed as a
poorly financed, odd-woman-out, one-issue candidate. Yet her political record
was viewed positively, and her status as a representative of disaffected women
was constantly emphasized by the media. Moseley-Braun won the Democratic
primary election with 38 percent of the vote, followed by Alan Dixon with 35
percent and Albert Hofeld with 27 percent. Fifty-one percent of Moseley-
Braun's vote came from the city of Chicago, compared to 30 percent for Dixon
and 19 percent for Hofeld. Moseley-Braun's total vote count of 298,664 from
the city of Chicago was more than the combined total of 284,373 for Dixon
and Hofeld. Moreover, as a result of heavy crossover voting from Republican
women in the Chicago suburbs, Moseley-Braun received 110,910 or 39 percent of the Chicago suburban vote as compared to 76,889 (27 percent) for
Dixon and 93,357 (33 percent) for Hofeld. Moseley-Braun carried 7 out of the

state's 102 counties. During the primary election she did not receive the endorsement of the only other African American public official who had won a statewide office, Attorney General Roland Burris. She also was not endorsed at that time by Paul Simon, a Democrat and the state's other U.S. senator.

The Election

After her primary victory, Moseley-Braun became an instant celebrity as the populace felt the possibility that history could be made. Whereas the primary campaign was dominated by the two white male candidates attacking each other's character and by Moseley-Braun's campaign on gender and economic issues, her general election campaign was encompassed by the themes of the 1992 presidential election campaign. All other issues, including those of gender and race, were subsumed under the tightly managed Clinton-Gore campaign that focused on economic issues.

Senate contests, as a unit of analysis, are influenced by a wide variety of factors including personalities, candidates' characteristics, political characteristics of states, and national political conditions.[2] The personality factor played a major role throughout the 1992 Illinois general election. Moseley-Braun benefited as the first viable woman and African American candidate for the U.S. Senate since Republican Edward Brooke last served in that body (1967–79). Moseley-Braun's Republican opponent, Richard Williamson, was seen as a strong supporter of the Reagan-Bush economic policies that had become unpopular in a state heavily affected by the recession and twelve years of Republican presidential administrations.

In a year in which voters put a high priority on change and diversity, Moseley-Braun was the right candidate with the right political profile at the right time. The state's political characteristics benefited Moseley-Braun from the outset. From the beginning of the general election campaign, Moseley-Braun held a commanding lead over Williamson in every geographical area except the heavily Republican five suburban collar counties immediately surrounding the city of Chicago. Seventy-seven percent of the voters said race was not an issue. Party preference polls indicate that 86 percent of Democrats, 55 percent of self-described Independents, and 24 percent of Republicans voted for Moseley-Braun. Women in all areas of the state backed Moseley-Braun by 61 percent compared to 20 percent for Williamson. Moreover, she was favored by 53 percent of all men compared to 30 percent for Williamson. Overall, she was preferred by 89 percent of black voters and by 53 percent of white voters.

Even though party preference polls fluctuated between the primary and general election, the foundations of Moseley-Braun's lead were built upon several factors: an overwhelming black vote with the support of nine out of every ten black voters; a better than three to one margin of victory in the city of Chicago; a two to one advantage in southern Illinois; and a 20 percent point margin of victory among women voters across the state. Williamson maintained a solid lead among suburban voters throughout the campaign and received one-third of Chicago's white ethnic vote.

Carol Moseley-Braun won the Illinois U.S. Senate election with 2,631,229 votes (53 percent) to Rich Williamson's 2,126,833 votes (43 percent) (Figure 3–1). A third-party candidate, Chad Koppie, received 100,422 votes (2 percent). In gaining 2.5 million votes statewide, Moseley-Braun carried 58 of the state's 102 counties, as compared to carrying 7 counties in the primary. Exit polls showed Moseley-Braun with a monolithic 95 percent of the black vote statewide, including 99 percent of the votes in some black wards in Chicago (as was true for Harold Washington when he was elected mayor of Chicago in 1983 and 1987 and for Jesse Jackson in the 1988 Democratic presidential primary).

Moseley-Braun received a 504,000 vote plurality in Chicago, taking forty-four of fifty wards, as well as almost 50 percent of the votes in six southwest and northwest side wards that traditionally were not receptive to African American or Latino candidates. In the Cook County suburbs, Moseley-Braun received 47 percent of the vote and carried nine of the thirty townships.

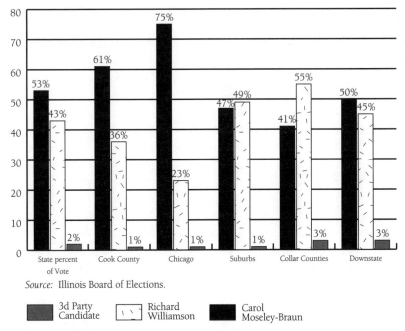

Figure 3–1. Illinois Senate Election Data, 1992.

Although she failed to win the five suburban, predominantly white-collar counties of DuPage, Kane, Lake, McHenry, and Will, she did get 43 percent of the vote there, denying Williamson the kind of Republican plurality in the suburban region that Republicans needed to win statewide. Moseley-Braun carried the ninety-six-county downstate region with 53 percent of the vote and fared well as a Democrat in urban and university counties such as Peoria, Madison, St. Clair, Rock Island, DeKalb, and Champaign.

In dozens of rural counties, she sliced out narrow victories or held Williamson to slim margins. For example, Williamson swept the six-county western Illinois cluster of Adams, Brown, Schuyler, McDonouth, Warren, and Mercer Counties by an average of just 73 votes each. Fifty-two counties were decided by margins of fewer than a thousand votes, including eleven in which the winner carried the county by fewer than a hundred votes. Exit polls showed that Moseley-Braun won 78 percent of the white vote and 58 percent of the female vote in her historic victory.

During the campaign, she repeatedly criticized Williamson for the Republican "trickle-down" economic policies of the twelve years of the Reagan-Bush administrations. More than four in ten voters identified economic issues as the most important in their voting decisions, and nearly two-thirds of them rejected her opponent. Moseley-Braun did not embrace purely social themes in the election, yet she dealt with such issues head-on when they confronted her. For example, although she kept her friend and ally Jesse Jackson at arm's length as she emphasized her agenda and economic issues over race, while at a campaign stop on the eve of the election, she rebuked the criticism of a man who criticized her for refusing to condemn Jackson or Louis Farrakhan by stating that all her life she had been a person who wanted to build bridges. Her campaign staff defined her victory as one of coalition politics rather than racial politics.

Placed in the context of Moseley-Braun's own description of herself as a "civil rights activist" throughout her political career, it would not seem appropriate to classify her candidacy as deracialized. From a traditional viewpoint, an examination of her victory finds that her massive three-to-one margin in the city of Chicago, combined with an even split in the Cook County suburbs, was more than enough to overcome Rich Williamson's strong showing in the collar counties. The extra 95,000 vote margin provided by downstate was merely an addition to her victory.

In the eighty-four downstate counties (28 percent of the vote) where minorities make up 10 percent or less of the population (less than the average minority population for downstate), Moseley-Braun ran just about even with Williamson. Interestingly, in these counties she did her best, running 8 percent ahead of Williamson in completely white counties where less than 1 percent of the population are other than non-Hispanic whites

*Percentage
of Votes*

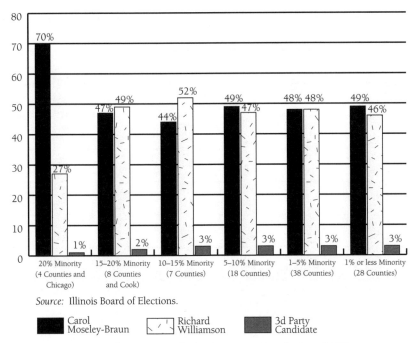

Source: Illinois Board of Elections.

Figure 3–2. Senate Election Results by Minority Population, 1992.

(Figure 3–2). In the city of Chicago, where the minority population is 62 percent, Moseley-Braun won by a margin of better than three to one. In DuPage County, where minorities are 12 percent of the population, Williamson won by a 21 percent margin (59 percent to 38 percent).

In the thirteen smallest counties (1 percent of the vote), with less than 10,000 population (Figure 3–3), Moseley-Braun ran just slightly below her statewide margin (these counties are also completely white). In the eighty-one downstate counties (33 percent of the vote) where the county population ranges from 100,000 to 200,000, Moseley-Braun ran just slightly ahead of Williamson. In the eight counties with a population of over 200,000 (67 percent of the vote), for all intents and purposes Cook County and the collar counties, overall Moseley-Braun ran ahead of Williamson by 15 percent.

In terms of median household income (the state average is $32,252), as might be expected, in the poorest eleven counties of the state (2 percent of the vote), Moseley-Braun had a large 16 percent margin of victory (56 percent to 40 percent) (Figure 3–4). She won ten of these eleven counties. In thirty-eight counties (9 percent of the vote) with a median household income of $20,000–25,000, her margin of victory was 6 percent (51 percent to 45 percent). In counties with a median household income of $25,000–32,252 (48

*Percentage
of Votes*

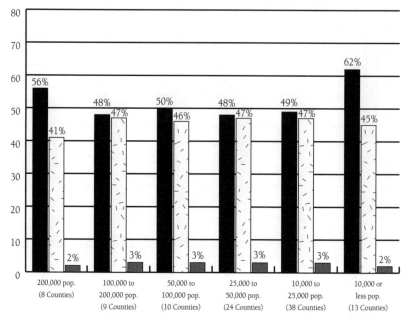

Figure 3–3. Senate Election Results by County Population, 1992.

*Percentage
of Votes*

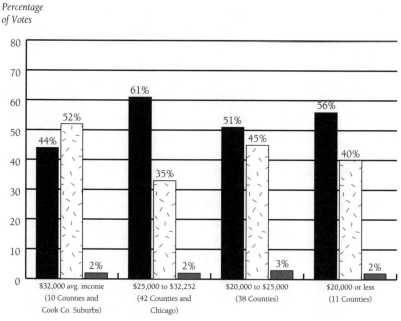

Source: Illinois Board of Elections.

Figure 3–4. Senate Election Results by Median Household Income, 1992.

percent of the vote), Moseley-Braun's margin of victory was about the same as her margin of victory in the thirty-eight counties with a median household income of $20,000–25,000, with Chicago of course providing her a far larger margin of victory. In the ten counties and the Cook County suburbs where the median household income was above average (41 percent of the vote), overall Williamson garnered a margin of 8 percent (52 percent to 44 percent). He won all of these ten counties and the Cook County suburbs.

In terms of the percentage of the population below the poverty line, as might be expected, there is a fairly obvious trend. When a county had 20 percent or more of its population below the poverty line (basically, Chicago), Moseley-Braun's margin of victory was 50 percent (Figure 3–5). At 15–20 percent below the poverty line, Moseley-Braun's margin over Williamson was 12 percent. At 11.9–15 percent below the line (the state average is 11.9 percent), her margin was 5 percent. Finally, her margin was 3 percent when 9–11.9 percent of a county lived below the poverty line. In affluent areas where less than 9 percent are below the poverty line (with the median household income being at least $28,000), Williamson won by 9 percent.

Overall, Moseley-Braun's victory was broad-based, somewhat surprising for the first African American woman elected to the U.S. Senate. In general, she ran ahead of or at least even with her opponent everywhere except in the white, wealthy, highly educated, staunchly Republican collar

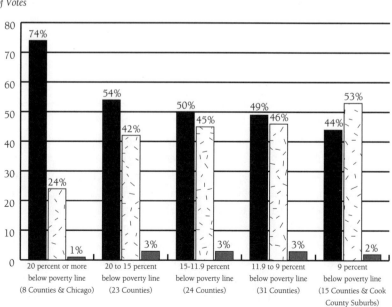

Figure 3–5. Senate Election Results by Population below the Poverty Line, 1992.

counties. Other than in the city of Chicago, Moseley-Braun's margin seems to have had little or nothing to do with minority population strength. She did slightly better (62 percent) in completely white, rural Calhoun County in the southwestern part of the state than she did (60 percent) in impoverished, 34 percent minority Alexander County in the state's southern tip. Moseley-Braun's voting strength seemed to be relatively consistent in both rural and urban areas (with an obvious bias in favor of Chicago). She maintained a lead, or in some cases a dead heat, with Williamson in all but the most affluent, well-educated populations.

Moseley-Braun's strength seems to be divided into two camps. About half of her voting strength came from Chicago and the Cook County suburbs. Ironically, a substantial part of the other half came from a conglomeration of counties that were on the opposite end of the state. These counties are characterized by a white population that is less well educated, lower income, and largely rural. Williamson received support largely in the northeastern affluent, well-educated, suburban counties.

Moseley-Braun's senatorial victory crossed all geographical areas of the state of Illinois and all racial groups. Areas with incomes above the state median income level did not provide a majority vote for Moseley-Braun. In addition, the six white ethnic wards on the southwest and northwest sides, with vehemently antiblack voting patterns, did not provide majority support for the Moseley-Braun election. Altogether, her primary victory swept her into a national whirlwind driven by the fact that an imminent electoral victory was possible and that she could become the first African American female senator in U.S. history. The very strong support of the national and state Democratic party, as well as African American and women's groups, was instrumental to Moseley-Braun's victory.

A Critique of the Deracialization Concept

The election of first-generation black mayors in large cities in the late 1960s was the combined outcome of changing demographics and the pressure of U.S. political and social movements. The basis for these elections was always in the African American population. As time progressed and black political participation expanded, the base from which black politics emanated became more diversified. As the locus of the political environment changed, many big city politicians maintained their leadership styles as well as the solidified base of support established in their initial elections to office.

Students of black politics built their conceptual framework for explaining black political life almost exclusively around the election of black big city mayors. While these studies have made significant contributions to the literature of modern political science and provided a valuable source of ideas and expertise for improved understanding of black politics, they also led to the development of a dominant paradigm that focused almost exclusively on political behavior in majority black urban districts and jurisdictions.

The nature of American political culture and the need to replace dwindling economic resources to serve a more deprived constituency forced black mayors to adopt governmental and policy priorities increasingly at odds with business leaders, institutional managers and property owners, and a dwindling middle-class taxpaying base. Changes in national priorities, wholesale reductions in federal transfer payments and entitlements for urban areas, migration of newly arrived racial and ethnic groups, changes in political district lines, development of more sophisticated community organizations for people of color and whites, and the gradual emergence of a new African American post–civil rights political leadership changed the nature of leadership in black political life.

This second generation of black political leaders was skillful in the art of politics within and outside of African American political communities, experienced in interest and pressure group competition, and able to communicate their campaign programs across a wide variety of racial and ethnic groups. While individual African American politicians, such as Ronald Dellums of California and Edward Brooke of Massachusetts, represented racially mixed electoral districts in earlier decades, the diversity of this second-generation of politicians differs in that the earlier group's base largely came from within black communities. The second generation's approach to electoral politics includes political bases in which black populations are a majority constituency in most cases and a plurality in others. Their approach to electoral mobilization emphasizes expanding political bases and electoral coalitions across racial and ethnic lines. Their vision of public policy formulation and implementation often differs from the traditional black leaders.

An example of the emerging second-generation leadership is the late Mayor Harold Washington of Chicago. The basis of Mayor Washington's first mayoral victory was overwhelmingly African American, with strong, vocal black nationalist support. White and Latino votes provided the margin of victory for Washington. Yet one of Mayor Washington's first priorities was to build a multiracial coalition to govern the city of Chicago. This coalition, buttressed by a vigilant black electorate, provided the strong support for Mayor Washington as he set out to reform a long-standing machine structure and win reelection to a second term before his untimely death in November 1987.

Mayor Washington's style contrasts with that of Mayor W. W. Herenton, the first black mayor of Memphis, Tennessee. Herenton proposed in late 1993 that his city merge with the surrounding suburbs in Shelby County. Herenton's idea immediately "ran into the political reality of

established government structures, as well as suburban whites jealously
guarding their racially and economically homogeneous enclaves, and urban
blacks benefitting from a rising tide of political power."[3] The city's business
community provided early support for the proposal. The premise of Herenton's proposal, given that he was facing reelection at the time of his proposal and had won his earlier term by a slim margin of 140 votes, was that he
could win the electoral support of the white voters in the areas that would be
annexed to the city and could thus win the upcoming mayoral election.

An example of a black mayor governing in a city in which blacks are a
minority voting population is Mayor David Dinkins of New York City.
Dinkins won his first term by less than 2 percent of the vote but lost his
second term in 1993 when a significant percentage of the white population
supported a white Republican candidate. Mayor Dinkins had pursued a moderate and conciliatory governance stance. Latinos and Jews did not desert
Dinkins in large numbers and the black turnout was perhaps not as significant as had he been a more racially symbolic mayor.

These mayoral careers point out that the issue of race for second-
generation black mayors is a two-edged sword. On the one hand, they must
appeal to a broader white population while holding on to their black political
base. Their ability to do so is a common factor in mainstream politics with
mainstream candidates. For first- and second-generation black politicians,
this factor remains an ominous variable.

Carol Moseley-Braun's campaign is a classic example of the combination of first- and second-generation politics. While she ran a political campaign emphasizing economic issues, coalition building, and garnering support from mainstream party officials, she received overwhelming black
support and described herself as a product of the civil rights movement. Her
strong support from the city of Chicago, progressive women, and white
groups undoubtedly was an important factor that enabled her to project such
a stance. Moreover, the unique manner in which she entered the race, as well
as its context, played a very significant part.

Analysis of senate contests must consider personalities, candidates'
characteristics, political characteristics of states, and national political conditions. The ideal deracialized election is defined as an electoral activity consisting of African American candidates running in majority white districts,
usually against white opponents, and strongly appealing for white support.
Within the context of these broad categories, Moseley-Braun's campaign and
election meet the minimal requirements for the deracialized election. However, her election also meets requirements for the unit of analysis established
for senatorial campaigns. The antecedent variable making the election both a
deracialized and senatorial contest is the fact that Moseley-Braun is African

American and that an overwhelming amount of her electoral support came from the African American population.

An important heuristic question exists for the emerging discourse on deracialization. The question lies in the ability of scholars in this emerging area to clearly delineate the theoretical and substantive variables in each case across the complete political and electoral spectrum. This will require a broadening of the traditional paradigm for analyzing black electoral politics, and it will enable the discourse to include a more penetrating analysis and understanding of the interconnections of race, politics, and power motivating electoral behavior in these black and multiracial districts.

The concept of deracialization has an important part to play as black and American politics move toward more elections in which black candidates will compete outside the boundaries that limited first-generation black politicians. If deracialization is to have theoretical reliability and validity, scholars must recognize the political history and culture, structure of power relations, and the choices that black and opposition candidates face in these jurisdictions. This would enable them to provide a more balanced set of hypotheses that may lead to a paradigm for this area of study in American politics.

Notes

I would like to thank Jim Cotton, my research assistant, for his excellent assistance in the completion of this chapter.

1. Joseph McCormick II and Charles E. Jones, "The Conceptualization of Deracialization: Thinking through the Dilemma," in *Dilemmas of Black Politics: Leadership, Strategy, and Issues,* edited by Georgia A. Persons (New York: HarperCollins, 1993), 69. Hereinafter cited in text by page number.

2. Alan I. Abramowitz, "Explaining Senate Election Outcomes," *American Political Science Review* 82 (1988): 385–403.

3. Ronald Smothers, "City Seeks to Grow by Disappearing," *New York Times,* Oct. 18, 1993, A8.

II

Deracialization in City and State Politics

4

The Election and Governance of David Dinkins as Mayor of New York

J. Phillip Thompson

In 1989, David N. Dinkins narrowly won election to the mayor's office in New York City. He defeated former U.S. Attorney Rudolph Giuliani, a Republican, by a scant 47,000 votes out of 1.8 million cast. More than half of Dinkins's votes came from African Americans, and another sixth of the votes came from Latinos. Dinkins's remaining votes came from whites, including nearly 30 percent of the Jewish vote, one-quarter of the white Catholic vote, and more than 40 percent of the liberal white vote.[1] Dinkins, a Democrat, won with the support of the city's Democratic political establishment, including New York Governor Mario Cuomo, county Democratic party leaders, and former Mayor Ed Koch, whom Dinkins defeated in a hotly contested race in the mayoral primary. Dinkins's primary victory had a different coalitional basis than his general election victory. He won 50.8 percent of the primary vote compared to Koch's 42 percent. African Americans constituted more than two-thirds of the Dinkins vote in the primary. The coalition of African Americans, Latinos, labor union members, and liberal whites that supported Dinkins in the primary—his "primary election coalition"—provided 70 percent of his votes in the general election.

The remaining thirty percent of Dinkins's votes in the general election came from former Koch voters, Independents, Republicans, and Democrats who did not vote in the primary. These voters comprise the second group of voters that elected Dinkins mayor—his "general election coalition." This coalition was more conservative, less supportive, and included more whites than his primary election coalition. In fact, had the election been held one week later, it is questionable whether Dinkins would have won. In an early October 1989 opinion poll, Dinkins led Giuliani by twenty-four points. While avoiding explicit references to race, Giuliani attacked Dinkins's inability to manage his personal finances as well as his so-called "softness" on crime. Racially based mistrust of Dinkins led many whites who normally voted Democratic to defect by election day.[2]

The fact that Dinkins was able to win a third of the white vote in the general election was remarkable, given the racial polarization in the city before the election. Koch initially governed the city primarily supported by an electoral base of Jews and middle-class white Catholics. Over time he expanded his base to include the Democratic party organizations of Queens and the Bronx, big businesses and real estate developers, and Latino voters. Koch was hostile to liberal white "ideologues," municipal unions, and African Americans—whose leaders he labeled in 1977 as "poverty pimps."[3] Koch's rhetoric and leadership style contributed to racial polarization in an already racially troubled city. Thus, Dinkins campaigned for office in a racially charged atmosphere.

David Dinkins was initially persuaded to run against Ed Koch by the very groups excluded from Koch's governing coalition. Dinkins had strong support for his candidacy among African Americans, and he won early and enthusiastic union support.[4] Koch's popularity declined due to the deteriorating quality of life in the city—most evident in the city's growing crime rate and its homeless crisis—and due to heightening racial tension. Liberal, white "ideologues," personified by Koch critic City Councilwoman Ruth Messinger, grew in influence. In addition, Jesse Jackson's strong support from Latino voters during his presidential campaign in 1988 bode well for an African American/Latino alliance in the 1989 New York mayoral race. Finally, Koch was hurt by the scandal surrounding the Bronx and Queens Democratic organizations. These two former powerhouses of support for Koch were in a state of disarray. Both organizations were the subject of an investigation involving the acceptance of bribes by Bronx party chairman Stanley Friedman, who was later convicted, and by Queens party chairman Donald Manes, who committed suicide.

After the hard-fought primary, Koch surprised many observers by strongly supporting Dinkins in the general election. No doubt Koch relished the opportunity to oppose Rudolph Giuliani, who as U.S. Attorney in New York led the investigations against Koch's political supporters in the Bronx and Queens. Koch's support was valuable in both winning moderate Jewish support for Dinkins and avoiding a split in the Democratic party that could have given momentum to Giuliani.

Dinkins had also been a shrewd campaigner. He studiously avoided personal attacks on Koch during the primary election, making it easier for Koch to support him in the general election. Dinkins's low-key, pragmatic, and accommodating style also made it difficult for Giuliani to characterize him as leading a "black takeover" of New York—a problem that has characterized the first-time election of other African American mayors.[5] Dinkins emphasized racial harmony and unity, a theme that won considerable white support against Koch's race-baiting tactics.

Dinkins's leadership style was similar to that of J. Raymond Jones, a pioneer Harlem political strategist and the first African American Democratic county chair in New York City. Jones disliked ideological or charismatic political leadership, although he believed that charismatic leaders (such as Adam Clayton Powell) could be utilized to mobilize voters.[6] Jones believed in organization, patronage, compromise, and making deals—the hallmark qualities of machine politics. These qualities served Harlem politicians well in the early 1930s, when the Manhattan political machine (more popularly known as Tammany Hall) crumbled, undermined by the influence of liberal white reformers (mainly Jewish professionals) who challenged the Italian-led machine. Leaders such as Jones, Percy Sutton, and later Dinkins were adept at leveraging the African American vote to form alliances with competing white factions. They won important county positions at a time when African Americans never represented more than 25 percent of the vote. They are the original African American "crossover" politicians.

As the Italian-led machine deteriorated, Manhattan politics came to be dominated by reform-minded whites and African Americans. Unlike white reformers, the Harlem brand of politics did not emphasize issues, particular policies, or ideological debate. It was aimed strictly at the accumulation of power and patronage. In fact, Dinkins's lack of a liberal reform policy agenda cost him liberal white support in his early campaigns for borough president of Manhattan.[7] Eventually, he developed a liberal reform policy agenda. In his successful 1985 campaign for borough president of Manhattan and in that position, Dinkins advocated major reforms in the city's homeless and criminal justice programs. He gained crucial liberal white support by persuasively arguing that Koch's policies were cost-ineffective and inhumane. Coming into office as mayor, Dinkins was contradictorily recognized both as a liberal reform leader and a pragmatist.

Dinkins as Mayor

Dinkins's mayoralty began on January 1, 1990, with a weak mandate based on a fragile electoral coalition. He won white support in the primary and general elections, but African American/white relations in the city were severely strained. Another problem was that Dinkins's union support created skepticism among his business supporters, as well as from Koch.

Moreover, Dinkins faced an immediate budget crisis with a revenue shortfall and a host of immediate service and infrastructure problems. The city's roads, water system, and many of the more than two thousand bridges were in a state of disrepair. Despite a production rate of more than five thousand new or renovated low- and moderate-income housing units per year, the city's homeless population was increasing. The city's educational system was in a state of crisis with a high dropout rate, crumbling buildings, and demoralized teachers. The city was also plagued by an AIDS epidemic. Drugs and crime topped the list of concerns, and many New Yorkers looked to Dinkins to fulfill his campaign promise to be "the toughest Mayor on crime the city has ever seen."

Dinkins's first action as mayor was to assure all elements of his general election coalition that he was attentive to their concerns. He did so by appointing a staff that reflected the key elements of his election coalition. As corporation council, the city's top legal position, he appointed Victor Kovner. A former law partner of Koch, Kovner is a well-known figure in the business community, media, and Jewish leadership circles. Dinkins appointed Norman Steisel as first deputy mayor. Steisel was a commissioner of sanitation under Koch and later became a Wall Street financier. Through these first appointments, Dinkins clearly wished to allay fears that he would be fiscally irresponsible.

Dinkins's other appointments included Bill Lynch as deputy mayor for Intergovernmental Relations. Lynch had a long history in the labor movement and in black politics. As deputy mayor for Finance and Economic Development, Dinkins appointed Sally Hernandez-Pinero, a Puerto Rican attorney and former Financial Services commissioner under Koch. Barbara Fife, a longtime Democratic party insider and leader of New York "good government" groups, was named deputy mayor for Planning and Development. Dinkins also appointed Milt Mollen, a former judge and Brooklyn Democratic party leader, as deputy mayor for Criminal Justice.

Dinkins's top appointments touched most sectors of his general election coalition: business, labor, women, Puerto Ricans, African Americans, and Jews. In selecting such a diverse staff, Dinkins avoided criticism that he was concerned only about African Americans and showed that he intended to include all New Yorkers in his administration. On the other hand, Dinkins's appointments reflected the contradictions, ambiguity, and lack of direction of his own election campaign.

Dinkins knew that to govern New York City, where African Americans are less than a quarter of the population, he would have to make compromises and share power. Dinkins's style is to mediate conflict; however, this style has some major drawbacks. Mediating conflict is inherently reactive.

Ideologues, or charismatic leaders, inflame latent conflicts when they need to agitate and call to action their constituency. Ideologues have the ability to define issues and mobilize political constituencies to force their issues into public discourse. Mediators react to the issues and conflicts that others generate. Mediation works well if the mediator has the power to enforce his or her decisions and has an understanding of his or her desired direction. When a mediator lacks clear authority and direction, others will attempt to impose their will. This is what happened to Dinkins. Viewing him as a weak and reactive leader, labor leaders, state and city politicians, and business leaders lost little time in attempting to assert themselves. City council president Andrew Stein went so far as to announce his candidacy for mayor only one year after Dinkins took office.

With a strong political machine behind him, Dinkins would have had the support of the city council and a strong voice in the state legislature.[8] Lacking a machine, Dinkins was assured of neither. Unlike a machine leader or a popular African American mayor in a city with a plurality of African American voters, Dinkins entered office with weak political authority. In order to strengthen his authority, he had to maintain his electoral base in the absence of formal mechanisms and find the means to translate his electoral base into influence over the city council and state legislature. In short, to lead effectively Dinkins needed the ability to mobilize and leverage his base. He had been able to assemble his primary election coalition primarily because Koch was widely perceived as racist, antiunion, and ineffectual in addressing quality-of-life issues. As mayor, Dinkins needed to establish his own program and direction to maintain his primary political base, but no direction emerged. The Dinkins administration allowed his primary electoral coalition to falter and with it his potential political strength.

The major issues Dinkins addressed in office were crime, the budget, city council relations, and race relations. His handling of these interrelated issues demonstrates the importance of establishing strong political authority to be an effective mayor in New York.

Crime

In July 1990, eight months after Dinkins's election, the media highlighted a string of four child killings in nine days, all caused by random gunfire. These deaths came on top of the slaying of nineteen cab drivers that year and four murders by a serial gunman called the "Zodiac" gunman. The crime wave was the lead story in the press for six weeks. Media attention reached a crescendo when a young white tourist from Utah was murdered during a robbery attempt on the subway. The *New York Post* linked the crime wave to Dinkins's hesitation to massively expand the police force. In one trenchant front-page story, the *New York Post* led with a huge banner headline, "DAVE, DO SOMETHING!"

The negative press had an immediate effect on the mayor's public standing. A Gallup poll showed a 20 percent drop in whites' support of Dinkins, although he maintained support among African Americans.[9] Dinkins reacted angrily to the results of the poll, drawing a negative comparison between his continued African American support, despite high black-on-black crime rates and his fledgling white support after a series of highly publicized killings of whites. Addressing a mostly African American radio audience, Dinkins said, "You are aware [that] the problems of crime and violence in our community are not new. We've had this problem, and now I guess it has gone beyond our borders and others have become concerned. Fact of the matter is, we have been concerned since day one."[10]

Dinkins's most vocal critic was former Mayor Koch. Koch was featured in a weekly television show, wrote a regular newspaper column in the *New York Post,* and had his own morning radio talk show, all of which focused criticism on Dinkins. Dinkins had to choose between a costly increase in police hiring—in a period of expected mammoth budget shortfalls, attendant increases in taxes, and cuts in social services—and continued politically damaging attacks by the press. In political terms, Dinkins had to choose between salvaging his fragile election coalition and safeguarding the budget to support social service programs important to his primary election coalition. After weeks of hesitation, Dinkins announced that he would proceed with an increase of nearly eight thousand police officers, three thousand jail beds, and $150 million for education and youth programs aimed at crime prevention. The total bill for these initiatives was $650 million per year.

Dinkins's anticrime initiatives momentarily quieted the press. The episode revealed, however, that his administration lacked a long-term political and policy agenda. By acquiescing to demands for more police, Dinkins had essentially let the media set public policy. The police department already had a notoriously bloated budget with uniformed officers performing clerical tasks best left for lower paid civilians. By not insisting on cost-cutting and efficiency within the police department, but rather embracing expensive police expansion, Dinkins lost the initiative to reform the police bureaucracy. The price tag of the anticrime initiatives also precipitated an inevitable tax-increase versus social-services-cuts battle. The same voters who lost confidence in Dinkins's crime fighting ability were likely to oppose tax increases to pay for more police. Rather than refocusing the debate from "more cops" to "reforming police bureaucracy," Dinkins was caught between an unpopular tax increase and cutting back on city services important to his primary election coalition.

Budget

Since the New York City fiscal crisis in the mid-1970s, city finances have come under the watchful eye of the Financial Control Board (FCB, formerly called the Emergency Financial Control Board). The FCB is composed of the governor, state comptroller, mayor, city comptroller, and three additional members appointed by the governor. The FCB has the power to reject the city's expense and capital budget, although in practice it has mainly limited itself to insisting that the city has a balanced budget.[11] The FCB was created to avoid a second city financial collapse after the city went bankrupt in 1975.

From the day Dinkins took office, the budget was a matter of primary concern. The city was faced with an immediate $75 million shortfall in the fiscal year (FY) 1990 budget. In March 1990, Dinkins was forced to cut new drug treatment programs, school maintenance and computers, one hundred transportation maintenance jobs, 40 percent of the Department of Sanitation's "clean team," and hospital supplies.[12] He was confronted with continually revised revenue forecasts, each predicting a larger than expected budget shortfall. He was in the unwelcome position of announcing more bad news almost every week. To close the budget gap, Dinkins and the city council agreed to $260 million in service cuts and $453 million in new taxes, including $263 million in real estate and property taxes.[13] Dinkins and the city council, which was handling major budget responsibilities for the first time under the new city charter, were both anxious to demonstrate their ability to manage the budget. Both sought to resolve the budget problem quickly to avoid any outside interference from FCB.

Dinkins's lack of policy prioritization made matters worse and prompted anonymous grumbling in the press from several city commissioners. Agencies were simply asked to make across-the-board cuts in services, with little dialogue with the mayor's staff as to which programs the mayor wanted to keep. The lack of prioritization in cutting the budget denied Dinkins an opportunity to publicize the service and development programs to which he was absolutely committed and squandered an opportunity to salvage his credibility with his primary election coalition. Dinkins's seemingly blind adherence to balancing the budget gave the impression that he was more preoccupied with satisfying the city's bondholders than he was concerned about the city's poor and its municipal employees, the two main elements of his primary election coalition.

Despite his budget cuts, Dinkins funded some model programs in low-income communities. In Harlem, he funded an eighteen-hundred-unit low- and moderate-income housing construction/rehabilitation initiative called the "Bradhurst Plan." Under it, the city would relinquish ownership of vast tracts of land to a coalition of churches and community groups. The coalition would be funded by the city and would be allowed to develop, market, and manage the property. The city would work with the coalition in a consultant capacity to help the coalition develop a plan for comprehensive service delivery and neighborhood economic development. The Bradhurst Plan is touted as the largest community-run development plan ever attempted in the United States, and it is the type of initiative Dinkins's primary election coalition expected of him as mayor. However, Dinkins's staff approached the budget from the narrow technical perspective of satisfying the bondholders, missing opportunities to take political bows for innovations such as Bradhurst. The lack of publicity directed toward Dinkins's primary election coalition, despite some substantive attention to their concerns budgetarily, fostered the image that Dinkins had abandoned his base of support.

The lack of political focus in budgetary matters by the Dinkins administration was also evident in its relationship with labor unions. The first mistake in this regard was that the city's labor negotiator settled the teachers' contract before settling the contract with the unions representing other city workers. The United Federation of Teachers (UFT) is a powerful political force but was among the last unions to endorse Dinkins in the primary election. The contracts for District Council Local 37 of the American Federation of State, County, and Municipal Employees (DC 37 of AFSCME) and Teamsters Local 237, two of the earliest union supporters of Dinkins in his primary election coalition, came up immediately after the teachers' contract. Dinkins granted the UFT a 4.5 percent increase, which was considerably lower than the 20–30 percent sought by UTE Dinkins argued that the city was in danger of losing good teachers and that 3 percent of the increase would come from adjustments in city pension assumptions. The other 1.5 percent increase would come from tax revenue funds. Dinkins then offered DC 37 and Teamsters 237 increases of 1.5 percent.

Stan Hill and Barry Feinstein, the leaders of DC 37 and Teamsters 237, respectively, were embarrassed that after working early and hard for Dinkins's election, their unions were offered less than the teachers' union. Moreover, Hill complained that he learned about the Dinkins administration's plans to lay off city workers from reading the morning newspapers during the middle of contract negotiations with the administration. Eric Smertz, Dinkins's embattled labor negotiator and longtime Koch adversary, bitterly complained that labor negotiations were being run by Dinkins's union-hostile budget staff. He publicly stated that labor negotiations were undermined by the city's budget director, Phil Michel, whom he accused of making secret contingency agreements with bond-rating agencies to lay off city workers. Smertz was dismissed soon thereafter by Dinkins, who believed that Michel had informed Smertz of the secret agreements.

This episode demonstrates that Dinkins's staff was divided over how to handle the unions. Moreover, the hostile manner by which negotiations were handled did not seem to reflect Dinkins's style as a mediator. Former New York Mayor Robert Wagner, perhaps the closest to Dinkins in personal style, had always taken pains to make the union leadership feel important (despite contract differences) and never initiated labor policy without first clearing it with labor.[14] Labor expected Dinkins to do the same.

Dinkins eventually conceded to rough parity between the teachers and other unions, but this required pushing for reductions in the teachers' contract.[15] In consequence, all of the unions were angry at the Dinkins administration, and business leaders were sharply critical of the wage increases. In the end, Dinkins came through with reasonable contracts, but his administration's lack of political sensitivity in dealing with the unions had badly antagonized labor. After the negotiations, Dennis Rivera, head of Local 1199, the health and hospitals workers' union, said publicly that he would not support Dinkins again in 1993 unless Dinkins shifted to the left.[16] The hostility generated among the unions subsequently also cost Dinkins in his dealings with the city council.

City Council Relations

City council members found themselves in a new position in 1990. In 1989, New York's voters approved a new city charter that eliminated the Board of Estimate, the city's main governing body in the twentieth century.[17] The charter gave the mayor and the city council, previously a rubber stamp for the Board of Estimate, control of the city budget as well as control of city land use. Thus, the council became a powerful body for the first time.

The charter required an expansion of the council from thirty-five to fifty-one seats, primarily to increase minority representation. Although the city was more than 50 percent minority at the time of the charter change, only eight council members were minorities: six African Americans and two Latinos. The charter mandated a redistricting of the council and a special council election in 1991, as well as another election on the regular four-year cycle in 1993.

Since the council does not have responsibility for administering agencies, the main area of its influence is the city's budget. Thus, the budget and council elections became the council's two main issues. For FY1992, Dinkins presented the council with a proposed increase of $776 million in property taxes, targeted especially at the city's relatively undertaxed single-family homeowners.[18] Single-family homeowners in New York tend to reside primarily in white neighborhoods in outer Queens, Staten Island, and the southeast parts of Brooklyn, areas where Dinkins's support was weakest. Dinkins's justified the tax increase as necessary to maintain city services, especially social programs. In crass political terms, the issue was one of taxing white homeowners to fund programs beneficial to low-income minorities. The revenue package was particularly onerous for the council leadership, including council speaker and majority leader Peter Vallone, whose core constituents were single-family homeowners. Moreover, 1991 was an election year and council members were hesitant to raise taxes.

Although Dinkins had a hard sell from the beginning, two things were in his favor. As New York's first African American mayor, he commanded respect and admiration in African American communities throughout the city. His popularity among African Americans could have been translated into pressure on the six African American council members to support his tax package. This was especially true since the programs Dinkins proposed to fund were essential to the city's African American and Latino communities. Dinkins's other potential advantage was his relationship with the unions. Unions, especially DC 37, have substantial influence on the city council. Union jobs stood to be lost if Dinkins did not win his proposed tax increase.

Dinkins did not use these two potential sources of assistance to strengthen the chances that his tax increase proposal would be approved by the city council. As a result, he lost the council vote on the budget. Even African American council members, whose districts stood to gain from Dinkins's budget proposal, did not vote in favor of the budget proposal. The final agreement was a "compromise" with the council to raise property taxes by $400 million. But for Dinkins, who staked so much on winning the $776 million increase, it was a severe defeat. He was forced to make service cuts and lay off ten thousand city workers.

Dinkins not only lost the tax increase vote in the city council, he was also outmaneuvered. In a last minute political ploy, he announced a list of programs that would be cut if he did not win his proposed tax increase. The cuts included a number of popular programs such as the Central Park Zoo, libraries, and museums. The council then outsmarted Dinkins by restoring funding for the popular programs he had cut and then threatening to cut $330 million from agencies such as the Corporation Council and City Planning, which lack political constituencies but are important to the effective governance of the mayor's office.[19] Dinkins was forced to come to terms with the council.

His last minute budget flop highlighted the absence of a unified political strategy in his administration. The hostile treatment of the unions by Dinkins's budget staff had weakened his political hand with the council. It also seemed incredible that African American council members would so boldly oppose Dinkins on such an important issue. It was apparent that Deputy Mayor Bill Lynch, who as Dinkins's campaign manager had built a minority/labor coalition, played a minor role in budget and labor negotiations. The press speculated that a rift between First Deputy Mayor Steisel, considered hostile to labor, and Lynch may have been a factor in the tax proposal defeat. Near the end of the budget approval process, Dinkins called on Lynch for crisis management assistance. The day before the budget deadline, Lynch organized agencies to prepare sheets identifying the impact of the budget cuts on local communities and had staff rally community advocates to lobby the council. But these efforts were too little too late.

Unions and community advocates were slow to adapt to the new power relationships between the mayor and council. DC 37 and Teamsters 237 criticized Dinkins in the media, rather than supporting his efforts to increase property taxes and avoid layoffs. Community advocates also focused their lobbying efforts on the mayor, as they had in the past, not realizing that their greatest opposition was the city council and that the council had the final authority on the budget. Ironically, one of the main selling points of the revised city charter had been that an increased number of smaller districts would make it easier for community groups to influence council members. Council members were vulnerable to community pressure, but they were not subjected to any. Community advocacy groups in New York City are creatures borne of politics at the citywide level. They are generally skilled at manipulating the press but are newcomers to grassroots political organizing.

Had Dinkins enlisted the support of unions and community groups from the beginning, he might still have lost the budget battle with the city council. However, he would have at least maintained the support of his primary election coalition, and he would have laid the groundwork for a formidable challenge to uncooperative council members in the 1991 council elections.

Needing to rebuild his political base, Dinkins allowed Deputy Mayor Lynch to form a political coalition with progressive trade unionists, elected officials, and community groups to run candidates in the 1991 council elections. The coalition, which was named the "Majority Coalition," was formed in July 1991. It ran candidates in eighteen districts, winning in five. In addition, the coalition ran competitive races in several other districts. Earlier attention to building the Majority Coalition structure probably would have generated greater results. The Majority Coalition was not reticent in its opposition to conservative council members and council members beholden to council speaker and majority leader Peter Vallone. For a deputy mayor to openly campaign against council incumbents was an unprecedented bold move in New York City politics. After the budget experience of 1991, Dinkins showed an awareness of the need for a supportive council and displayed a new willingness to aggressively pursue council support.

Race Relations

In his study of southern politics in the 1940s, V. O. Key maintained that race lurked beneath the surface on almost every issue. Key's observation in this regard is equally applicable to New York City in the 1990s. Dinkins was elected to office largely because of his ability to mediate conflicts between African Americans and whites, particularly between African Americans and Jews. This often means walking a fine line between the two groups, as they are wary of each other.

Dinkins was among the first to denounce the anti-Semitic remarks made by Rev. Louis Farrakhan in 1984. At the same time, Dinkins stayed on as a leader in support of Rev. Jesse Jackson's presidential campaign, despite Jackson's well-publicized anti-Semitic slurs during his 1984 presidential campaign. Dinkins also walked a fine line between African Americans and Jews in his response to the racially inflammatory tactics of African American community activists Al Sharpton and Alton Maddox, Jr. Never directly criticizing them, and acknowledging an insufficient fight against racism in the city, Dinkins addressed dozens of young African American audiences with a message of self-help, personal responsibility, and discipline that won a warm reception among both African Americans and whites.

Dinkins displayed more leadership in mediating racial conflict than perhaps any other mayor in New York City's history. Yet he did not develop a common and specific agenda around which he could rally all ethnic groups. He initiated appeals to specific ethnic groups that may have had merit but that tended to antagonize other ethnic groups. Dinkins's invitation to Nelson Mandela to visit New York in 1990, for example, evoked tremendous support from African Americans but had a negative impact on African American/Jewish relations. The visit highlighted Mandela's support for Yassir Arafat as well as Israel's military ties to South Africa. Dinkins countered Mandela's trip with a highly publicized visit to Israel during the Persian Gulf war in February 1991. The trip neutralized doubts about Dinkins's commitment to Israel and about his stance on Jewish issues in general, but it generated skepticism among some African Americans.[20]

The most serious African American/Jewish conflict erupted in August 1991 when a Hasidic Jewish driver accidentally struck and killed a young African American boy playing on the sidewalk in the predominately black Crown Heights section of Brooklyn. The killing provoked several days of rioting and charges of favored treatment given to Hasidic Jews by the police and city agencies. During this period, a young Hasidic man was stabbed to death in apparent retaliation. Dinkins called the murder of the young Hasidic man a "lynching" and at the same time promised to investigate charges of favoritism directed toward Hasidic Jews. Dinkins's handling of Crown Heights won him respect for his ability to calm racial tensions. More importantly, his staff organized youth programs and involved both African American and Hasidic young people in developing a common youth agenda.

Dinkins's relationship with the Latino community, in contrast with his relationship with Jews, declined considerably after his election. Latino leaders have often seemed out of "the loop" on major initiatives by the Dinkins's administration, provoking criticism from the Latino community. Dinkins expressed support for an imprisoned Irish Republican nationalist, for example, but refused to allow formerly imprisoned Puerto Rican nationalists (considered heroes among Puerto Ricans) into a meeting of political activists with Nelson Mandela. Latino political leaders also complained that they lack patronage in the Dinkins administration. Although Dinkins appointed a Puerto Rican woman as deputy mayor for Finance and Economic Development and a Cuban as head of the Health and Hospital Corporation, neither had a political background in New York City and they were not viewed as likely channels for local patronage.

Latino leaders and the Latino press condemned Dinkins for the work of the City Council Redistricting Commission. Latino leaders claimed that Latinos were cheated by Dinkins's African American appointees on the commission. They claimed that although Latinos and African Americans are roughly the same proportion of the city population (about 25 percent), the commission created twelve so-called "winnable" seats for African American candidates but only eight Latino winnable seats.[21] Dinkins responded that the number of winnable Latino seats was limited by Latino demographic dispersion, low voter registration, and the comparative youth (younger than the voting age) of Latinos in the city.

In fact, Dinkins had limited leverage on the commission. The commission was controlled primarily by the city council, which appointed eight of its fifteen members. Nonetheless, criticism of Dinkins only subsided after U.S. Representative Jose Serrano from the Bronx and union leader Dennis Rivera called for an end to the bloodletting between African Americans and Latinos. They appealed for a united front "against those who would benefit from [their] division," an allusion to Andrew Stein, the city council president, who had already announced his intention to run against Dinkins. The statement by Rivera and Serrano was actually stronger and more direct than any appeals made to Latinos by the Dinkins administration. The split with Latinos revealed that parts of the Latino leadership were so displeased that they might try to break the African American/Latino alliance that helped elect Dinkins.

Conclusion

Much of the literature on black mayors focuses on their election to office. This literature has focused on the nature of coalition building in black electoral campaigns, the racial animosity aroused among conservative whites by black candidacies, and the level of black voter mobilization. Studies have also addressed the effects of black mayors on policy. Rufus P. Browning, Dale R. Marshall, and David H. Tabb report that African Americans have made significant gains in employment and policy preferences as a result of the election of black mayors. However, their study is limited to ten small cities in California, and their data were collected before the conservative policies of the Reagan administration took effect. Kenneth R. Mladenka, and Albert K. Karnig and Susan Welch found that black mayors have had a limited impact on policy.[22] Karnig and Welch cite possible conservatism or incompetence of black mayors, along with external factors, as explanations for their limited impact. Many scholars assert that black mayors are unable to have a significant impact on policy, citing external economic constraints, regressive federal policies, and institutional racism.[23] Charles V. Hamilton and Clarence N. Stone have described dynamic models of black governance. Hamilton holds that the more often black officials produce tangible policy products, the more participation and support they will generate from their political base.[24] Stone argues that in order for black mayors to change policy priorities, they have to mobilize groups not traditionally part of the "governing coalition" to play an active part in the policy process.[25]

This chapter suggests that Dinkins had a limited impact on policy, though not because of external constraints, conservatism, technical incompetence, or a lack of interest groups to support policy change. Dinkins lacked a political strategy for governance. Like Stone's analysis of Atlanta, this chapter emphasizes that black mayors have to mobilize nonelite interest groups (usually the same groups that supported their mayoral campaigns) in order to implement policy changes. Unlike Atlanta, nonelite groups (such as unions and minority associations) are well developed in New York City and are relatively easy to mobilize.

Ultimately, Dinkins's ability to affect policy depended largely on his ability to influence the city council. Major policy initiatives that affect the budget or land use require the approval of the council. City council members are influenced by labor, business groups (particularly real estate), the media, community advocates, and by ideas and ideology. Influencing the council to implement new policies requires a political strategy, organization, and mobilization of resources not unlike an electoral campaign.

In a city with the size and complexity of New York, the mayor's selection of executive staff is often the key to policy and political outcomes. Dinkins organized his staff in the opposite manner in which he organized his campaign. As mayor, he gave the most power to representatives of groups that supported him the least. He relied on them to develop his governance strategy. Not surprisingly, this generated conflict. With clearly defined political and programmatic priorities from the beginning, Dinkins's decision to hire a diverse staff would have been received as a shrewd maneuver to build support for his program. Lacking such direction, Dinkins's selection of staff generated internal bickering. The absence of direction led to a view that Dinkins was a weak political leader.

Notes

1. For a demographic analysis of voting in the 1989 primary and general elections, see John Mollenkopf and J. Phillip Thompson, "The Shifting Electoral Base of New York City Politics: The David Dinkins Coalition," paper presented at the annual meeting of the American Political Science Association, 1991.
2. Democrats outnumber Republicans by a four-to-one ratio in New York City. For an analysis of racially based mistrust in the 1989 general election, see Asher Arian, Arthur Goldberg, John Mollenkopf, and Ed Rogowsky, *Changing New York City Politics* (New York: Routledge, 1991), esp. chaps. 6 and 7.
3. For an analysis of the Koch coalition, see Martin Shefter, *Political Crisis/Fiscal Crisis: The Collapse and Revival of New York City* (New York: Basic, 1985).
4. Stan Hill, leader of DC 37 of AFSCME, Dennis Rivera, head of Local 1199, and Barry Feinstein, head of the local Teamsters union, were early strong supporters.
5. For a discussion of this issue in Coleman Young's election, see Wilbur C. Rich, *Coleman Young and Detroit Politics* (Detroit, Mich.: Wayne State University Press, 1989), 104.
6. For an account of J. Raymond Jones's rise in New York politics, see John C. Walter, *The Harlem Fox: J. Raymond Jones and Tammany, 1920–1970* (Albany: State University of New York Press, 1989).
7. Dinkins ran for Manhattan borough president three times, in 1977, 1981, and 1985 when he won. Councilwoman Ruth Messinger, the popular progressive representative of Manhattan's Upper West Side, endorsed Andrew Stein against Dinkins in his 1981 campaign for Manhattan borough president. Dinkins lost the election by one percentage point.
8. For an interesting comparison of the relationship of political machines to mayors' control of fiscal policy, see Ester R. Fuchs, *Mayors and Money: Fiscal Policy in New York and Chicago* (Chicago: University of Chicago Press, 1992).
9. See William Murphy, "Mayor Reacts to Poll: Whites Should Give Him Some Time," *Newsday,* Sept. 29, 1990, 3.
10. Todd S. Purdam, "Dinkins Talks of Crime Fear and of Race," *New York Times,* Sept. 20, 1990, sec. B, p. 1, col. 5.

11. See Shefter, *Political Crisis/Fiscal Crisis,* 169.
12. See "Statement by Mayor David N. Dinkins at Press Conference to Announce
    $75 Million in Actions to Keep the City's 1990 Budget in Balance between Now
    and June 30," news release, Monday, March 26, 1990.
13. From "Dinkins-Vallone Statement on the FY1991 Budget," news release, July 1,
    1990.
14. See David R. Eichenthal, "Changing Styles and Strategies," in *Urban Politics: New
    York Style,* edited by Jewel Bellush and Dick Netzer (Armonk, N.Y.: M. E.
    Sharpe, 1990), 70.
15. The UFT eventually agreed to defer 20–30 percent of its wage increase to pre-
    vent layoffs. The settlement was thereby reduced to roughly 4.5 percent. Infor-
    mation was provided by the New York City Office of Collective Bargaining.
16. See Michael Tomasky, "Public Enemies," *Village Voice,* July 9, 1991, 11.
17. The Board of Estimate had apportioned one vote to each of the city's five bor-
    ough (county) presidents, two votes each to the city comptroller and city council
    president (who ceremoniously presides over the city council), and two votes to
    the mayor.
18. New York has a four-tier property tax structure divided among homeowner (up
    to three-unit single-family homes), other residential, commercial, and utility
    properties. The four categories of property can be legally taxed at different rates.
    Although nominal tax rates are roughly equal, homeowners are generally as-
    sessed at only 8.34 percent of market value, while other properties are assessed
    in the 50 percent range. The result is a relative windfall for homeowners and a
    heavy tax burden for apartment renters. Homeowners in New York tend to be
    white, while the vast majority of African Americans and Latinos dwell in multi-
    family units. For a critical analysis of New York City's property tax system, see
    Gerald C. S. Mildner, "New York's Most Unjust Tax," *NY: The City Journal*
    (Summer 1991): 21.
19. David Seifman, "Beat the Clock," *New York Post,* July 1, 1991, 4.
20. "Interview with Victor A. Kovner," *Newsday,* Oct. 8, 1991, 87.
21. In the primary election, African Americans won twelve seats and Latinos won
    nine seats. In its primary election analysis, the Institute for Puerto Rican Policy
    called the election a "major gain" for Puerto Ricans and other Latinos.
22. See Kenneth R. Mladenka, "Blacks and Hispanics in Urban Politics," *American
    Political Science Review* 83 (1989): 172–75, 185; Albert K. Karnig and Susan
    Welch, *Black Representation and Urban Policy* (Chicago: University of Chicago
    Press, 1980), 151–52.
23. See Ronald W. Walters, *Black Presidential Politics* (Albany: State University of
    New York Press, 1988), for a description of institutional racism in the two main
    political parties as a barrier to African American mayors. For an analysis of con-
    servatism on the part of the federal government as an obstacle to African Amer-
    ican mayoral success in Atlanta, see Gary Orfield and Carole Ashkinaze, *The
    Closing Door: Conservative Policy and Black Opportunity* (Chicago: University of
    Chicago Press, 1991). For a discussion of economic constraints to black gover-

nance, see Robert C. Smith, "Black Power and the Transformation from Protest to Politics," *Political Science Quarterly* 96 (Fall 1981): 1–43.

24. See Charles V. Hamilton, Foreword, in *The New Black Politics: The Search for Political Power,* edited by Michael B. Preston, Lenneal Henderson, Jr., and Paul L. Puryear, 183.

25. Clarence N. Stone, *Regime Politics: Governing Atlanta, 1946–1988* (Lawrence: University of Kansas Press, 1989).

5

The Election of Norman B. Rice as Mayor of Seattle

Mylon Winn and Errol G. Palmer

Much of the scholarly attention given to the election of African Americans in the 1989 elections has focused on the elections of David Dinkins as mayor of New York City and L. Douglas Wilder as governor of Virginia. Though equally important, Norman B. Rice's election as mayor of Seattle, Washington, has received less attention than Dinkins's and Wilder's elections. Rice, Dinkins, and Wilder are the first African Americans elected to the top executive position in their respective cities and state. Rice's election is particularly noteworthy because African Americans constitute just 10 percent of Seattle's population.

Albert K. Karnig and Susan Welch contend that African American candidates win elections more often when the black population is the majority than when it is the minority.[1] Karnig and Welch's contention suggests that Seattle's 10 percent African American population is too small to have a decisive impact on a citywide election. Hence, a nonracial, or deracialization, election strategy must be employed by African Americans to win elections in cities like Seattle.

Deracialization as a formal concept is new to African American politics. Its origin can be traced to Charles V. Hamilton's advice to the Democratic party for the 1976 presidential election.[2] Hamilton argued that Democratic candidates should present issues that appeal to both African American and white voters. When candidates use a deracialization strategy, their competence and compassion are stressed. Race-specific issues are avoided or deemphasized. Hence, voters are not subjected to a campaign that they perceive as racially based and threatening to their interests.

Thus, the issues discussed during deracialized elections are fashioned to appeal to all voters. When African Americans are the majority, an African American candidate can support race-specific issues. This involves responding to African American voters' concerns about racial discrimination in employment, education, housing, and other domains. Therefore, campaigns must be responsive to race and social concerns. Conversely, African American candidates facing a white majority electorate must take a stance on race-neutral issues like cutting taxes, reducing government's size, decreasing spending, and improving government efficiency.

This chapter examines whether Norman B. Rice used a deracialized campaign strategy in his race for mayor of Seattle, Washington. We discuss the strategy that Rice used to successfully challenge a white candidate who supported issues that appealed to racial prejudice. We also examine how Rice used an issue-based campaign that distinguished between issues that responded to the concerns of citizens and rhetoric that appealed to racial differences. How did Rice encourage whites to vote for him? Rice's success demonstrates that African American candidates can win an election in a city with a large white population.

The chapter is divided into eight sections. They examine (1) the emergence of electoral politics as a strategy among African American candidates, (2) race and deracialization, (3) African Americans in Seattle, (4) Rice's emergence in Seattle politics, (5) the mayoral campaign, (6) deracialization as a campaign strategy, (7) Rice's governance style, and (8) the implications of Rice's election.

African Americans and Electoral Politics

The civil rights movement was a morally based effort to pass laws preventing racial discrimination in education, employment, access to public and private facilities, and voting. In the 1950s and 1960s, demonstrators protested against segregation laws and customs. This changed in the 1970s when the number of African Americans holding elected office increased. Rather than relying on protest, African Americans turned to electoral politics to attempt to create desirable social change. Robert C. Smith suggests that starting in the 1960s, African American politics became an agent for social change.[3] Over time, African American political mobilization has been transformed from a movement outside the system to electoral politics within the system. In both cases, the objective was to remove racial barriers to social and economic opportunities. These objectives focused on social responsibilities.

This strategy was aided by the 1965 Voting Rights Act, which significantly increased the number of African Americans participating in the political process. Enacting this law eliminated barriers to registering black voters, which opened the door to organizing African Americans politically. Michael B. Preston argues that this new strategy meant African Americans had decided to use electoral politics to improve the social and economic positions of blacks and that they seemed to believe that more would be gained from working within the system than outside of it.[4] In other words, African Americans have come to believe that "political power" is better than "street power."

Preston contends that stressing "ballot power" assumes there is power in numbers. Karnig and Welch point out that African American candidates "won in fewer than 30 percent of the cities with lower black population levels, but won in 88 percent of the cases with black majorities in the electorate."[5] Hence, Preston is correct: a large African American voting population is crucial to electing blacks to public office.

Candidates who stress improving opportunities and benefits are likely to gain the electoral support of blacks.[6] Support is based on a candidate's attitude toward educational reform, eliminating crime and drug problems, and improving relations with the police. The latter was a problem in Philadelphia during Mayor Frank Rizzo's administration.[7]

William R. Keech contends that the ballot is not enough to create change that will benefit African Americans.[8] Voting is a step in getting benefits, but there is more to fomenting social change than participating in or having enough votes to win elections. William E. Nelson and Philip J. Meranto suggest that political power (the ability to influence the allocation of governmental resources), insofar as it flows from electoral action, is achieved only if numbers are augmented by "group cohesion, leadership, political consciousness, and organization."[9] To some degree, this has happened in cities where African Americans have used bloc voting to elect and reelect black candidates. Birmingham, Alabama, and New Orleans, Louisiana, are cities where bloc voting was successfully used to elect Mayor Richard Arrington and reelect former Mayor Ernest Morial, respectively.[10]

Political participation should empower African Americans. This assumes that once blacks are elected, they can remove racial barriers that limit education, employment, housing, and business opportunities available to African Americans. The black political literature embraces this goal by advocating electoral strategies that create group consciousness and cohesion—a socially responsible position that implicitly considers the importance that African American voters assign to eliminating racial barriers. Empowerment involves creating electoral cohesiveness, but it may be pointless in a campaign where African Americans are a small number of voters and candidates are appealing to racist beliefs.

Race and Deracialization

The limited electoral success that Karnig and Welch discovered indicates that African American candidates must satisfy different expectations when black voters are the minority. African American candidates in such cases need blacks as their base of voter support. To this end, candidates must appeal to those African American voters who value racial sensitivity and social responsibility. This base is expanded by attracting white voters. This involves developing positions that appeal to those white voters who value fiscal conservatism and improved government performance. These are competing expectations when African Americans are dependent on government for services and white voters want a smaller government that is spending less on social programs. This creates a difficult situation for African American candidates who must demonstrate to black voters that they are sensitive to social issues and appeal to white voters by espousing a philosophy of fiscal prudence and governmental efficiency.

Ideally, competing expectations are eliminated by minimizing racial affiliation as a criterion for voting decisions. However, research has shown that the ideal and actual practices are different. Race continues to be a determining factor in individuals' voting decisions. Research by Jack Citrin, Donald Philip Green, and David Sears supports this observation.[11] They examined the 1982 California governor's race between Tom Bradley and George Deukmejian to determine whether Bradley's race was a factor in how white voters cast their ballots. They found that Bradley's campaign did not emphasize nor did his opponent stress Bradley's race. Deukmejian's decision to avoid the issue of race in the campaign did not mean that race was not a factor in the election.

Citrin, Green, and Sears used a *Los Angeles Times* survey to determine whether race was a factor in the California governor's election. While Bradley's personal image was favorable, survey data demonstrated that white voters held negative opinions of African Americans and that some believed that blacks were getting too much favorable treatment from government. These two factors reduced Bradley's support among white voters.[12]

Citrin, Green, and Sears also examined the race between Wilson Riles, an African American incumbent candidate, and William Hoenig, a white candidate, for state superintendent of schools in California, an election won by Hoenig. Hoenig was relatively unknown to voters; Riles did not enjoy high name recognition among voters, although he had served as superintendent of schools in California for sixteen years before the election. They held similar views on education. Riles's campaign deemphasized his race and focused on education issues. Yet the main difference between the candidates was their race.

Citrin, Green, and Sears concluded that race was an indirect factor in Bradley's defeat and a direct factor in Riles's defeat.[13] The deracialization strategies used by Bradley and Riles did not preclude race from becoming a factor that influenced how whites voted. One possible inference from these two campaigns is that a deracialized strategy should attempt to make whites uncomfortable about voting against African American candidates simply because of race.

Joseph P. McCormick contends that white voters are not dependable supporters of the electoral interests of black candidates. He points out that David Dinkins in New York City and L. Douglas Wilder in Virginia barely won their respective elections. McCormick states that white candidates did better among African American voters than Dinkins and Wilder did among white voters, indicating that white candidates are more appealing to black voters than black candidates are to white voters. With this observation, McCormick cautions that white electoral support for African American candidates "should be regarded as soft."[14] If he is correct, it does not matter whether African American candidates are less threatening: they will not be supported by a significant number of white voters. A serious consequence is that deracialization is likely to cause black politics to become unresponsive to "racism and its lingering socioeconomic effects on African Americans."[15]

Politics does not have to be a zero sum process for African American and white voters. The ability to satisfy the interests of both is especially important when the black population is the minority. A campaign strategy that appeals to the interests of both black and white voters can satisfy different racial expectations.[16]

African Americans in Seattle

Seattle's attractiveness as a city is based on its reputation for offering economic opportunities and a desirable place to reside. Since 1984, approximately 284,000 jobs have been created in King County, where Seattle is located. The creation of new companies accounts for some of the growth, and the expansion of companies like Boeing Aircraft Company and others in retailing, computer software, and timber products account for the remainder.

Minority companies have fared well by doing business with King County, but there are some problems. In 1989, $85 million in contracts were awarded in King County. Minority businesses received $14.9 million of the total awarded. Receiving contracts is offset by problems caused by the difficulty of obtaining capital from lending institutions. Banks are unwilling to lend money to some African American companies. Consequently, blacks are forced to rely upon more expensive alternative sources to obtain money to take advantage of business opportunities.

An added dimension is Seattle's reputation as one of the more desirable U.S. cities in which to live. While fishing, hiking, and many cultural amenities may provide Seattle residents with an attractive lifestyle, its reputation is somewhat marred by high unemployment rates and some blacks' difficulty in obtaining capital to finance business ventures. The negatives of Seattle are outweighed by the positives of employment, business opportunities, and the city as a desirable place to reside.

Seattle is an ethnically diverse city of 516,259 (1990 U.S. Census). Racial and ethnic groups constitute 26.3 percent of the total population: 50,918 (9.9 percent) African Americans; 6,674 (1.3 percent) American Indians, Eskimos, or Aleut; 59,141 (11.5 percent) Asians or Pacific Islanders; and 18,349 (3.5 percent) of Hispanic origin. Whites constitute 380,423 (74 percent) of the city's population. This diversity has not proven to be a source of racial conflict, instead lending itself to racial interaction.

The largest population of African Americans are located near downtown Seattle in a community called the Central Area. The rest of the black population is diffused throughout Seattle and King County. The Central Area is an ethnically diverse community because it is also populated by whites and Asians.

Racial division has not characterized political contests. Instead, voting decisions have been based on the candidate's party affiliation and stance on issues. This perception was challenged by Shelby Scates after the 1985 mayor's election in which Norman Rice, an African American candidate, was defeated by Charles Royer, the white incumbent. Scates, a *Seattle Post-Intelligencer* reporter, argued that race influenced the decision of white voters to support Royer rather than Rice. He concluded that white voters in Seattle were not ready to elect an African American as their mayor.[17]

Scates's allegation was an afterthought, rather than an issue discussed during the mayoral campaign. His contention applied only to the office of mayor. African Americans had been repeatedly elected in citywide elections to Seattle's city council. Thus, the significance of Scates's position is that he introduced the possibility that the mayor's office in Seattle was unattainable for African Americans.

Research indicates that most African American officials are elected in district elections (as opposed to at-large elections) where blacks are the majority.[18] The argument that large numbers of black voters are needed to elect African American candidates does not apply in Seattle. Seattle's small black population dictates using a race-neutral campaign strategy. By doing so, candidates do not have to rely on African American voters to win an election.

Moreover, in districts with a small black population, a viable black candidate must assemble a broad electoral coalition.

Citywide elections have not prevented African American candidates from being elected to the Seattle city council. During the past eleven years, two African Americans (Sam Smith and Norman Rice) have served on the city council. They could not have been elected and reelected without significant electoral support from white voters. The small African American population (and thus even smaller number of black voters) means that Smith and Rice have depended on white voters to get elected to public office.

The Emergence of Norman B. Rice in Seattle Politics

Rice was first elected to the Seattle city council in 1978 and was twice re-elected. He chaired the finance and public safety committees and was president of the city council during one of his three terms. He developed a reputation as a person who knows the importance of working with people and getting a consensus among competing groups. Rice has been described as a "solid performer" who is "accessible" and listens to the people. He had a leading role in helping the city manage the financial crisis caused by federal budget reductions during the Reagan administration. This made him an important player in Seattle city council politics.[19] His performance and reputation made him a likely candidate to run for mayor of Seattle.

Supporters wanted Rice to run for mayor in 1989. Polls indicated that he had a good chance of winning. His previous campaigns had made him one of the best-known local politicians in the Seattle area. A major supporter was Rice's minister, Rev. Samuel McKinney, pastor of Mount Zion Baptist Church, a prominent African American church in Seattle. Rev. McKinney talked with Rice about the importance of his running for mayor and urged him to enter the race. When Rice finally decided to run, Rev. McKinney and other black supporters contacted several influential liberal white Seattle residents and pointed out that they were expected to support Rice's candidacy, in return for previous support of liberal white candidates from African Americans.[20]

The Mayoral Campaign

Rice delayed entering the mayoral race until he was sure of his decision. He was concerned that none of the declared candidates were addressing important issues facing the city, such as homelessness, health care, crime, drugs, and a declining quality of life for the city's residents. He was worried about what he called "voices of division" along racial lines that had been introduced into the race for mayor. The source of the division that concerned Rice was Initiative 34, part of which sought to eliminate mandatory busing. Doug Jewett, already a candidate for mayor, had coauthored Initiative 34. The initiative also would require the city to give the school district $4.3 million to create magnet schools that students could choose to attend. Rice hoped another candidate (there were twelve candidates in the race) would emerge who would speak against the racial division he believed the initiative was causing. When no one surfaced, Rice entered the race.

The perception that Initiative 34 introduced racial division into the campaign set the 1989 race for mayor apart from the 1985 contest.[21] Rice declared his candidacy on July 19, 1989, just minutes before the filing deadline. Hubert Locke speculated that Initiative 34 motivated Rice to enter the mayor's race because the other candidates had failed to take a stance on this divisive issue.[22] Indeed, Rice presented himself as the candidate who was willing to oppose Initiative 34, which he called "a terrible new ingredient in the city's already strained racial fabric."[23] This position was intended to appeal to a population that was liberal about racial issues.

Rice portrayed himself as the only candidate who unequivocally endorsed unity and rejected racial division. This stance made all of his primary opponents (except Doug Jewett) appear as if they were not being forceful enough in speaking out against Initiative 34. Jewett's support of Initiative 34 meant that he could be portrayed as the candidate who chose racial division over unity.

Deracialization as a Campaign Strategy

Rice's candidacy increased the field of candidates to thirteen. Doug Jewett, Randy Revelle, Norman Rice, Dolores Sibonga, and James Street were the top contenders in the open primary. Jewett and Revelle had raised the most money, and therefore were able to run well-financed, competitive campaigns. Growth in the metropolitan area, crime, drugs, schools, busing, and children's programs were issues discussed during the primary. All were important issues, but mandatory busing received the most attention. This was sparked by Jewett's decision to focus his campaign on the passage of Initiative 34.

Preprimary polls indicated that there was support for Initiative 34. Jewett's candidacy benefited from this support but at a cost: his campaign was accused of having racial overtones. He was undeterred and tried to make busing the central issue in the mayoral race. In contrast, Rice discussed growth in the metropolitan area, crime, drugs, and children's programs. He stressed that he was concentrating on issues that concerned all Seattle voters. In sum, Rice used a deracialization strategy.

Jewett and Rice finished first and second, respectively, in the primary and advanced to the general election (Rice received 20 percent and Jewett 24 percent of the primary votes). Jewett continued to focus on Initiative 34 during the general election campaign. He argued that his stance on Initiative 34 was an indicator of his leadership. By championing Initiative 34, Jewett argued that he was forcing Seattle's leaders to "deal" with the most important problem affecting the Seattle school district. While he discussed affordable housing, drug-related crime, the need for a treatment program for children who were addicted to drugs, and hiring more police officers, Jewett's support of Initiative 34 was the central focus of his campaign.

Rice focused on broader issues: crime, affordable housing, and employment. He emphasized his role in adding one hundred police officers between 1986 and 1989, creating anticrime teams in neighborhoods, and working with community leaders to make sure their residents were supportive of the police. Rice also took a position on the busing issue: he favored gradually eliminating mandatory busing. He also favored working with the school board to improve education, after busing had been eliminated. He was quick to point out that he was campaigning for mayor of Seattle, not for a position on the Seattle school board. This was Rice's way of emphasizing that he was concentrating on issues that were the responsibility of the city.

Jewett's strategy, which worked during the primary, was not as successful during the general election. In less than two months, from September 20 to November 2, 1989, the lead that Jewett had at the end of the primary had disappeared. A November poll indicated that 50.5 percent of the respondents would or were likely to vote for Rice and 42 percent would or were likely to vote for Jewett.[24] Another poll indicated that the city was practically deadlocked over Initiative 34, with 41 percent in support and 40 percent opposed.[25] Rice took advantage of the Democratic majority in Seattle. He also succeeded in tacitly labeling Jewett a one-issue (busing) candidate and his campaign as divisive.

The controversy that Initiative 34 introduced into the campaign created significant interest in the election, resulting in a voter turnout of 60 percent. Rice benefited from the high voter participation of mainly Democrats. He received 93,491 votes to Jewett's 67,276 votes. Rice was supported regardless of the race of voters. Support varied by precinct (Figure 5–1): where white voters were under 80 percent, Rice received 73 percent and Jewett 27 percent of the votes.[26] In precincts in which white voters were between 80 and 95 percent, Rice received 59 percent of the votes to Jewett's 41 percent. In precincts in which the percentage of white voters was 95–100 percent, Rice received 48 to Jewett's 52 percent of the votes. As the proportion of whites in precincts increased, the support for Rice decreased. Hence, Rice's campaign was more effective in precincts that were more heterogeneous.

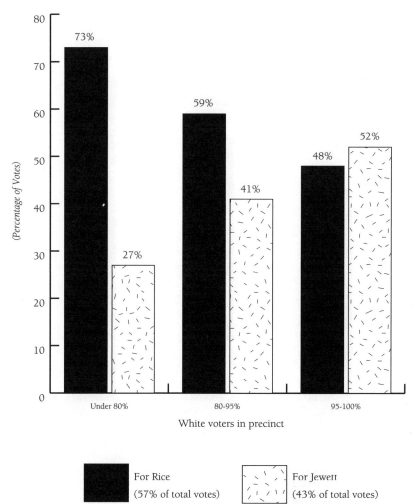

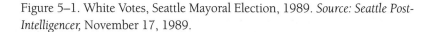

Figure 5–1. White Votes, Seattle Mayoral Election, 1989. *Source: Seattle Post-Intelligencer,* November 17, 1989.

African American voters generally rejected Jewett's candidacy (Figure 5–2). In precincts in which black voters were under 5 percent, Rice received 55 percent to Jewett's 45 percent of the votes. In precincts in which black voters were between 5–35 percent, Rice received 68 percent to Jewett's 32 percent of the votes. In precincts in which black voters were over 35 percent, Rice received 84 percent to Jewett's 16 percent of the votes.

While there was generally a positive response to Rice's campaign, this does not mean that race was not an implicit factor in the campaign. Racially tolerant white voters were challenged by Rice's deracialization strategy. Rice

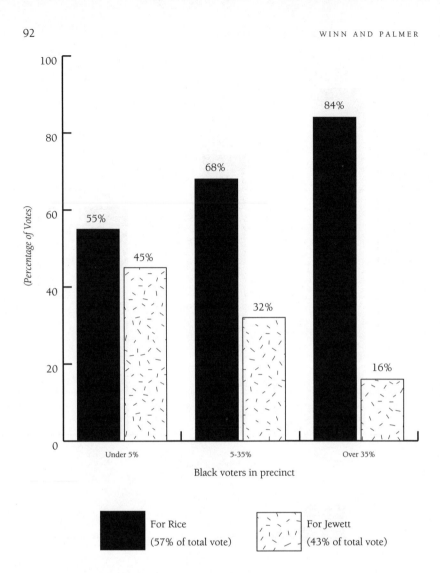

Figure 5–2. Black Votes, Seattle Mayoral Election, 1989. *Source: Seattle Post-Intelligencer,* November 17, 1989.

identified himself as a loyal Democrat who was concerned about the same issues as other good Democrats.[27] This is a deracialization strategy that identifies the common position on issues shared by Rice and black and white voters. Moreover, Rice adroitly used the implicit introduction of race into the campaign to enhance his chance for being elected. Rice's strategy in this regard was sophisticated and effective.

Rice's Governance Style

Rice hired an ethnically diverse staff of minorities, women, and white males as department heads and members of his executive staff. Rice contends that when people come to city hall and see minorities and women in decision-making positions, they feel confident about their government. Rice believes that citizens feel comfortable dealing with a staff that is representative of Seattle's ethnically diverse population. He believes that this influences citizens to feel that they have greater access to his administration.[28]

Developing an education program was Rice's first major policy initiative. To this end, the Family and Education Levy was developed and presented to the voters. The overall purpose of this tax was to significantly improve public education in Seattle—specifically, to improve early childhood development, create school student/family services, develop student health services, establish nonschool-hour activities for elementary-aged latchkey children, and enhance select educational programs.[29] The levy passed by a yes vote of 57 percent—at a time when Seattle residential property taxes were skyrocketing. In most cases, the assessed values of property doubled the previous values. The adamant opposition of many citizens to raising taxes made passing the education levy a noteworthy accomplishment for Rice's administration. Rice pointed out that he used the political resources of the mayor's office to support the levy.[30] This was the first time that a mayor of Seattle had used his office's political resources to support a school-related levy.

Conclusion

Future African American candidates can learn about the conditions that determine the success of a deracialized campaign from Rice's election. Rice's election demonstrates that blacks can successfully challenge white candidates who support issues that appeal to racial prejudice. To this end, Rice used an issue-based campaign that appealed to voters who were able to distinguish between issues that responded to the concerns of citizens and rhetoric that appealed to racial differences. This strategy deracialized the campaign by limiting the appeal of racial issues. This was possible because Seattle does not have a pronounced history of racial division.

Rice's strategy encouraged whites to vote for a well-known African American candidate. This strategy was supplemented with an appeal to voters along party lines. Rice's stance on Initiative 34 took the high ground. This proved to be successful and created a problem that his opponent could not resolve. Rice's success demonstrates that African American candidates can win an election in a city where whites are an overwhelming majority of the registered voters.

Notes

We are indebted to Randell Goo, Dorothy "Dottie" Pearson, Rose Richard, Zakiyah Spencer, Megan Stearns, Adel Smith, and Nancy J. Winn for their assistance, and especially to Huey L. Perry and Wilbur Rich.

1. Albert K. Karnig and Susan Welch, *Black Representation and Urban Policy* (Chicago: University of Chicago Press, 1980).

2. Charles V. Hamilton, "Deracialization: Examination of a Political Strategy," *First World* 1 (Mar./Apr. 1977): 3–5.

3. Robert C. Smith, "Recent Elections and Black Politics: The Maturation or Death of Black Politics?" *PS: Political Science and Politics* 23 (June 1990): 160.

4. Michael B. Preston, "Black Politics and Public Policy in Chicago: Self-Interest versus Constituent Representation," in *The New Black Politics: The Search for Political Power,* edited by Michael B. Preston, Lenneal J. Henderson, Jr., and Paul L. Puryear (New York: Longman, 1987), 159.

5. Karnig and Welch, *Black Representation,* 56.

6. See Huey L. Perry and Alfred Stokes, "Politics and Power in the Sunbelt: Mayor Morial of New Orleans," in *New Black Politics,* edited by Preston et al., 1987, 250–51; Wilbur C. Rich, "Coleman Young and Detroit Politics, 1973–1986," in *New Black Politics,* edited by Preston et al., 1987, 208–9.

7. Bruce Ransom points out that Mayor Rizzo's "law-and-order" emphasis, when he was police commissioner, created strained relations with Philadelphia's African American community. Police brutality and racism charges created mistrust that spilled over into Rizzo's tenure as mayor ("Black Independent Electoral Politics in Philadelphia: The Election of Mayor W. Wilson Goode," in *New Black Politics,* edited by Preston et al., 1987, 258–60).

8. William R. Keech, *The Impact of Negro Voting: The Role of the Vote in the Quest for Equality* (Chicago: Rand McNally, 1972).

9. William E. Nelson, Jr. and Philip J. Meranto, *Electing Black Mayors: Political Action in the Black Community* (Columbus: Ohio State University Press, 1977), 26.

10. Huey L. Perry, "Black Politics and Mayoral Leadership in Birmingham and New Orleans," *National Political Science Review* 2 (April 1990): 154–60.

11. Jack Citrin, Donald Philip Green, and David Sears, "White Reaction to Black Candidates: When Does Race Matter," *Public Opinion Quarterly* 54 (1990): 81–94.

12. Ibid., 87.

13. Ibid., 91.

14. Joseph P. McCormick II, "The November Elections and the Politics of Deracialization," *New Directions* 17 (Jan. 1990): 27.

15. Smith, "Recent Elections," 161.

16. Charles Green and Basil Wilson, *The Struggle for Black Empowerment in New York City: Beyond the Politics of Pigmentation* (New York: Praeger, 1989), 107.

17. Shelby Scates, "Subtle Factor in Royer-Rice Contest," *Seattle Post-Intelligencer,* Nov. 10, 1985, F2.

18. Susan Welch, "The Impact of At-Large Elections on the Representation of Blacks and Hispanics," *Journal of Politics* 52 (1990): 1050; Peter Engstrom and Michael McDonald, "The Election of Blacks to City Councils," *American Political Science Review* 75 (1981): 344; Karnig and Welch, "Electoral Structure and Black Representation on City Councils," *Social Science Quarterly* 63 (Mar. 1982): 99; Theodore Robinson and Thomas Dye, "Reformism and Representation on City Councils," *Social Science Quarterly* 59 (June 1978): 131–41.

19. Mark Murry, interview on Rice's leadership of the Seattle city council's finance committee.

20. Rev. Samuel McKinney, interview, Seattle, Washington, July 14, 1990.

21. Larry Gossett and David Olson, interviews, Seattle, Washington, July 16 and 17, 1990.

22. Hubert Locke, interview, Seattle, Washington, July 15, 1990.

23. Susan Gilmore and Ross Anderson, "Rice Pursues a Calling in Mayoral Race," *Seattle Times,* Sept. 13, 1989, D1.

24. Neil Modie, "Norm Rice Clings to 9 Percent Lead Over Doug Jewett in Mayoral Race," *Seattle Post-Intelligencer,* Nov. 2, 1989, A1.

25. Mike Meritt, "Anti-Busing Initiative Now a Virtual Dead Heat," *Seattle Post-Intelligencer,* Nov. 2, 1989, A1.

26. The data for Figures 5–1 and 5–2 were provided by Scott Maier.

27. Rice, interview, Seattle, Washington, Nov. 29, 1990.

28. Ibid.

29. "Just the Beginning: A Report of the Commitments to Strengthen Our Schools and Our Children," June 16, 1990.

30. Rice, interview, Seattle, Washington, Nov. 29, 1990.

6

The Rise and Fall of Deracialization: Andrew Young as Mayor and Gubernatorial Candidate

Carol A. Pierannunzi and John D. Hutcheson, Jr.

In recent years, the concept of deracialization has been applied to many electoral contests. The term generally refers to a particular campaign style that deemphasizes racially divisive issues. In some instances, a deracialized strategy has facilitated the formation of successful electoral coalitions, as was the case in L. Douglas Wilder's gubernatorial election in Virginia.[1] In other settings, black candidates have been successful without adhering to a deracialized strategy,[2] and some deracialized campaigns have been unsuccessful. This chapter focuses on Andrew Young's use of deracialization as a political strategy. While Young, as mayor of Atlanta, successfully forged a governing coalition with the city's business elite, his attempt to develop a deracialized statewide electoral coalition in his campaign for governor of Georgia was notably unsuccessful and, in some ways, may have contributed to his defeat.

Young's political career has brought him name recognition well beyond the city of Atlanta and the state of Georgia. He was elected to the U.S. House of Representatives, served as U.N. ambassador during the Jimmy Carter administration, and was a well-known civil rights activist during the 1960s and 1970s. He has remained in the spotlight as an advocate for the selection of the city of Atlanta as the site for the 1996 Summer Olympics and has been widely credited for the success of that effort. Although residents of Georgia outside Atlanta had never been represented by Young, they certainly were aware of him as a political force in the state when he declared for governor.

Mayor Young's Deracialized Governing Coalition

Young actively sought support from Atlanta's business elite in order to secure a governing coalition as mayor. Clarence Stone defines the coalition of formal and informal power by which a community is governed as a regime.[3] Regimes focus more on managing conflict and response to social change and less on formal power. In Stone's view, electoral victory is necessary but insufficient for political leaders to govern. Stone's examination of the governing regime in Atlanta suggests that Young sought to place himself in a pivotal position within the city's governing regime, a regime that has been largely concerned with economic development issues.[4] During his mayoralty, Young advocated highway development, the construction of a convention facility, the restoration of Underground Atlanta as a tourist attraction, and the construction of a domed stadium within the city. In addition, he was noted for his support of a one-cent sales tax increase, the creation of a rail-truck "piggyback" switching facility, and airport expansion. He was a vocal proponent of the selection of Atlanta as a site for the 1988 Democratic National Convention, and his efforts to create an image of Atlanta as an international city were well publicized. His most recent economic development project, the selection of the city as the site for the 1996 Summer Olympics, underscores his commitment to such image building and economic development.

All of these projects required Young to maintain strong ties to the city's business elite. The deracialization strategy achieved great success for Young as leader of Atlanta's governing coalition. Yet such development projects were not without their detractors. Low-income residents of the city were displaced by the construction of the domed stadium, and there was strident controversy over the construction of the rail-truck piggyback switching facility, which increased large truck traffic and noise pollution in several residential areas. The two major highways that Young advocated were also highly controversial.

After the selection of Atlanta as the site for the Olympics, neighborhood organizations objected to the development of large sports facilities in their residential areas. Residents of an affluent neighborhood were able to fend off the construction of the tennis facilities in a nearby public tennis area. The site of the Olympic stadium in a poor neighborhood attracted public opposition from a newly created neighborhood group. However, the Atlanta Organizing Committee (the organization that proposed Atlanta as the site for the Olympics) was unshakable in its resolve to have the stadium built on the site in the poor community. Residents of the affected neighborhood were informed that the stadium would be built in their community despite their objections and that therefore they should make the best of the situation.[5] Many of these same residents had been affected by the construction of the existing stadium during the heyday of urban renewal in Atlanta.

In contrast to its successes in economic development, Young's administration gave little attention to social problems and was seen as unresponsive to the needs of the city's low-income residents.[6] Young himself was not popular with many residents of public housing projects. He was picketed by advocates for the homeless, and his policies were opposed by numerous neighborhood associations.

A neighborhood planning program developed by Young's predecessor, Maynard Jackson (who reassumed the mayoralty following Young's tenure), was largely disassembled by the Young administration. Jackson, who did not formally endorse the Young gubernatorial candidacy, was viewed as oriented more toward neighborhood concerns than was Young,[7] who was more often viewed as part of the establishment.[8]

Critics charged that Young spent too much time overseas while in office and that he did not pay enough attention to the social service delivery issues that concerned Atlanta residents. When critics referred to Young as not being a hands-on type of mayor, he responded that he had his "hands on economic development."[9] Young defended his frequent trips overseas as an effort toward making Atlanta an "international city" and attracting more foreign investment. Those who supported Young noted economic development as his strong point. The *Atlanta Constitution*'s editorial endorsement of Young read: "Ask the city's Chamber of Commerce if it has ever seen a more effective salesman" (July 26, 1990).

Thus, as he entered the race for governor, Young had a history of support for economic development. He did not, however, have a reputation for advocacy of housing, employment, education, and other issues more salient to many black voters. His low-key style and focus on economic development were designed to attract white voters. Young was at the apex of deracialized politics, and his staff was intent on keeping race out of the gubernatorial campaign. But a coalition of the type that Young had successfully assembled in Atlanta was untested in statewide electoral politics in Georgia.

Deracialization and the Gubernatorial Campaign

While Young attempted to deemphasize race as a campaign issue, others were quick to note it. As he traveled the state, Young attracted attention as the first major black candidate for governor of Georgia. His international reputation and the symbolic importance of his candidacy drew reporters from national publications, such as *Time* and *U.S. News and World Report,* and garnered him an appearance on the *Today* show. Young maintained his strategy of quietly trying to get African Americans to the polls while doing nothing to alienate white voters. In one telling remark early in the campaign, Young indicated that racism, once like a cancer, was now like acne. Zell Miller, Young's successful opponent, responded that racism was increasing.[10] Young's low-key approach did little to encourage black turnout. At one point, addressing an audience in a rural, black majority county where unemployment was high, he told the crowd that he would be able to improve employment opportunities through his "clout" with business leaders,[11] not exactly what low-income blacks would expect to hear from a black candidate.

Although Young received overall support from many black leaders, he encountered opposition from some black leaders. Several influential African American ministers, a city councilman, and an outspoken state senator openly criticized Young for his ties to the business elite.[12] Maynard Jackson, the mayor of Atlanta both before and after Young's mayoral tenure, withheld endorsement of Young's gubernatorial candidacy, as did the city council, until just days before his defeat in the runoff election.

At times, Young's campaign seemed undirected. Frank Greer, Young's media advisor, was the only member of the campaign staff who had statewide electoral campaign experience. Although there was a consultant position planned, disagreement within the campaign hierarchy prevented filling the position. Goals were unclear, and the staff was misdirected, if not dysfunctional.[13]

Young campaigners claimed that they were actually running two campaigns, one for black voters and one for white voters. The appeal to blacks focused on campaigning from the pulpit, using leaflets, and making personal appearances, while the appeal to whites focused more on the media.[14] Zell Miller, Young's principal opponent, focused heavily on media politics.

Young also seemed to be running two campaigns for financial support. His close ties to the Atlanta business elite failed to produce early campaign support. Three months before the July primary, Young had raised $1 million from various donors, including such Atlanta corporate giants as Delta Airlines, Coca-Cola, and the architect John Portman, but the amounts were smaller than anticipated and many expected contributions did not materialize.[15] So Young sought and received financial support from outside of Georgia. Of thirteen donors who contributed $10,000 or more to his campaign, nine were from out of state. His largest contributions came from Bill Cosby (who donated $50,000 to the campaign) and Anne Cox-Chambers (also a $50,000 contribution) of Cox Enterprises, a communications corporation that publishes the *Atlanta Journal* and the *Atlanta Constitution*. One other sizeable contribution ($10,000) came from a Washington, D.C., law firm of which Cox Enterprises is a client.[16] Passing attention was given to the fact that Young received contributions from several firms that had been awarded city contracts during his mayoral terms.[17]

Perhaps the greatest flaw in the Young campaign, however, was its lack of excitement. Black voter apathy was higher than expected. There was no compelling reason to vote for Young—no single issue that distinguished him from his opponents as the primary neared. In contrast, Miller's central theme focused on a proposal for a state lottery. He appealed to the voters through a highly organized media campaign that addressed issues such as boot camp prisons, reduced auto insurance rates, and the lottery. Young's only potential weapon, his pro-choice abortion position, was quickly diffused by Miller, who said that although he personally did not favor abortion, he would take no action to restrict it further. Moreover, Young's international image may have benefited him less than expected, especially when contrasted with Miller's lengthy career in state politics. As the primary neared, Young and Miller emerged as front-runners in a very conservative field of five candidates that included former segregationist Governor Lester Maddox.

Preprimary polls indicated that Young's support was drawn largely from black voters, urban areas (especially in and around Atlanta), and voters who were not native-born Georgians, especially those who were not native-born southerners. A comparison of two preprimary polls taken in May and June indicates that Miller had gained 7 percent during the interim while Young had gained only 1 percent. The May poll found that the two candidates were in a virtual tie (at 30 percent each). The June poll indicated that Young had only 8 percent of the vote outside the metropolitan Atlanta area and was running slightly higher among female voters.[18] At this point in the campaign, Miller had outspent Young in media expenses ($1,760,912 to $654,575; the three other candidates had spent a combined total of $1,523,199 on media advertising).[19]

The primary turnout was much higher than expected, about 35 percent. Young believed the high turnout was almost a referendum on the highly popular lottery issue,[20] the issue on which Miller built his campaign. Overall, Young garnered only about 15 percent of the white vote. Miller received 13 percent of the statewide black vote, but he did better among blacks in the metropolitan Atlanta area (about 20 percent). Young did better among black voters who were less acquainted with his ties to the business elite and his strong support for economic development projects. White support for Young was strongest near Atlanta and weakest in rural areas. He narrowly won the five-county area closest to the city. When all the votes were counted, Miller had received about 42 percent of the vote and Young about 29 percent. Roy Barnes, a conservative state representative also making his gubernatorial bid, put more pressure on Young than expected, receiving about 20 percent of the vote. Young and Miller were left to face each other in a runoff.

The primary results suggest several interesting points. First, although neither Young nor Miller could be described as liberal candidates, the voters rejected the more conservative politics of the other candidates (e.g., Lester Maddox received only about 3 percent). Second, the high turnout for the primary was going to be a factor for the runoff. Recent black victories in other elections had occurred when white turnout had been lower.[21] Moreover, black turnout had been rather disappointing.[22] Some interpreted the higher than expected turnout in rural white areas as an awareness among rural whites that a black candidate was on the ballot and that they should vote for a nonblack candidate.[23] Higher than expected turnout among rural whites was especially typical of areas where, in addition to Young being on the ballot, local elections included black candidates.

Finally, it was apparent that the Young campaign needed a change of strategy to garner the votes of those who had voted for other candidates no longer in the race. Young began by courting the powerful speaker of the Georgia House of Representatives, Tom Murphy. However, Murphy did not endorse Young in the runoff, saying that his choice, Lauren "Bubba" Mc-Donald, had been defeated in the primary and that he did not have a second choice. Murphy, a longtime opponent to the lottery, then reversed himself on the lottery issue, saying that he had "called it wrong," effectively indicating his support for Miller. McDonald formally endorsed Miller the evening after the primary.[24]

In the last few days before the runoff, with polls indicating that Miller's lead was widening,[25] Young decided to adopt a negative advertising campaign and to attempt to identify himself with civil rights issues.[26] A heated televised debate, generally conceded to be a draw, failed to spark voter interest, and, as the runoff neared, the Young campaign was still floundering without either a central issue or the near unanimous black support that typically characterizes a viable black candidate running against a white opponent. It seemed unlikely that the Young campaign would produce the miracle it was hoping for as Young rushed, in a final campaign push, from pulpit to pulpit on the Sunday before the runoff.

Young's defeat in the runoff was more crushing than anticipated. He received only 38 percent of the vote. Moreover, in heavily black areas in Atlanta, Miller received 20 percent of the black vote. In predominantly white counties, Miller acquired much of the support that had been given to other candidates in the primary. For example, in Forsyth County, which has very few black residents, Miller received 60 percent of the primary vote and 85 percent of the runoff vote.[27]

Black turnout overall was disappointing. The deracialized strategy that had served Young so well during his mayoral administration failed him as a gubernatorial candidate. Only in the final days of the campaign, as he began to revive his ties to the civil rights era, did Young cast off the deracialized rhetoric for which he had been so well-known in Atlanta. During this time, Young was asked whether race had played a role in the campaign. He responded, "I haven't had anyone call me a name and I haven't had anyone shoot me a bird."[28]

In an editorial following the runoff, John Head noted that had Young addressed himself directly to Georgia's African Americans he would have "drive[n] away white voters in droves." Head also suggested that the lack of cohesive black support for Young may have been due to his neglect of poor blacks in the past. Both Head's editorial and another observer[29] asked what blacks who did not support Young were left with after Young was defeated in the runoff. In fact, black voters would have been hard pressed to find representation on issues such as housing and social programs from the candidates who remained. Maynard Jackson and Young both expressed support for Miller as he prepared for the general election, which he eventually won—but little remained of any discussion of black representation at that point. Young devoted himself to his Olympic Committee duties and prepared for private life. The campaign left him $700,000 in debt.[30]

Deracialization Is Not Enough

Charles E. Jones and Michael Clemons argue that deracialization is only one of a number of factors that may contribute to the success of black political candidates in majority white districts.[31] Assuming that race continues to be a predominant influence in American politics, Jones and Clemons propose a model of racial crossover voting that, in addition to deracialization, includes factors such as political apprenticeship, party apparatus, a racial ombudsman function, and a "wild card." These variables are viewed as "critically important" in African Americans' attempts to win elections in nonblack majority districts "since they can mitigate the impact of race in interracial political contests."[32]

L. Douglas Wilder's election as governor of Virginia illustrates the utility of Jones and Clemons's model and serves as a useful comparison for this analysis. While Wilder's margin of victory (0.37 percent) was the narrowest in the history of gubernatorial campaigns in Virginia, his campaign has been described as a "Herculean" effort, one in which he did everything right.[33] Wilder's long apprenticeship in state government contrasts sharply with Young's lack of experience in state government. While Young had represented Georgia's only black majority congressional district and had served as U.N. ambassador and as mayor, he had no state legislative experience. His political background did not prepare him to deal adroitly with statewide issues, and he admitted that he was "uneasy campaigning for governor among rural whites."[34]

Furthermore, Young's administrative abilities and his attention to day-to-day administrative details had been widely criticized during his tenure as mayor. In contrast, Wilder had been elected to the Virginia Senate in 1970 where he served for sixteen years and where he was chair of three standing committees before being elected lieutenant governor in 1985. Thus, Wilder had amassed some twenty years of legislative and administrative experience in state government before running for governor.[35] In fact, Wilder himself, in commenting on Young's defeat, expressed the opinion that lack of state-wide experience, rather than race, was the more prominent factor in Young's defeat.[36]

While Wilder enjoyed the support of the Democratic party apparatus in Virginia,[37] Young's principal opponent, Zell Miller, as lieutenant governor and a leader of the Georgia Democratic party (owing to the lame duck status of the then current Democratic governor), had statewide campaign machinery in place, and prominent elected officials (Senators Sam Nunn and Wyche Fowler as well as Atlanta Mayor Maynard Jackson) remained neutral. This, of course, can be attributed to differences between the primary and the general election, but there is little doubt that Miller, having run several statewide campaigns and enjoyed a long-term prominent position within Georgia's Democratic party, held an advantage through his access to the Democratic party machinery. Moreover, Miller had direct access to traditional sources of Democratic campaign financing while Young had to rely heavily on funding sources outside the state.

Other differences in the Wilder and Young gubernatorial campaigns were more subtle. While the media did not promote race as a divisive factor in the Georgia election, and while both Miller and Young avoided racially divisive campaign tactics, the only major newspaper to endorse Young was the *Atlanta Constitution*. On the other hand, the media acted as "racial ombudsman" in the Virginia election by minimizing the racial factor in the campaign.[38] To some degree, this too was the case in Georgia. However, unlike Young, Wilder was successful in achieving the support of the print media. Additionally, Wilder capitalized on what Jones and Clemons refer to as a "wild card factor," in this case the abortion issue, made more salient by the 1989 *Webster v. Reproductive Health Services* decision (106 L.Ed.2d. 410). This decision created a storm of political activity that ultimately advantaged Wilder.[39] Young, however, was unable to clearly distinguish himself from Miller on any issue. While Young's pro-choice position was somewhat more aggressive than his opponent's, Miller successfully defused the issue by suggesting that he would not take any restrictive action regarding abortion rights.

Thus, the Wilder and Young efforts to capture racial crossover votes in majority white districts appear more dissimilar than alike. One common component was deracialization. Jones and Clemons conclude that Wilder's strategy "exemplified the multidimensional nature of the deracialized political strategy" and that his "utilization of this approach helps to account for the extraordinary level of white support (39 percent) he received."[40] Wilder projected a moderate image; and, as in the Young campaign, Jesse Jackson and other prominent black politicians were not asked to assist. Similarly,

Young carefully cultivated a moderate image throughout his tenure as mayor, portraying himself as the economic development candidate while avoiding controversial issues. Unlike Wilder's opponent, Young's opponent avoided negative campaigning.

What perhaps is most clearly suggested by the comparison of the Wilder and Young campaigns is that deracialization may be necessary for a black candidate to win in a majority white district or jurisdiction, but it is obviously insufficient to guarantee a win. Young's lack of familiarity with state government, his relative lack of access to the statewide party campaign apparatus, and his inability to clearly distinguish and capitalize on differences in policy preferences with his principal opponent were deficits that would have severely disadvantaged any candidate, black or white.

The Future of Black Politics in Georgia

Young's gubernatorial defeat was not uniformly observed as an indication that black candidates in Georgia could not win in predominantly white districts and jurisdictions. The same election that produced the Young defeat also provided some promising cues. While Georgia currently has only one African American representing a majority white district in the state legislature (the district encompassing the University of Georgia in Athens), in a majority white rural district a black woman came within 250 votes of gaining a legislative seat, and a black candidate for a state judgeship in a majority white district near Savannah was defeated by only 80 votes.[41] Young's defeat can be explained by the presence of factors other than race.

Andrew Young was the first black to get as far as a runoff in a statewide election in Georgia. African Americans currently serving in the state legislature and in elected offices in county government may be preparing themselves to run for statewide elected office. Perhaps with legislative experience and the strength of the Democratic party behind them, they will be more successful than Young was in his effort to become the first black elected to a statewide office in Georgia.

Notes

1. Alvin J. Schexnider, "The Politics of Pragmatism: An Analysis of the 1989 Gubernatorial Election in Virginia," *PS: Political Science and Politics* 23 (June 1990): 154–56.

2. See, for example, Mary Summers and Philip Klinkner, "The Daniels Election in

New Haven and the Failure of the Deracialization Hypothesis," *Urban Affairs Quarterly* 27 (Dec. 1991): 202–15.

3. Clarence Stone, *Regime Politics: Governing Atlanta, 1946–1988* (Lawrence: University of Kansas Press, 1989), 6.

4. Ibid, 110–11.

5. Bert Roughton, "Fight Vowed Over '96 Stadium Site," *Atlanta Constitution,* Nov. 19, 1990, A1.

6. Stone, *Regime Politics,* 143, 166–67.

7. Carol Pierannunzi and John D. Hutcheson, Jr., "Electoral Change and Regime Maintenance: Maynard Jackson's Second Time Around," *PS: Political Science and Politics* 23 (June 1990): 151–53.

8. Adolph Reed, "A Critique of Neo-Progressivism in Theorizing about Local Development Policy: A Case Study from Atlanta," in *The Politics of Urban Development,* edited by Clarence N. Stone and Heywood Sanders (Lawrence: University of Kansas Press, 1987), 199–215.

9. May, "Young Hoping to Outwit Conventional Wisdom," *Atlanta Constitution,* July 14, 1990.

10. "Role Reversal: Look Who's Crying Racism Now," *Atlanta Constitution,* May 22, 1990, A12.

11. May, "Candidates Go to Pulpit for Votes," *Atlanta Constitution,* July 9, 1990, A1.

12. Ibid.

13. Deborah Scoggins, "Democratic Candidates Taking Different Tacks," *Atlanta Constitution,* July 29, 1990, D1.

14. Ibid.

15. David K. Secrest and Charles Walston, "Young, Berry Find Atlanta Business Coffers Aren't Thrown Open," *Atlanta Constitution,* May 7, 1990, B1.

16. Peter Mantius, "Miller in Lead, Dollarwise," *Atlanta Constitution,* July 9, 1990, A1.

17. Secrest, "Runoff Foe Likely to Press Young on Donors," *Atlanta Constitution,* July 6, 1990, D1.

18. May, "Miller Gains Steam in Race against Young," *Atlanta Constitution,* June 17, 1990, A1.

19. May, "Miller Is Clear Front-Runner for Primary," *Atlanta Constitution,* July 14, 1990.

20. Tom Baxter and A. L. May, "Issues Outweigh Race More for Atlanta Blacks," *Atlanta Constitution,* July 23, 1990, B1.

21. Baxter, "Numbers Game Begins for Miller, Young," *Atlanta Constitution,* July 19, 1990, B1.

22. Baxter, "Fight for His Life: Young Has Big Hurdle in Miller," *Atlanta Constitution,* July 18, 1990, A1.

23. Baxter, "The Legacy of Young's Campaign," *Atlanta Constitution,* Aug. 12, 1990, G1.

24. Scoggins, "McDonald Endorses Miller for Governor," *Atlanta Constitution,* July 31, 1990, B3.

25. May and Scoggins, "Miller Has 20-Point Edge in Final Week," *Atlanta Constitution,* July 30, 1990, B1.

26. May, "Civility toward Young Masks Racial Fissures," *Atlanta Constitution,* Aug. 5, 1990, A1.

27. May, "Loud and Clear: It's Zell," *Atlanta Constitution,* Aug. 8, 1990, A1.

28. Ibid.

29. May, "Miller's Grip on Black Voters May Be Slipping," *Atlanta Constitution,* Oct. 27, 1990, C1.

30. Gary Pomerantz, "Young Faces Turning Point," *Atlanta Constitution,* Aug. 9, 1990, D1.

31. Charles E. Jones and Michael Clemons, "A Model of Racial Crossover Voting: An Assessment of the Wilder Victory," in *Dilemmas of Politics: Issues of Leadership and Strategy,* edited by Georgia A. Persons (New York: HarperCollins, 1993).

32. Ibid., 4.

33. Ibid., 33.

34. Mike Christensen, "Young Admits It Was Hard Wooing Rural White Voters," *Atlanta Constitution,* Nov. 29, 1990, A6.

35. Jones and Clemons, "Model of Racial Crossover Voting," 137.

36. Cynthia Durcanin, "Virginia Governor Doubts Young's Race Caused Defeat," *Atlanta Constitution,* Aug. 9, 1990, D3.

37. Jones and Clemons, "Model of Racial Crossover Voting," 19.

38. Ibid.

39. Ibid., 29.

40. Ibid., 24.

41. Baxter, "Legacy of Young's Campaign."

7

The Election of Troy Carter
to the Louisiana House
of Representatives

James L. Llorens, Sharon K. Parsons, and
Huey L. Perry

On November 16, 1991, Troy Carter's election to the Louisiana
House of Representatives in District 102 ushered in a "new
brand of politics" to Algiers in New Orleans.[1] A large neighborhood with a
strong historical identity, Algiers is located across the Mississippi River from
downtown New Orleans. In that election, Carter defeated Steven Ruiz, a
white opponent, and became the first black elected to a political office in Algiers. The 102d District was created by the state legislature as part of the
House redistricting following the 1990 census. The redistricting plan adopted
by the legislature included eleven new black majority districts, although the
102d was not one of them.

African Americans constituted 49.7 percent of the registered voters in
the district at the time of the election. The actual number of black registered
voters exceeded that of white registered voters by 263, but the district also
contained 332 voters classified as "other." This level of registration reflected
an increase in registration as a response to the gubernatorial candidacy of
David Duke. Duke's candidacy led to record levels of voter registration among
blacks and whites in Louisiana. The actual level of black voter registration in
the 102d District was lower than 49.7 percent at the time the district was created. The newly created district contained much the same population as the
former district. The former representative of the district chose to seek a state
senate seat rather than to run for reelection from the newly created district.

Prior to Troy Carter's decision to run for the vacant legislative seat in
the 102d District, he was a New Orleans city official appointed by Mayor
Sidney Barthelemy. Carter had not held elective office prior to his election to
the state legislature. He was young, with strong family ties in the black community of Algiers. Carter's electoral strategy was critical to his success. Our

analysis reveals that his efforts fit the category of a deracialization strategy.[2] This style of electoral race refers to African American candidates employing a campaign strategy that downplays racial themes in order to attract white voter support.

Carter's campaign provides an opportunity for analyzing the successful application of a deracialized strategy in a unique arena—a state legislative campaign in the South. The Louisiana primary election, which is a truly "open primary" (all candidates appear on a single ballot and the two candidates who receive the most votes, regardless of party, run against each other in the general election), presented a field of nine candidates for the 102d District in 1991. There were five white and four black candidates. In the primary, Steven Ruiz received the highest number of votes and Carter received the second highest number of votes. This chapter examines Carter's campaign in the primary and general election and explores, in particular, the link between his campaign activities and the electoral behavior of the voters in the 102d District. Interviews with Carter and the election results are analyzed to determine the source of Carter's support and, more specifically, the source of his support from whites.

The Theoretical Framework

Charles E. Jones and Michael Clemons offer a theoretical construct to explain black political success (or failure) in districts with a white majority.[3] While this model was applied to analyze racial crossover voting in L. Douglas Wilder's gubernatorial election in Virginia, it is also extremely helpful in examining Carter's win in the 102d District. The model consists of five major components: (1) political apprenticeship, (2) party apparatus, (3) a media/racial ombudsman role, (4) the wild card factor, and (5) a deracialized political strategy. Jones and Clemons suggest that the critical importance of these components lies in their potential to mitigate the impact of race and the adroitness with which this is accomplished.[4] In the following section, we assess each component's applicability and relative importance to Carter's success.

Political Apprenticeship

Political apprenticeship refers to political qualifications. Jones and Clemons emphasize that prior experience in an elected office is especially important for black candidates. The absence of such requisite political credentials can provide a convenient reason to dissuade certain white voters from supporting black candidates lacking such experience as well as can fuel negative media attention. Political apprenticeship did not have a substantial impact on

Carter's election. Indeed, the absence of an incumbent in the race resulted in a number of candidates with no prior political officeholding experience. Moreover, political experience can be obtained without having held elective office. Carter had obtained some political experience as a New Orleans municipal employee and member of the political organization of Mayor Sidney Barthelemy.

In the general election, Carter's opponent, Steven Ruiz promoted himself as a businessman. Ruiz had not held an elected office and generally lacked basic political credentials. Although neither had Carter held an elective position prior to winning the House seat, he was not new to the New Orleans political scene. His campaign strategy stressed his education and his experience as New Orleans deputy legislative coordinator for the mayor (he lobbied the state legislature on behalf of Mayor Barthelemy) and executive aide to Mayor Barthelemy. Carter's few years of appointed political apprenticeship may have softened the potentially fatal impact of a lack of prior political officeholding experience on a black candidate's electoral prospects to the point where it was not a major factor in this election.

Party Apparatus

The party apparatus provides support for a candidate in the form of political endorsements, resources, and mobilization of party supporters. The endorsement of the party machinery can enhance the credibility of a black candidate and lessen the race factor.[5] In a nonstatewide election, political endorsements can be the major show of party support. In the general election, Carter and Ruiz, both Democrats, received their share of political endorsements. Ruiz was backed by the white leaders of Algiers[6] and endorsed by state senator-elect Francis Heitmeier, whose former House seat included much of the new 102d District, District Attorney Harry Connick, and Councilwoman Jackie Clarkson.[7]

Carter won with little support from the white political elites in Algiers. New Orleans Mayor Barthelemy and his executive assistant Al Stokes, both African Americans, not only endorsed Carter, but Stokes also directed his campaign. Carter was also backed by some white political leaders, including former Mayor Moon Landrieu, Councilman Joe Giarrusso, and former Algiers Councilman Mike Early. In Carter's election, political endorsements were crucial, but equally important was the use of the "resource" of political guidance and advice. Party apparatus may be influential in statewide elections, but it is probably considerably less influential in nonstatewide elections. This is especially true in Louisiana, which is still predominantly a one-party state in which the majority party is not highly organized.

Often in Louisiana, two Democrats oppose each other in general elections. Party apparatus is less important than independent political organizations and factions within the Democratic party. In local elections, endorsements may cross party lines or, as in the Carter-Ruiz race, both candidates may be in the same political party.

Media/Racial Ombudsman

Media/racial ombudsman involves the role of media in mitigating racial conflict in political campaigns and elections. In this role, the media can serve to condemn any race-baiting attempts or the introduction of any racially tainted campaign tactics.[8] The Carter-Ruiz contest was relatively free of any attempt to exploit the issue of race. In this election, the media played a traditional and influential role. The *Times-Picayune,* New Orleans's major daily newspaper, reported vitae, political endorsements, and candidates' stands on certain issues without apparent bias. The day before the election, the *Times-Picayune* endorsed Carter. A newspaper endorsement can be especially critical in convincing a certain percentage of white voters of a black candidate's "acceptability," as the media is still perceived as an articulator of white interests.

Wild Card Factor

The wild card factor can take the form of an external and unanticipated event or issue. Jones and Clemons caution that the impact of the wild card is "double edged in that it can either siphon off critical support or provide the electoral cushion needed for a victory."[9] In Carter's election, the wild card factor proved to be an influential component and partly explains his political success. Indeed, two factors evident in the 102d District election could be considered "wild cards." The first wild card occurred before the campaign, and it provided a more level playing field in the election. The incumbent in the 102d District, Francis Heitmeier, chose not to seek reelection from the House district, opting instead to run for a seat in the state senate. Therefore, one wild card in this election was an open contest; Carter did not have to oppose an incumbent.

The second wild card factor was the gubernatorial election in which former Governor Edwin Edwards, a populist Democrat, opposed Representative David Duke, widely known for espousing a racist platform. Duke's success in the primary election precipitated an unprecedented surge in voter registration in Louisiana. Record numbers of black and white voters registered to cast their ballots in the general election. The gubernatorial election drew national interest and resulted in a record turnout in the election, especially among black voters determined to prevent Duke from being elected governor. This factor lessened the need for candidates such as Carter to concentrate on voter turnout in the general election. It also focused black voters on supporting black candidates.

An African American candidate may find difficulty in successfully employing a deracialized strategy when facing a white candidate in the South.[10]

Carter understood the nature of the battle against an incumbent and declared that he would not enter the race if Francis Heitmeier decided to run for re-election.[11] With a base of political support, no opposition from an incumbent, and high voter turnout, Carter's success pivoted on the skillful use of a deracialized strategy.

Deracialized Political Strategy

The first component of a deracialized political strategy, according to Jones and Clemons, is that candidates must adopt positions on timely issues with strong cross-race appeal. Expanding on the earlier work of Charles V. Hamilton,[12] Jones and Clemons advocate a multifaceted approach in viewing a deracialized political strategy that emphasizes not just issues but also political style and campaign tactics.[13] Carter's use of deracialization as a political strategy is by far the most influential factor in understanding his election. His well-crafted campaign strategy emphasized issue positions that were timely and had strong appeal across racial lines. Any race-sensitive issues adopted by Carter (for example, minority set-aside programs) were also part of his opponent's platform. Ruiz's slate of issues included education, crime, and the formation of an enterprise zone as a method of decreasing the city's unemployment. The major issue positions adopted by Carter focused on crime, education, economic development, and abortion.

Both candidates stressed similar positions on campaign issues, except on one issue: abortion. Ruiz did not state a position on abortion, indicating that if elected, he would "vote according to the majority of registered voters" on this matter if it came up in the legislature during his tenure.[14] In contrast, Carter, early in his campaign, announced a pro-choice abortion position. He felt that his position on abortion attracted white, female, middle-class voters—votes lost by Ruiz because of his reluctance to take a position on the issue. Carter's pro-choice stand on abortion may have been especially significant in the election because of the restrictive nature of Louisiana's abortion laws. The state's restrictive abortion laws could have provoked a strong negative response among women living in the 102d District, which is in the largest urban center in the state.

Abortion has effectively been used as a crossover issue in other elections featuring a deracialized campaign strategy. Georgia A. Persons cites abortion as one of the issues that readily transcends race.[15] L. Douglas Wilder, in his successful 1989 campaign for governor of Virginia, recognized the need to attract the vote of younger white women and vigorously pursued their vote by incorporating a pro-choice position in his platform. Abortion became a focal point of the election. Wilder's opponent, Marshall Coleman, adopted a pro-life stand and avoided difficult questions on his position. The two candidates' different positions on abortion were viewed as critical to the outcome of the election.[16]

The second aspect of a deracialized strategy is the use of a political style that is nonthreatening and reassuring to white voters. Carter does not fit the confrontational mold of the traditional black politician. His style is best described in terms he used to depict his campaign efforts—enthusiastic, systematic, and scientific.[17] Carter's political style is aided by his personal qualities. He has been described as intelligent, articulate, and genuine. In Wilder's campaign for governor of Virginia in 1989, he was viewed as having personal qualities similar to those attributed to Carter: competent, intelligent, and trustworthy. However, campaign strategy cannot rely on the persuasion of such personal attributes; voters often already assume, as in Wilder's campaign, that candidates possess such personal qualities.[18] An additional factor in Carter's campaign was the use of a white media consultant who was a former state legislator and well-known in the New Orleans area.

The third and final aspect of a deracialized political strategy is the campaign strategy used to mobilize the electorate. Jones and Clemons advise that these tactics should be free of overt racial appeals, otherwise a black candidate could risk alienating white voters.[19] Carter's campaign avoided race-based tactics and instead attempted to appeal to more educated, middle-income groups of blacks and whites as well as elderly citizens in the district. This appeal resulted in Carter receiving over 20 percent of the white vote.

While the deracialization concept is useful in understanding Carter's success in gaining white votes, the concept is insufficient in explaining the black votes received by Carter. Jones and Clemons's discussion of the three elements of a deracialized political strategy does not explore any special considerations of the "primary support base" for African American candidates. Thomas Cavanaugh and Denise Stockton caution that black candidates using a deracialized strategy must maintain a delicate balance between not alienating white voters and solidifying their natural black electoral base.[20] Andrew Young, in his unsuccessful campaign for governor of Georgia in 1990, discovered that the deracialization strategy is a two-edged sword. In his overzealous attempt to attract white voters, he alienated significant numbers of black voters.

Troy Carter won in a district where the racial balance was approximately a fifty-fifty ratio. He was successful not just because he employed a strategy that facilitated the courting of white voters; equally important, he did so without losing the base of support among black voters. In Carter's case, solidifying his natural black electoral base necessitated a skillful strategy to assure not only keeping the support of black voters but also mobilizing them to vote. African American candidates using a deracialized campaign must implement a multifaceted approach with their black constituency. They must be attentive to black voters and not risk ignoring or alienating the black electorate, a mistake that can cost an election, especially in a district or jurisdiction with a sizeable black population. Black candidates also must utilize a strategy to stimulate black voter turnout.

To mobilize voter turnout, Carter used an extensive grassroots effort, coffee parties, nightly phone banks, targeted mailings, door-to-door campaigning, and radio and television spots. He depended on a massive volunteer effort by neighborhood political groups, churches, youth organizations, and women's groups.[21] This type of personalized candidacy and contacts[22] and grassroots door-to-door campaigning[23] is more effective in low voter turnout neighborhoods and can sharply increase the likelihood of voting among blacks.

Even though many view the African American electorate as cohesive, predictable,[24] the strongest partisan identifiers (Democrats),[25] and a built-in base of support for black candidates,[26] an African American using a deracialized campaign strategy cannot assume that the black electorate will simply give that support unearned. Typically, strong black support is essential to a successful deracialized strategy. Los Angeles Mayor Tom Bradley, in his unsuccessful 1982 campaign for governor of California, discovered the perilous position of running in a white majority setting and being accused of ignoring black voters, resulting in a dampened minority turnout. As indicated previously, Andrew Young was also unsuccessful in his use of a deracialized strategy because of his inability to walk the tightrope of appealing for white voter support while keeping intact the support of the black electorate.

Carter's employment of a personalized campaign and grassroots efforts through various civic and neighborhood organizations and churches promoted the viability of his candidacy among African American voters. In his campaign, Carter also mentioned that his grandfather was a respected minister in the area. His emphasis on campaigning in black churches is also a campaign tactic used by L. Douglas Wilder in his 1989 Virginia gubernatorial candidacy. At one point in Wilder's campaign, some prominent black leaders believed that he was being "too coy" with his black constituency. Wilder started attending a wide variety of churches as well as community forums. By the time of the election, most of the complaints had been silenced. To explain the impact of Wilder's strategy of not taking the black vote for granted, it is important to understand the continuing social and political importance of the African American church, particularly in the South.

Proof of Carter's success in effectively courting the black electorate was a record 70 percent voter turnout in the Fischer public housing development, which historically had the lowest black voter turnout in the city. Additional proof of his success in this regard was that black turnout exceeded white turnout in Algiers.[27] While Carter's success in this regard was undoubtedly aided by David Duke's bid for governor, his effective campaigning for the support of black voters was also a significant factor in the record turnout of black voters in the 102d District.

An Analysis of Carter's Issue Positions

Applying to Carter's election the theoretical assumptions of the deracialization concept, we conclude that Carter ran a deracialized campaign. Carter's
own assessment of the issue positions he took in the campaign provides additional support for our theoretically based conclusion.

Carter contends that black candidates are more appealing to white
voters today because they are usually more qualified than white opponents.
According to Carter, this leads to an increased willingness on the part of white
voters to vote for black candidates.[28] Carter not only ran a deracialized campaign—he ran a sophisticated campaign that allowed him to appeal to white
voters while maintaining his natural support among black voters. To keep his
support among black voters, Carter indicates that whenever black issues were
raised, he stood up for them. As an example of this, he cites affirmative action
and set-aside programs.[29] To appeal to black and white voters, Carter also addressed race-neutral issues such as crime, education, abortion, senior citizen
neglect, and economic development. He considered his strong stance on
crime unusual for a black elected official.

Carter believes that deracialization is an important political concept
and strategy. He stated that deracialization is a positive strategy since there are
problems and issues that transcend race, such as the environment and the
economy. Carter stated that even in majority black districts and jurisdictions,
it is important for African American candidates to focus on issues of concern
to all voters.

Election Analysis

Carter received 8,164 of 14,650 total votes cast (56 percent). Turnout in the
election was 78 percent. African American voters in the district represented
50 percent of the total number of voters in the district, 9,397 of a total 18,890
registered voters. The turnout by precinct ranged from 59 percent to 84 percent. Seventeen of the thirty-three precincts in the district had a majority of
black registered voters, with the percentage of black registered voters ranging
from 54 to 98 percent. In the primary election, Carter received a plurality of
the votes in eleven of the seventeen black precincts. In the general election, he
received a majority of the votes in all of the majority black precincts. In the
nonblack majority precincts, Carter's percentage of votes in the general election ranged from 14 to 50 percent.

An analysis of the election results indicates that Carter was successful
in attracting enough of the white vote in the 102d District to secure a victory.
The precinct returns indicate that Carter benefited from the record turnout in

the black precincts where his percentage of the vote ranged from 56 to 96 percent. The majority white precincts also showed support for Carter, much more than did the majority black precincts for his opponent. An important factor in analyzing Carter's success in attracting white voters is to attempt to identify which white voters he was successful in attracting. Carter identified his white support as middle- to upper-income, professional, and new to the district. While precinct demographics are not available, there appears to be one variable available by precinct that helps to identify those voters: the percentage of Republican voters in the district.

The "old guard," as Carter characterized the established political group in the 102d District, is solidly Democratic, as are most voters in the district and the state of Louisiana. The "old guard" is also heavily blue-collar. Carter realized that it would be difficult for him to penetrate that bloc of voters. Moreover, his opponent in the election was the choice of the Democratic political establishment in the district. Carter's political support, primarily from Mayor Sidney Barthelemy and his organization, had bases outside the 102d District. Carter's strategy was to identify newcomers in the district that were not supporters of the establishment politicians, because that group of voters would be more likely to demonstrate independence in their voting decisions. The "independent" group of voters Carter wanted to identify were more likely to be Republican.

Republican voters comprise 19 percent of the total registered voters in the district. The percentage of registered Republicans in the district by precinct ranged from 3 to 43 percent. Understandably, the higher levels of Republican voters appear in the majority white precincts and the lower levels appear in the majority black precincts. A measure of support for Carter in majority white precincts correlates significantly with the level of Republican voters in those precincts. This correlation is significant in a nonstatewide election in Louisiana or anywhere in the South.

A deracialized strategy can be operationalized as a shift toward a more conservative ideological direction from that of what is perceived as a racialized strategy. One exception to that assumption is the successful employment of a pro-choice position by candidates employing deracialized strategies. While the pro-choice position is normally considered a liberal stance, there is evidence that this position can attract conservative female voters. This move toward a conservative strategy could then attract voters in the Republican party to African American candidates. Apparently, this is what happened in the 102d District. The cautionary note here is that Louisiana operates a different primary system than other states, as previously indicated. We are less likely to observe this phenomenon in states where candidates from the two major parties oppose each other in the general election, rather than run on the same ballot as is the case in the Louisiana open primary system.

In an attempt to identify the likely source of Carter's nonblack support, we constructed an index that measures the level of support for Carter that exceeded the level of black voting strength in each precinct. That index is measured by the following formula: $I = CV/BRV$, where "CV" equals the percentage of total votes received by Carter in the general election in the precinct, and "BRV" equals the total number of black registered voters in the precinct.

A value of 1.0 for the index would indicate that the number of votes received by Carter in the general election was equal to the number of black registered voters in that precinct. We could assume that a value of 1.0 would occur when the turnout among black voters in that district was 100 percent and all of those voters cast ballots for Carter. Obviously, a value of 1.0 could be attained when a number of whites equal to the number of black registered voters in the precinct cast ballots for Carter (with no blacks voting for Carter) or a combination of white and black support for Carter equaled the number of black registered voters. A simple analysis of the distribution of voters in the precincts cancels out these possibilities. The assumption can also be made that analysis of the voting results indicates that the majority of support for Carter came from African American voters.

A value of less than 1.0 would indicate that Carter received fewer votes than the total number of black votes eligible to be cast. This would be the result of either a less than 100 percent turnout, or black votes being cast for Carter's opponent. For purposes of this study, the critical values of this index are those values above 1.0. An index value above 1.0 would indicate that support for Carter exceeded the number of black registered voters in that precinct, which translates into white support for Carter. The higher the index value above 1.0, the greater the nonblack support for Carter. Table 7–1 presents the values of the index measured by precinct.

The values for the index presented in Table 7–1 for majority black precincts approximate the average turnout of voters in the election. This is indicative of almost total support for Carter among African Americans voting in the general election. In twelve of the sixteen precincts with a majority of white registered voters, the value of the index exceeds 1.0. The overall range of values for the index is 0.72 to 8.56. In the black precincts, the range of values is 0.72 to 0.88. The range of values in majority white precincts is 0.93 to 8.56.

Clearly, Carter was successful in attracting white support for his candidacy. The South has a history of racial bloc voting,[30] and African American candidates generally have not been successful in attracting white voters when their opponents are white candidates in districts with less than a significant majority of black voters. This obviously was not the case in Carter's election. Who were Carter's white supporters? While there is not sufficient demographic data to unequivocally answer that question, further analysis of the available data lends itself to some justifiable conclusions.

TABLE 7–1

Carter Election Results by Race and Party, 1991

Precinct	BRV %	CV %	REP %	Index
1	16	41	27	1.81
2	24	36	20	1.04
3	22	40	25	1.32
4	61	56	19	.88
5	90	86	3	.78
6	93	90	4	.72
7	83	81	6	.73
8	76	74	6	.75
9	78	80	5	.79
10	89	88	5	.75
11	99	96	5	.70
11A	92	85	3	.70
12	54	61	12	.83
12A	77	74	5	.76
13	58	57	10	.71
13A	43	50	11	.96
13B	88	93	9	.78
14	13	19	23	1.16
14A	8	31	43	2.93
14B	13	24	42	1.43
14C	17	29	32	1.31
14E	66	76	13	.77
14F	13	27	38	1.44
15	67	69	11	.75
15A	16	20	21	.92
15B	4	14	34	2.66
16	33	39	23	.93
17	2	23	47	8.56
17A	4	16	37	2.79
17B	2	16	35	5.53
18B	31	43	27	.94
19	99	96	3	.78
19B	95	95	5	.80

Source: Office of the Secretary of State of Louisiana.

BRV = Percentage of black registered voters in precinct

CV = Percentage of votes received by Carter in general election

REP = Percentage of registered Republicans in precinct

Index = Measure of white support for Carter

The 102d District contains a considerable proportion of Republicans among the white electorate. Table 7–1 indicates that in the white majority precincts, the percentage of Republicans among registered voters ranges from 11 to 47 percent. In the black majority precincts, the percentage of Republicans among registered voters drops dramatically, from 3 to 19 percent. Thus, the greater the percentage of black registered voters, the lower the percentage of registered Republicans. The data in Table 7–2 and Figures 7–1 and 7–2 allow further analysis of the relationship between Republican voters in the 102d District and the election of Carter.

Table 7–2 presents the correlations between variables. There is high correlation, positive and negative, between those variables that measure characteristics of the white and black populations of the district and the votes received by Carter. There is little variation in the measures, which indicates almost solid bloc voting. The table of correlations allows the inference of relationships between Carter's support and voter characteristics, but the high correlations limit the use of ordinary least squares regression analysis. We still, however, attempt to further analyze the relationship between Carter's support and Republicanism in the district, with the caveat mentioned above.

Figure 7–1 presents the relationship between the percentage of votes Carter received in the general election and the percentage of Republicans in the district. A bivariate regression was computed and plotted. There is a significant negative correlation of –.89 between the percentage of registered Republicans and the percentage of votes received by Carter in the general election. The greater the percentage of registered Republicans, the lower the number of votes for Carter. This relationship is expected when analyzing the overall results of the election, considering the relatively high (for Louisiana) percentage of Republicans in the district. However, the relationship changes in Figure 7–2.

In Figure 7–2, we compute and plot a bivariate regression using our constructed index as the dependent variable and the percentage of Republicans as the independent variable. We now see a significant relationship in the opposite direction from that of Figure 7–1. The measured correlation is a significant .67. This interesting reversal supports our hypothesis that a critical variable in Carter's white support is the percentage of Republicans in the 102d District. The results in Figure 7–1 indicate that Carter's overall support is not dependent on Republicans in the 102d District. On the other hand, Figure 7–2 indicates that the white support he received is significantly related to the percentage of Republicans in the district. The bivariate regression's R square value of .45 indicates that 45 percent of the variance in the index is accounted for by the percentage of Republicans in the district.

This is a limited analysis because of limited data. The 102d is a small district, and the analysis by precincts presents us with a small N (33), which

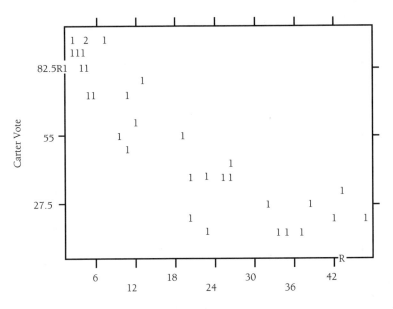

Correlation = −.89036
R Square = .79275
Sig. = .0000
Note: R on horizontal and vertical axis indicates best fit line of regression.

Figure 7–1. Registered Republicans and Votes for Carter.

TABLE 7–2
Correlations for Carter Vote, 1991

	PCTBRV	PCTWRV	PCTCV	TRNOUT	PCTREP	INDEX
PCTBRV	1.000	—	—	—	—	—
PCTWRV	−1.000**	1.000	—	—	—	—
PCTCV	.9852**	−.9852**	1.000	—	—	—
TRNOUT	.2404	−.2404	.2200	1.000	—	—
PCTREP	−.9243**	.9243**	−.8904**	−.3130	1.000	—
INDEX	−.5645**	.5645**	−.5234**	−.0878	.6708**	1.000

N = 33.   1 tailed sig.: * = .01; ** = .001.   PCTBRV = Percentage of black registered voters in precinct.   PCTWRV = Percentage of white registered voters in precinct. PCTCV = Percentage of Carter vote.   TRNOUT = Voter turnout.   PCTREP = Percentage of registered Republicans in precinct

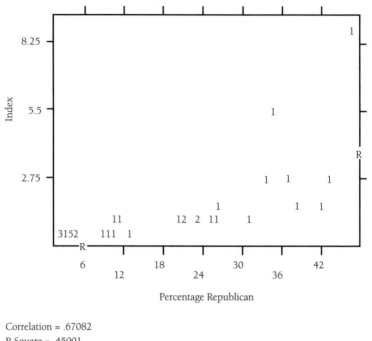

Correlation = .67082
R Square = .45001
Sig. = .0000
Note: R on horizontal and vertical axis indicates best fit line of regression.

Figure 7–2. Index of White Support and Registered Republicans.

results in fewer degrees of freedom. This proves especially difficult in at-tempting analysis through the use of ordinary least squares multiple regres-sion. Nevertheless, we believe it is worthwhile to attempt to analyze the elec-tion results through regression in order to identify significant variables. Table 7–3 reflects the regression analysis that constitutes the centerpiece of our empirical analysis of Carter's successful application of the deracialization concept.

Table 7–3 presents the results of a model that utilizes the index mea-sure as the dependent variable. This model is designed to measure the vari-ables that contribute to Carter's support over and above his support in the black electorate. Our major hypothesis for this model is that the primary con-tributor to Carter's support would be Republican strength in the precincts. The findings support this hypothesis.

The adjusted R square for this highly significant model is .47. The only statistically significant variable is the percentage of registered Republicans. It is expected that white registration and Republican registration would have a

TABLE 7–3
Regression Model for Index Support for Carter, 1991

Variable	Coefficient (SE)	Beta	Sig
BMAJ	1.999 (1.210)	.637	.109
TRNOUTG	.087 (.049)	.272	.086
PCTREP	.132 (.040)	1.14	.002
PCTWRV	.007 (.023)	.162	.746
(Constant)	−8.941 (4.620)		.063

R square = .5385.   Adj. R square = .4726.
Significance = .0002.   SE = Standard error.
BMAJ = Black majority precincts.
TRNOUTG = Turnout in general election.
PCTREP = Percentage of registered Republicans in precinct.
PCTWRV = Percentage of registered white voters in precinct.

positive impact on the dependent variable. Both variables perform as expected. However, Republican registration is highly significant (.002) and is the largest factor in the equation, with black majority districts being the second highest contributor, though statistically nonsignificant. Our hypothesis that Republicans in the 102d District constituted a significant contribution to Carter's support among the white electorate is supported. This finding is surprising in a state such as Louisiana, which experiences significant racial bloc voting and in which the Republican party is considered the most conservative bloc of the white electorate.

Conclusion

The purpose of this chapter was to analyze the election of Troy Carter to the Louisiana House of Representatives from the 102d District in New Orleans. Carter successfully employed a deracialized campaign strategy. This is especially significant because it occurred in an election that was neither state- nor citywide. It also occurred in a state in the deep South where racial bloc voting has consistently occurred. The district at the time of the election was not considered a black majority district, and it was assumed that the successful candidate would have to attract voters from the candidate's opposite racial group. The general election provided an excellent opportunity to test our hypothesis because it presented an election between a white and a black candidate with somewhat equal qualifications. If people in the 102d District had voted solely along racial lines, then the key variable would have been voter turnout among each group. As it turned out, the level of turnout was fairly equal. The difference was in the black candidate's ability to attract white voters.

In the introduction to this book, Perry outlines the ongoing scholarly debate on the impact of deracialization strategies on the election of African Americans. Based upon the experience in this one election, we are tempted to answer in the affirmative. Carter's election victory provides support for all of the arguments for using a deracialization strategy. Carter himself asserts that deracialization is a useful and important strategy for black candidates. He was able to identify a probable source of support among the white electorate in his district and successfully attract their support. In this instance, a deracialized strategy accounts for a black elected official, while a nonderacialized strategy could have resulted in a white being elected from that district.

Many other variables would have to be considered before we can support the contention that deracialized strategies absolutely result in more black elected officials. The critical variable is the distribution of black voters in the district. It is likely that Carter would have been unsuccessful had the percentage of black voters been significantly less than 50 percent. The crossover of white votes was not large enough to ensure victory in that situation.

Another critical variable is region. The South has not provided many instances of successful deracialized campaigns. Thus, the variable of the distribution of black voters interacts with the factor of region. In order for black candidates to wage successful deracialized campaigns, there must be a close-to-majority percentage of black voters. Racial crossover voting among the white electorate in the South is not substantial enough to provide an environment for successful deracialized campaigns in districts and jurisdictions with significantly less than a majority black population. The Carter election demonstrates that an African American candidate can be successful in the South by employing a deracialized strategy in a district with a 50 percent black population. There is not enough support at this time, however, to demonstrate that this can happen on a large scale in the South.

Notes

1. Clancy DuBos, "Enthusiastic Amateurs: Troy Carter," *Louisiana Political Review* 2 (Nov./Dec. 1991): 31.
2. Huey L. Perry, "Deracialization as an Analytical Construct in American Urban Politics," *Urban Affairs Quarterly* 27 (Dec. 1991): 181–91; Georgia A. Persons, "The Election of Gary Franks and the Ascendancy of the New Black Conservatives," in *Dilemmas of Black Politics: Issues of Leadership and Strategy*, edited by

Georgia A. Persons (New York: HarperCollins, 1993), 194–208.

3. Charles E. Jones and Michael Clemons, "A Model of Racial Crossover Voting: An Assessment of the Wilder Victory," in *Dilemmas of Black Politics,* edited by Persons, 128–46.

4. Ibid., 129–30.

5. Ibid., 131.

6. DuBos, "Enthusiatic Amateurs," 31.

7. Leslie Williams, "Two Candidates Carry Share of Endorsements," *New Orleans Times-Picayune,* Nov. 14, 1991, B-1, B-3.

8. Jones and Clemons, "Model of Racial Crossover Voting," 132.

9. Ibid., 134.

10. Huey L. Perry, "Deracialization as an Analytical Construct," 27.

11. "Scuttlebutt," *Gambit,* Aug. 13, 1990, 8.

12. Charles V. Hamilton, "Deracialization: Examination of a Political Strategy," *First World* (March-Apr. 1977): 3–5.

13. Jones and Clemons, "Model of Racial Crossover Voting," 132–33.

14. Williams, "Two Candidates Carry Share."

15. Persons, "Election of Gary Franks," 31.

16. Jones and Clemons, "Model of Racial Crossover Voting," 142–43.

17. DuBos, "Enthusiastic Amateurs."

18. Jones and Clemons, "Model of Racial Crossover Voting."

19. Ibid., 133.

20. Thomas Cavanaugh and Denise Stockton, *Black Elected Officials and Their Constituencies* (Washington, D.C.: Joint Center for Political Studies, 1983).

21. DuBos, "Enthusiastic Amateurs," 31.

22. Dianne Pinderhughes, "Political Choices: A Realignment in Partisanship among Black Voters," in *The State of Black America,* edited by J. D. Williams (New York: National Urban League, 1986), 85–113; Christopher G. Ellison and David A. Gay, "Black Political Participation Revisited: A Test of Compensatory, Ethnic Community and Public Arena Models," *Social Science Quarterly* 70 (Mar. 1989): 101–19.

23. G. H. Kramer, "The Effects of Precinct-Level Canvassing on Voting Behavior," *Public Opinion Quarterly* 34 (1971): 560–72.

24. Lenneal J. Henderson, Jr., "Black Politics and the American Presidential Elections," in *The New Black Politics: The Search for Political Power,* edited by Michael B. Preston, Lenneal J. Henderson, Jr., and Paul L. Puryear (New York: Longman, 1987), 3–27.

25. Pinderhughes, "Political Choices," 85–113.

26. Persons, "Election of Gary Franks," 194–208.

27. DuBos, "Enthusiastic Amateurs," 31.

28. Troy Carter, interview by Huey L. Perry, New Orleans, La., May 1991.

29. Ibid.

30. See Bernard Groffman and Chandler Davidson, *The Impact of the 1965 Voting Rights Act* (Princeton, N.J.: Princeton University Press, 1994).

III

Critical Perspectives on
Deracialization

8

The Election and Governance of John Daniels as Mayor of New Haven

Mary Summers and Philip A. Klinkner

Many observers have concluded that the 1989 gubernatorial and mayoral elections in Virginia, New York City, Cleveland, Seattle, and New Haven, among others, represent important advances in the ability of African American candidates to gain acceptance by white voters. Several political scientists have explained the success of these candidates in terms of their ability to "deracialize" their campaigns by avoiding specific racial appeals and stressing their personal qualifications and political experience.[1] Some analysts have concluded that these campaigns prove "that race can be overcome . . . with a mainstream centrist appeal."[2] While essentially agreeing with such characterizations of these elections, others have argued that because these candidates appealed to white voters, they could not address the needs of African Americans. Their success, therefore, offers merely the symbolic achievement of a few more "black faces" in elected governmental office.[3]

For all the recent attention, the concept of deracialization—as put forward by both proponents and critics—presents several conceptual and empirical problems. These problems raise serious questions about the usefulness of deracialization as an analytical construct for understanding black electoral politics. This chapter explores some of these problems through an analysis of the 1989 election and subsequent administration of John Daniels, the first black mayor of New Haven, Connecticut.

The Limitations of the Deracialization Hypothesis

Those who claim that victories like the Daniels election are the result of deracialization strategies assume that African American candidates usually run for office with direct appeals to black voters based on race-specific agendas that include affirmative action and minority set-aside programs. It is then taken as a sign of "the maturing of black politics" when black candidates try to win white votes. The theory is that they do so by downplaying racial identity;[4] the theory implies that white voters disregard the color of a politician's skin, if he or she successfully avoids all reference to racial issues.

Explaining black politics in these terms promotes an overly defensive and limited idea of racial identity and experience. Race-specific agendas embody a fairly conservative, essentially defensive strategy, embraced by politicians, judges, and activists who have seen no other means for changing the broader status quo. Their purpose is to gain access to its privileges for some members of minority groups. Such agendas have never embodied the totality of African American political goals and aspirations.[5]

No one can deny that racism influences American politics. The United States is a long way from deracializing any aspect of life, but examples from popular culture provide some evidence that black experiences can strike a resonant chord with whites. We should not be surprised that different types of "crossover appeals" are becoming increasingly possible in American political culture.

Even more problematic is the assumption of the proponents of deracialization strategies that the substantive interests of blacks and whites are mutually exclusive and that any attempt to build a multiracial coalition necessitates the abandonment of black interests. In the original formulation of the deracialization concept, Charles V. Hamilton called on the Democratic party to adopt deracialized solutions to the problems of poor blacks, such as full employment and national health insurance.[6] In his critique of deracialization strategies, Robert C. Smith claims that whatever the merits of Hamilton's proposal, "the routine issues" of the 1989 campaigns—"fiscal conservatism, mass transportation, education reforms, abortion, and wars on drugs and crime"—are "a far cry" from the "ideologically progressive" policies that Hamilton proposed.[7] Smith implies that there are no "ideologically progressive" approaches to the issues that currently concern voters and that if crime and fiscal conservatism matter to the electorate, then all would-be progressives should abdicate the political agenda to conservatives until a more enlightened electorate emerges.

Rather than assuming that recent African American electoral victories have resulted from centrist, establishment politics and conservative appeals to white voters—as opposed to progressive politics, grassroots organizing, and appeals to black pride—political scientists should analyze each election in its own particular context. A close look at the first Daniels campaign, for example, shows that black candidates can affirm their racial identity while advocating a progressive policy agenda that appeals to both blacks and whites.

The First Daniels Campaign

Deracialization theorists would initially find much in John Daniels's election to confirm their hypothesis. New Haven is approximately one-third black, which requires a successful African American mayoral candidate to attract a substantial proportion of the white electorate.[8] Daniels is an established politician who came up through the ranks of the Democratic party, holding public office as an alderman and then a state senator for more than twenty years. As a senator representing an area that was less than one-third black, he developed many ties with whites as well as blacks. He was widely respected as a decent, hardworking man, skilled in the arts of compromise and constituent service, with one of the most liberal voting records in the Connecticut legislature.

Throughout his campaign for mayor, Daniels made strenuous efforts to appeal to white voters. After considerable debate among his advisers, for example, the announcement of his candidacy took place not in a black church, but in one of the city's historic churches on the town green. Mobilizing against crime was his most central campaign issue, and he called on parents, young people, and teachers to help root out drugs and strive for excellence in their own families, schools, and neighborhoods.

Daniels succeeded in attracting both black and white voters. A February 1989 poll by the Democratic Town Committee showed the incumbent Mayor Ben DiLieto leading Daniels by ten points. At the end of March, DiLieto announced that he would not run for reelection, insisting that he simply wanted to spend more time with his family, but many observers noted that there had been little talk of retirement before Daniels declared his candidacy. Two new candidates, John DeStefano and James Perillo, entered the Democratic primary, the only race that matters in a city with an eight-to-one Democratic margin among registered voters. DeStefano, who had been chief executive officer and director of development in the DiLieto administration, received the mayor's endorsement. Perillo, head of the New Haven Coliseum, was supported by some Democratic party activists but dropped out of the race in August after the Democratic party convention endorsed DeStefano.

A poll by the *New Haven Register,* conducted three weeks before the Democratic primary, showed Daniels leading DeStefano among decided and leaning voters by a margin of 58 to 28 percent. Among decided voters, Daniels showed very strong support from blacks and Latinos, receiving 95 and 79 percent of their support, respectively. He also drew significant support from white voters, receiving 40 percent of their vote.[9] These figures seem to correspond with the actual primary election results in which Daniels won 59 percent of the vote—more votes than DeStefano and both Republican candidates combined.[10] He was elected mayor on November 7, 1989, with 68 percent of the vote, losing only two of the city's thirty wards.

The Daniels Campaign and the Deracialization Hypothesis

Both proponents and critics of deracialization strategies have grounds to argue that the Daniels victory was the result of a deracialized appeal to white voters in a campaign that reflected many of the "mainstream" issues and symbols of 1989. This explanation fails, however, to account for two significant aspects of Daniels's campaign: a massive mobilization and turnout in New Haven's black community, and the campaign's challenge to the party organization and the previous mayoral administration's downtown development priorities.

Deracialization theorists who want to contrast the "new breed" of successful African American politicians with the "old politics of protest" might claim that Daniels's victory resulted from his record as an established politician and loyal Democrat. But the Daniels campaign represented first and foremost an insurgent challenge. Daniels entered the race against a popular incumbent who was widely regarded as unbeatable. Moreover, Daniels took on the Democratic party establishment in a town known for the strength of its machine politics. His credentials certainly helped to make him a credible candidate, but his challenge to the political status quo was equally important to his victory.

There were no black elected officials or clergymen on stage at Daniels's announcement because the established "leadership" of the black community was too closely tied to the incumbent administration by all the carrots and sticks of machine politics.[11] Daniels's willingness to risk opposing DiLieto, however, made it possible to forge a coalition of black and white activists who had fewer ties with the administration and many different reasons for being outraged by its priorities for the city.

Contrary to the deracialization hypothesis, Daniels did not avoid references to his racial identity. In some ways, he was able to use his race to his advantage with all ethnic groups. His expressions of pride in his racial heritage created empathy with minority voters, but his sense of community also appealed to many whites. He talked about growing up in a New Haven housing project and attending local schools. Most voters could identify with a candidate who had grown up "on the poor side of town" and worked hard to achieve notable success. Much like David Dinkins in New York City, Daniels conveyed the message that his race would help him create a politics of inclusion and ease racial tensions.

Daniels made crime the focus of his campaign because it was the issue of greatest concern to voters throughout New Haven. He did not, however, offer a conservative "law and order" platform to appease white voters' fears that a black candidate would be soft on crime. Instead of calling for more police, he called for more imaginative, community-oriented policing—citing the work of Lee Brown in Houston (later hired by Dinkins to become New

York's police commissioner) as an example. He also consistently connected the rising crime rate with the DiLieto administration's "trickle-down" economics of downtown development at the expense of the city's neighborhoods and human resources. His call for parents and young people to help stop the spread of drugs and guns both spoke to the need for a politics of mobilization and empowerment in minority communities and suggested to whites that a respected black leader could successfully address the city's most serious problems.[12]

While critics of deracialization strategies seem to assume that the black community can be politicized *only* by direct racial appeals, the first Dinkins campaign in New York City suggested that viable black candidacies with a multiracial appeal can create higher voter turnout and support in the black community than those that rely primarily on racial identification.[13] The same was true of Daniels's election. The depth and breadth of Daniels's winning coalition can be judged by comparing his campaign to a race two years previously when Bill Jones, a black city official, challenged DiLieto. The Jones candidacy, supported primarily by black Democratic party activists and relying on mobilization of the black community, won only 24 percent of the primary vote and three of the city's thirty wards. In contrast, Daniels won 59 percent of the vote and twenty-two wards.

Additional differences between the two elections with respect to groups of voters are presented in Tables 8–1 and 8–2. In the city's predominantly

TABLE 8–1

Average Voter Turnout in Selected New Haven Wards, 1987 and 1989

	1987 %	1989 %
Black[1]	30	61
White[2]	43	63
Liberal[3]	17	46

1. Wards 20, 21, and 22 were 89, 97, and 81 percent black, respectively, according to the 1980 census.

2. Wards 17 and 18 were both over 98 percent white, according to the 1980 census. Traditionally, they have been the base of the DiLieto political machine.

3. Traditionally, Wards 1, 10, and 27 have been considered liberal white wards in New Haven. Ward 1 encompasses Yale University and most of its students. Ward 10 is home to many young professionals, Yale students and faculty, and reform-minded activists. Ward 27 is similar to Ward 10, in addition to having a large Jewish population.

TABLE 8–2
Average Voter Support for Black Mayoral
Candidates in Selected New Haven Wards,
1987 and 1989

	1987 %	1989 %
Black*	51	93
White*	5	14
Liberal*	19	65

* See notes for Table 8–1.

black wards, Daniels doubled the voter turnout and nearly doubled the rate of support as compared to the election in which Jones ran for mayor. Daniels also heavily increased turnout and support in liberal wards. He accomplished both of these tasks without causing a countermobilization in the more conservative white wards and actually drew a significant number of votes in those areas.[14]

The Daniels campaign, therefore, serves to confirm only the single most self-evident proposition suggested by deracialization theorists: African American candidates running in majority white districts must appeal to white voters. These candidates cannot rely exclusively on racial pride or race-specific agendas to win election. More importantly, however, the campaign suggests that, contrary to deracialization theorists, black candidates can appeal to white voters while still affirming their African American heritage. Progressive black candidates can, in fact, win a significant portion of the white vote.

The Daniels Electoral Coalition

The success of the Daniels campaign seems to challenge not only the deracialization hypothesis but also many other conventionally accepted political "realities." Why did so many white liberals support Daniels rather than one of the two white and at least nominally liberal candidates? How did Daniels raise more money than DeStefano, who as DiLieto's director of development had many business contacts, while still creating great enthusiasm among grassroots activists and students?[15] How did he mobilize blacks without alienating whites?

The answers seem to lie in the conjunction of three factors. First, an alliance developed between black Democratic party activists who had supported the Jones campaign in 1987 and grassroots organizers eager to involve young people in mobilizing blacks to assert their political power. Second, the city's problems with poverty, crime, homelessness, AIDS, and infant mortality created widespread dissatisfaction with the DiLieto administration's down-town development strategies. Third, the record and character of Daniels as an established politician willing to risk an insurgent campaign helped to unite people from different backgrounds with diverse aspirations—at least in part because he could give them a real hope of winning. These three crucial factors resulted in a rather rare phenomenon in American politics: a progressive coalition, led by blacks and supported by liberal whites and some business leaders, capable of winning an election in a majority white city.

Mobilizing the Black Electorate

There were several immediate precedents for the Daniels campaign with re-gard to New Haven's black electorate, including Jesse Jackson's presidential campaigns, especially in 1988, and Bill Jones's effort in 1987. In fact, Althea Tyson's campaign for registrar of voters in the spring of 1988 inspired many of her supporters, including Daniels, to think that a more serious challenge to DiLieto was both possible and necessary. Tyson was New Haven's first black assistant registrar of voters, and she made no secret of her desire to promote more intensive voter registration efforts in the black community. In the past, the Democratic party organization had endorsed the assistant registrar of voters to become registrar when that office became vacant—and the party's endorsement led automatically to election. However, in Tyson's case, when the registrar of voters retired, the party organization declared that Tyson had "personality problems" and endorsed a white candidate. Tyson's decision to challenge their nominee resulted in one of the hottest contests for a minor of-fice in New Haven's recent memory.

A group of black students from Yale and Southern Connecticut State Universities saw Tyson's campaign as an important opportunity to build on the excitement and organization created by Jesse Jackson's 1988 Democratic presidential primary victory in New Haven. They recruited high school stu-dents to help in door-to-door registration and get-out-the-vote efforts. They learned that DiLieto's hold over black elected officials was such that Daniels was one of the very few who gave Tyson any visible support. They were not able to produce a mass turnout in the black community even in a race that turned on a question of racial justice. Among those who did vote, however, Tyson did astonishingly well, not only in the black community, but also with Yale students and in the more liberal wards. She averaged 91 percent of the vote in the city's three predominantly black wards and 67 percent in the three traditionally liberal wards. In a race that depended primarily on organization, "the machine" came close to being out-organized, winning by only eight hun-dred votes. The race publicized the DiLieto administration's lack of "fairness" and proved that both blacks and white liberals would vote for a black candidate who ran on such an issue. Contacts, connections, and lessons learned in the Tyson campaign multiplied in the effort to elect Daniels.

Dissatisfaction with the DiLieto Administration

As New Haven's former police chief, Ben DiLieto admitted to illegally wiretapping antiwar and community activists in the 1960s. Despite the distrust this created among both liberals and blacks, in his ten years in office, DiLieto proved himself as much the master of "the executive centered coalition" as his well-studied predecessor Richard Lee.[16] DiLieto set an aggressive agenda for downtown development while keeping many different constituencies satisfied with a combination of patronage and symbolic gestures. For liberals, he appeared at peace marches and the New Haven-León "sister city" functions in support of Nicaragua. For blacks and Hispanics, he provided jobs, grants, and contracts in the human services sectors of the city's budget. He hired "the best and the brightest" professionals to devise packages of tax abatements and city assistance to encourage developers to build office towers and condominiums, spruce up shopping districts, and reopen two of the city's theaters.

The rhetoric of Mayor DiLieto and his staff reflected the same view of the city, its problems, and priorities that can be found in Paul E. Peterson's *City Limits*.[17] They continually emphasized that New Haven was in competition with surrounding suburbs for business investments and that the most important role for a city administration was to create a positive atmosphere for private sector development. DiLieto portrayed himself as the great defender of the city against the suburbs, a "mall buster" who paid a corporate law firm approximately $600,000 over six years to fight the opening of suburban malls in order to keep shoppers downtown. DiLieto's program was wrapped in trickle-down rhetoric with a populist appeal: this was the only way "to save the city's tax base" in order to provide services to the poor. These strategies allowed DiLieto to create a powerful political machine. With clear improvements downtown, token support for human services, and developers, contractors, and corporate lawyers contributing heavily to his campaigns, he won reelection four times by large margins.

The problem with DiLieto's program was that few benefits from his development strategies (or those of his predecessors) trickled down to the majority of New Haven's citizens. By 1989, New Haven had become the fourth poorest city in the United States. Life for the poor became more difficult as urban renewal programs eliminated low-income housing and rent prices escalated throughout the city.[18] In 1989 the infant mortality rate was the second highest in the nation. Crime rose at staggering rates. While DiLieto tilted at the windmills of suburban malls, New Haven's own mall, built with huge federal subsidies as the centerpiece for earlier urban renewal efforts, had become a hangout for teenagers with nothing to do—hardly a major attraction for suburban shoppers. The streets, schools, crime, and the lack of a skilled workforce made New Haven a less and less attractive place to live, work, invest, and spend money. The condominium market came to a standstill, and new office towers stood nearly empty. Despite the fact that the city had gained very little from many of these development projects, the DiLieto administration continued to respond to such problems by offering more tax abatements to encourage downtown development.

It was not only the poor, minorities, and liberals who became increasingly disillusioned with DiLieto's priorities. Lynn Fusco, a prominent white developer who had invested heavily in the city's first wave of office towers, was disgusted with an administration that was pushing for still more high-rise development as the solution to the city's problems. She played an important role in organizing early elite support for the Daniels campaign.

After DiLieto withdrew from the race, DeStefano, who lacked a strong personal political base, inherited the problems of DiLieto's record but few of the advantages of incumbency. This helped the Daniels organization grow into a genuinely multiracial campaign. Fusco worked with an African American banker in coordinating the Daniels fund-raising effort. Douglas Rae, the white chairman of the Yale University political science department, coordinated issues development, while Lisa Sullivan, a black Yale graduate student in political science, who had been active in Althea Tyson's campaign for voter registration, led field operations. Steve White, a twenty-six-year-old African American who had worked on Bill Jones's staff, was campaign manager. Khalid Lum, a black journalist for New Haven's most prominent "alternative" newspaper, became press secretary. Alma Ayala, a young Hispanic Yale graduate, was promoted from office manager to scheduler. Prominent black and white business people, professionals, and politicians served as the campaign's advisory committee.

Holding together such a coalition with its different objectives, styles, and priorities was never easy. There were ongoing conflicts between grassroots organizers and political professionals, insurgents and elites. There were tensions across various age, race, and ideological divisions. Everyone involved, however, knew that Daniels needed white votes and a massive turnout among blacks to win the election. While there were many arguments about how best to achieve both these goals, the diverse participants succeeded in developing a campaign that with its many difficulties had many strengths, including grassroots mobilization, sophisticated media and polling, and attention to the politics of both image and substance. The campaign cannot usefully be characterized by any of the models of deracialization.

The Daniels Administration and the Deracialization Hypothesis

Robert C. Smith criticizes black candidates who seek white allies, claiming that a deracialized electoral strategy may require blacks "to sacrifice their substantive policy agendas." He suggests that "the structure of ownership, financial institutions and investment that governs the economic prospects of cities . . . dominated by whites sharply constrains the agenda of black officeholders, effectively keeping the problems of poverty and the black underclass off the agenda of city government." He adds that electoral politics can have "little consequence" when it comes to dealing with the social and economic results of racism. Even African American mayors who do not seek white allies are unlikely to make much difference in the lives of their low-income constituents. Smith concludes, therefore, that electoral politics is good for little more than "politicizing people" and that "black leadership must act on the now well-understood limits of electoral politics, use it to 'politicize people' and undertake the arduous task of developing a movement style system challenging black politics."[19]

Daniels's tenure in office was indeed overwhelmingly dominated by the city's fiscal crisis. The DiLieto administration had left the city with a $12 million deficit. The area's severe recession meant that city welfare costs rose by one-third in 1989. The city's Standard and Poor bond rating dropped from AA– to BB–. A property tax reassessment (that the DiLieto administration had illegally avoided for a decade) increased taxes on some properties by as much as 400 percent and undermined the political support necessary for pursuing a more activist agenda.[20]

Contrary to Smith's claims, however, even with these severe economic and political constraints, the Daniels governing coalition effected some real changes in the city government's priorities, programs, and style of governing. For example, it dealt far more directly than past administrations with some of the social and economic effects of racism: police brutality, infant mortality rates, the spread of HIV among poor and minority populations, and city employment and service delivery practices. The Daniels record also suggests some of the problems with the assumption that African Americans inherently have "progressive policy preferences" and that "a movement style politics" will necessarily provide the progressive agenda that electoral politics misses.

In its rhetoric, distribution of jobs and contracts, and emphasis on human services, the Daniels administration generally embraced different priorities than its predecessors. Much more than previous administrations, it emphasized "fairness" and inclusiveness in political appointments and, in doing so, succeeded in diversifying the city workforce in terms of gender, ethnicity, and race.[21] The most prominent searches to fill positions in the Daniels administration were in the areas of law enforcement and human services, which the DiLieto administration had always used for uninspired patronage appointments.

With regard to its programmatic agenda, the Daniels governing coalition was certainly not without serious problems and contradictions. It was most effective on the one issue that also held together the electoral coalition: crime. But on many other important issues (e.g., housing, education, waste management, and development), the electoral coalition of liberals, developers, bankers, community activists, blacks, and Hispanics tended to fragment, and the administration failed to develop an aggressive agenda. As a result, many of the same elites that dominated (or ignored) these issues with the aid of the DiLieto administration continued to do so despite some friction with city hall. The Daniels governing coalition had many of the contradictions that Smith identifies as a result of multiracial alliances, but nevertheless they did address some problems related to urban poverty and racial inequities.

In order to evaluate Smith's claim that black candidates who seek white allies inevitably sacrifice their substantive policy agenda, we examine the Daniels administration's record with regard to the issues of crime, appointments, human services, fiscal management, and institutional constraints.

Crime

Crime and policing were the issues on which the Daniels campaign developed the most coherent theoretical and practical perspective, with a fairly elaborate critique of conventional policing's emphasis on using patrol cars to cut "response time" in answer to rising crime rates. Daniels embraced the concept of community policing as a way of working with individual neighborhoods in many different kinds of efforts to prevent crime.

For police chief, he appointed Nicholas Pastore, the one conceivable candidate who not only met the city charter requirements for supervisory experience on the New Haven police force but was also passionately committed to community policing.[22] With a mandate from Daniels to embark on a reform program, Pastore stopped such police tactics as sting operations, arguing that they served only as publicity stunts to boost arrest records, while actually increasing homicide rates as dealers were forced to compete for new turf.[23] He moved police supervisors from desk jobs to foot patrols. Pastore "left the mayor's inaugural ball . . . and spent three hours at a New Haven hospital with the families of several African American males who allegedly had been brutally beaten by some of (his own) cops."[24] He put a black officer in charge of developing an internal affairs bureau to investigate complaints of police brutality.

Pastore has been ready to face public controversy and the fury of his own department for his willingness to promote "dialogue" with gang members and militants, including, at a public forum on police brutality, embracing a man charged with shooting an officer. In efforts to improve police and community relations, he has called police out of "riot" situations—even wading in personally to shake hands and promote a nonviolent peace. He has argued repeatedly for the decriminalization of drug use and for more investments in social services and youth programs as the best weapons against crime. He has attempted strenuously to recruit more women and minorities, as well as involving young people in a police advisory commission that reviews department programs and personnel practices.[25] With strong support from Daniels, Pastore was able to face down rank and file protests of his changes in the department.[26]

Appointments and Human Services

Daniels made one of the most impressive appointments of his first year in office in human services. After instituting a national search for the head of the city's Human Resources Administration, he recruited Audrey Rowe, who had previously been social services commissioner of Washington, D.C., for eight years, followed by a year as a consultant for the Rockefeller Foundation. Rowe was widely praised for her ability to promote the delivery of effective human services and for her direct approach to both clients and social service workers.[27] The city's fiscal crisis and rising welfare costs meant that Rowe spent much of her time dealing with budget issues, but she successfully established a program of "family resource centers," based on the decentralized model of community policing, in ten of the city's poorest neighborhoods.[28]

Another important appointment was that of Vanessa Burns, an energetic African American who had been active in ward politics and city government, as head of the public works department, a traditionally white, male-dominated department. Even Paul Bass, a reporter for the *New Haven Advocate* and one of Daniels's sterner critics, agrees that the appointments of Burns, Rowe, and Pastore at the highest levels of city government made some significant difference in the day-to-day lives of many of New Haven's poorest citizens.[29] Despite severe fiscal constraints, the administration's obvious commitment to poor and minority citizens was a significant change from the past, not only in terms of its appointments but also with some relatively inexpensive, imaginative programs that literally saved lives.

Saving Lives: Community Policing

Crime is one of the most serious and intractable problems facing cities like New Haven. In response, Daniels established a program of community policing that began to show some success. Despite the dissatisfaction of some police officers, Chief Pastore managed to implement his innovative program, which is widely seen as an important factor in reducing the city's crime rate, both absolutely and relative to other comparable cities in Connecticut (Tables 8–3 and 8–4).[30]

Saving Lives: Infant Mortality

During the Daniels administration, New Haven witnessed a 43 percent drop in what was in 1989 the nation's highest infant mortality rate, from 18.5 deaths per 1,000 births to 11 per 1,000 in 1990, the lowest rate ever recorded for New Haven. No other city in Connecticut showed as dramatic a drop as New Haven.[31] This drop was widely attributed to the work of a commission on infant health, a consortium of the city's hospitals, clinics, and social service groups, established by the New Haven Foundation, a private, nonprofit funding agency with significant contributions from the Daniels administration. In 1986, as a state senator, Daniels had approached the New Haven Foundation about establishing such a program. His campaign for mayor highlighted infant mortality as one of the crucial issues demonstrating the need for new priorities for the city.

As mayor, Daniels created a Maternal and Newborn Health Division in

TABLE 8–3

Crime Statistics for New Haven, 1990–93

	Total Crimes	Murder	Rape	Robbery	Aggravated Assault	Burglary	Larceny	Auto Theft
1990	21,012	31	168	1784	2008	4476	9086	3459
1991	19,492	34	118	1355	2018	4146	8041	3780
1992	17,483	30	131	1227	1845	3672	7852	2726
1993	15,552	20	130	1238	1154	3417	7720	1873
% Change	−26.0	−35.5	−22.6	−30.6	−42.5	−23.7	−15.0	−45.9

Source: Data for 1990–92 from U.S. Department of Justice, *Crime in the United States, 1990, 1991, and 1992;* data for 1993 supplied by the Crime Analysis Unit of the New Haven Police Department.

TABLE 8–4

Changes in Crime Rate for Selected Connecticut Cities by Percentage, 1990–92

	Total Crimes	Murder	Rape	Robbery	Aggravated Assault	Burglary	Larceny	Auto Theft
New Haven	−16.80	−3.23	−22.02	−31.22	−8.12	−17.96	−13.58	−21.19
Hartford	−2.04	−31.58	−21.88	−13.61	−32.89	−16.32	7.54	25.03
Bridgeport	−8.85	0.00	−6.33	3.67	−5.91	−11.82	−16.71	−2.59

Source: U.S. Department of Justice, *Crime in the United States, 1990, 1991, and 1992.*

the City Health Department. With help from the Connecticut Department of Income Maintenance, the division grew to a staff of eight outreach workers and a supervisor by 1991. The outreach workers are residents of New Haven's poorest neighborhoods; they seek out high-risk pregnant women by going door to door and visiting homeless shelters and soup kitchens. They link these women, most of whom have no source of health care, with prenatal and pediatric care, nutrition and substance abuse programs, housing and transportation services; the volunteers continue to work with them after childbirth. With the program's focus on the needs of poor women, the most astounding drop in infant mortality rates took place among African Americans, from 26 deaths per 1,000 births in 1989 (a rate worse than that in many developing countries) to 11.7 in 1990.

Saving Lives: A Needle Exchange Program

The Daniels administration also implemented one of the nation's first needle exchange programs for drug addicts. Initially, the program was quite controversial among many religious leaders and politicians who feared that such programs endorsed drug use. Subsequent studies, however, have suggested that New Haven's program has reduced the transmission of the HIV virus among drug users. The program has been widely used as a model for other communities.[32]

Institutional and Fiscal Constraints

There is no question that on many issues Daniels was constrained by the institutional structures that govern the economic prospects of cities at the expense of poor and minority populations. Daniels outraged some of his former supporters, for example, when he ultimately sided with mass protests against a Housing Authority plan to aid project residents in buying homes in scattered neighborhoods throughout the city. Some black clergy felt that Daniels caved into pressure from whites when he declared that the plan had not been developed "democratically." While the vociferous opposition actually came from both black and white homeowners, it was clear that their mobilization carried far more clout in the electoral calculus of the administration than the needs and aspirations of welfare mothers and project residents.

Fiscal constraints shaped the agenda of the Daniels administration far more fundamentally than concerns with political popularity. Most significant was the dependence of Connecticut's desperately poor cities on local property taxes for funds for schools, recreation programs, and city services. In one of the richest states in the union, urban residents pay higher taxes without achieving anywhere near the level of services and funding enjoyed by their suburban neighbors.[33] Rather than mobilizing any serious challenge to these inequities, Daniels functioned as a good soldier within the system, slogging away at the impossible and thankless mission of balancing a budget.

Daniels alienated many supporters, as he and his advisors held to the principle that his personal and political integrity—part of the historical record of the first African American mayor of New Haven—required him to make balancing the city's budget his first priority. Unable to raise taxes further without almost certainly losing revenues as more and more businesses and homeowners left the city, the Daniels administration eventually declared that cutbacks were its only option—cutbacks that included programs crucial to Daniels's key constituencies: schools, libraries, parks, homeless shelters, and elderly centers.[34]

Moreover, the city's desperate fiscal status robbed Daniels of the opportunities enjoyed by every administration to reward friends and allies and solidify political support. Every city appointment and contract exacerbated tensions. Some of Daniels's allies were bitterly disappointed that his victory resulted in so few fruits for distribution. Others were angry that Daniels was willing to make any concessions at all to the politics of patronage when the city was fighting so hard to save its fiscal integrity.

The Strengths and Weaknesses of the Daniels Governing Coalition

In analyzing the Daniels administration, one could almost say that the chief problem with his governing coalition was that it held together too well. Blacks, whites, and Hispanics, business people and reformers, elites and activists were all present with their many contradictory objectives and aspirations. The administration failed to offer a compelling vision of the city and its future that could either weld these diverse forces into a greater whole or even energize some particular groups. Factions continued to complain about each other in an unwieldy governing process that seemed neither to drive anyone out nor move them forward. While Daniels was careful in at least some areas to seek out the best talent and to develop a broadly inclusive administration, his recruitment efforts and the budget crisis took up much of his first year in office. With all the individual employment searches, he never succeeded in pulling together a coherent governing team. It took two searches, for example, to recruit Yasha Escalera, an Hispanic with a background in developing low-income housing for Connecticut, as the city's director of development. Escalera did not start work until 1990, the second year of Daniels's two-year term, and resigned in 1992, as a result of tensions between himself and a new chief executive officer. Given the administration's failure to develop any coherent plans for development, the Chamber of Commerce's push for the Taubman Mall was the only show in town.

Mayor Daniels perceived that the lack of effectiveness in his first term cost him the endorsement of the city's major newspaper, the *New Haven Register*, in his reelection campaign in 1991. Daniels's opponent, Jonathan Einhorn, a white Republican lawyer, focused on the issues of crime and taxes, as well as on Pastore's controversial changes in the police department, calling for a return to "hard-line law enforcement" and the reinstatement of mass-arrest drug sting operations, police dogs, and the SWAT team. He also attacked Daniels's management of the city's budget and promised that he would allow no tax increases in the next year.[35] Einhorn's showing was the best for a Republican mayoral candidate since 1975. Voters cast their ballots much more along racial lines than in 1989: Einhorn carried thirteen of the city's mostly white wards. Daniels won 56 percent of the popular vote, carrying seventeen wards. He kept his overwhelming lead in Ward 1 among Yale students who voted for him 619 to 32. He held his own in integrated areas of the city, but his margin of victory clearly depended on the turnout in the city's black wards.[36]

In his second term, newspaper headlines focused on interstaff rivalries in Daniels's administration. Ongoing unrest over city budget cutbacks and increased taxes continued to erode his popularity. Some members of the administration continued to work hard to provide decent services and to get control over the budget process. But even where real success stories existed—like community policing and infant mortality—Daniels's divided, incoherent administration failed to publicize or take credit for them. Cynicism, depression, and distrust permeated the city's political atmosphere, rather than the spirited debate and mobilization one would hope to find with vibrant political leadership.

His 1989 opponent, John DeStefano, began capitalizing on the disaffection and sense of betrayal felt by many former Daniels supporters, collecting endorsements and funds for the next mayoral race from both whites and blacks (including such prominent political figures as Althea Tyson) with promises to provide a more efficient and caring administration. An African American, former Alderman John Artis Yopp, also declared his candidacy, backed by the controversial developer Wendell Harp, who was clearly dissatisfied with the results of his investments in Daniels's initial campaign. At the urging of many friends and advisors, Daniels finally decided not to run for a third mayoral term.

After Daniels announced his decision, DeStefano seemed virtually unstoppable in his drive for the office. Initially running against four minority candidates (Tomas Reyes, the president of the Board of Aldermen, Rev. Stanley Justice, minister of one of the largest black churches in New Haven,

James Newton, another former alderman, and Yopp) and a white maverick (the owner of an athletic shoe store, who had made a name for himself with banners urging drug dealers to take their patronage elsewhere), DeStefano received the endorsement of the Democratic party. All his opponents except Yopp pulled out of the primary race before election day; the last to withdraw, Rev. Justice, announced that he was doing so in order to avoid dividing the African American vote.[37] Despite such appeals for racial unity, DeStefano beat Yopp by an almost four-to-one margin (10,317 to 2,791) in a primary that had one of the largest pluralities and lowest turnouts in recent New Haven history. DeStefano carried such poor minority neighborhoods as the Hill and Fair Haven and lost in only three of the city's wards.[38]

Ironically, DeStefano's campaign embodied evidence that the Daniels coalition had changed New Haven's political rhetoric and governmental policies. The popularity of the urban populism that Daniels had endorsed in his first campaign for mayor was clear to all the candidates in the race, who vied with each other primarily in terms of their commitment to an inclusive administration that would speak especially to the needs of poor and minority communities. DeStefano, the former development director and second in command of the DiLieto administration, came out swinging against the plans for the Taubman Mall, calling it a white elephant that would suck up tax dollars while failing to meet the city's needs for neighborhood-based development.

Even more importantly, DeStefano's campaign crusaded against the injustices represented by the city's dependence on local property taxes. He set up a lawyers' committee to challenge the resulting inequalities between the city and its suburbs as a violation of the equal protection clause of the state's constitution, a case similar to an ongoing lawsuit (*Sheff v. O'Neil*) against the segregation and unequal funding of Connecticut's schools. While the success of DeStefano's efforts is far from certain, reforming the state's tax system to equalize its burden across regions represents one of the best options for allowing cities like New Haven to remain solvent while providing services that its citizens desperately need.

In reviewing the history of Daniels's election campaigns and administration, we conclude that while the failures of his governing coalition could be predicted by Robert Smith's theories of the weaknesses of deracialized campaigns and electoral politics, their achievements in fact challenge Smith's basic assumptions.

Race and Politics

The problems of the Daniels administration were not caused by white domination of a deracialized governing coalition. The administration's

characteristics suggest not that race determines politics but that politics determines politics. While some black and multiethnic administrations promote development policies similar to DiLieto's, the Daniels campaign built a
multiracial electoral coalition around a relatively progressive critique of
DiLieto's priorities. As a result, some of the blacks and whites in the Daniels
administration saw the need to address the problems of poverty more substantively than many more thoroughly black urban administrations. If anything, the multiracial nature of the Daniels administration actually helped to
promote a progressive agenda. However, this governing coalition could not
satisfy many of its own members and supporters with a program that did little
more than transfer jobs and contracts from one ethnic group to another.

Although Smith might say that the failures of the Daniels administration illustrate the superiority of "movement style" politics to electoral politics,
the opposite argument is more compelling. Many of those most involved in
the Daniels campaign were heavily committed to movement style politics,
and they saw the campaign primarily as a way of mobilizing and politicizing
people. Many were relatively vague about any concrete agenda; instead, they
wanted to be "out on the streets," "working with black youths," "bringing the
community together," and so on. Those who saw themselves as primarily
concerned with "issues" tended to define their concerns in absolute terms that
suggested little interest in achieving any specific objectives. Environmental-
ists, for example, generally preferred praising recycling and denouncing in-
cinerators over actually developing a workable plan for solving the city's trash
problems.

After Daniels's election, the developers, politicians, and business
people, black and white, who had supported him, beat a path to his door with
very specific requests for appointments and priorities. The progressives,
black and white, with the notable exception of those involved in establishing
community policing, infant health programs, and the needle exchange program, tended to go about their own particular organizing projects, sitting
back and waiting for the new administration to fail to meet their expectations,
to give them new reasons to engage in protest activities.[39]

While the Daniels administration can certainly be criticized for not
making better use of activists, activists can also be criticized for not making
better use of the administration. Progressives made an important contribution to Daniels's campaign with their critique of DiLieto's downtown development priorities, but they failed to take advantage of Daniels's election by
working to convert their ideas into governmental appointments, policies, and
actions. They had been taught by the conventions of left politics not to expect
any real change from the political system. They grew accustomed to thinking
of themselves as always in opposition, leaving to others the business of trying
to use governmental power to achieve desired policies.

Daniels's first electoral campaign suggests that a progressive, populist campaign platform and a multiracial coalition may actually be assets for winning an election. The record of his administration suggests that more thinking must be done to develop a progressive agenda for actually governing a city. Given the realities of federal cutbacks and a declining tax base, strategies for community mobilization and outreach represent one of the most necessary as well as politically attractive approaches to addressing serious urban problems. The ongoing struggle to establish community policing in New Haven highlights that such programs require clear thinking, specific agendas, and competent administrators who are willing to fight hard for them. A call for progressives to think seriously about how to win elections *and* govern our cities might better serve the development of such ideas, agendas, and administrators than vague appeals for more movement style politics.

Conclusion

The success of the Daniels campaign was not merely symbolic. New leadership in the police department, welfare administration, and public works resulted in some tangible differences in the lives of New Haven's poor and minority citizens. Community policing helped to reduce the city's crime rate and improved relations between the police and the community. The administration instituted hiring policies that began to substitute merit and inclusion for patronage and cronyism. Daniels also helped to shift political rhetoric away from tax breaks and quixotic development schemes to a focus on human services. The clearly impossible burdens faced by an administration attempting to provide decent services while being forced to make budget cuts highlights the need for tax reform within the region and across the state. Finally, with such innovations as the needle exchange program and efforts to fight infant mortality, the Daniels administration made the difference between life and death for some of New Haven's most vulnerable citizens.

Although the first Daniels campaign and administration had many of the characteristics cited by most theorists of deracialization, the deracialization hypothesis does not adequately describe or explain their achievements. Contrary to deracialization's assumptions, Daniels's victory owed as much to his challenge to the status quo as to his establishment credentials. Instead of deemphasizing race, he used it to appeal to both blacks and whites. Instead of taking conservative stands to attract white voters, he offered progressive policies that united blacks and whites on several issues. The record of his administration, which was not especially noted for its leadership or political courage, indicates that serious efforts to implement such policies can make some real difference in the lives of poor and minority citizens. Rather than

encouraging cynicism about the relevance of electoral politics and city governance for the lives of the poor, the story of the Daniels administration suggests
the need for much more intensive efforts to formulate and publicize political
initiatives aimed at solving urban problems.

Deracialization theory as formulated both by its promoters and its
critics does not provide an adequate framework for either analyzing or
changing the dynamics of African American politics. William Julius Wilson's
advice urging the Democratic party to adopt deracialized solutions to the
problems of poor blacks reflects the inadequacy of the concept.[40] Wilson's implicit assumption is that the problem with the Democratic party today is that
it has been dominated by a black and liberal leadership that has pushed a
race-specific agenda instead of broader programs that would be more attractive to white voters and provide more real benefits to the poor.

In fact, race-specific agendas have by and large represented the marginalization rather than the domination of black and liberal leadership within
both the Democratic party and American politics. The pursuit of these
agendas represents more a consequence than a cause of the Democratic
party's failure to develop more imaginative, far-reaching programs that would
challenge the economic status quo. Corporate elites and PACs, rather than
blacks and liberals, have stifled broader, progressive policy initiatives, such as
full employment, equitable taxation, and national health care and child
care.[41] To blame blacks and liberals for the party's failure to develop a popular
progressive agenda is only to join neoliberals and neoconservatives in
blaming the chief victims of the Democratic party's strategies.

The lessons of the Daniels administration fail to support those critics of
the deracialization hypothesis who assume that black politics would automatically be progressive were it not for attempts to work with whites. The political agendas of politicians, activists, and voters of all races are always social
constructs, developed by many people in the context of their different institutions, ideas, and circumstances. Black people's and white people's political
goals, and their sense of their limitations and possibilities, develop under the
influence of many of the same forces. In recent years, these forces have included deindustrialization and diminished federal funding for social programs. There have been few blacks or whites who have responded to these
circumstances with bold political programs to solve urban problems. In the
absence of any broader vision, both blacks and whites in city politics have defined their political goals primarily in terms of providing jobs and contracts
for their supporters.

The failure of analyses based on the deracialization hypothesis indicates the need to develop new analytical concepts to explain better what
may become a new trend in African American electoral politics—the election of African American candidates in majority white districts and jurisdictions. A more sophisticated analysis of black and white interests and the

range of options open to African American candidates should provide better explanations of electoral politics in general and African American politics in particular.

Notes

The authors would like to thank Paul Bass, Robert Dahl, Donald Green, Huey Perry, Douglas Rae, Adolph Reed, Raymond Seidelman, Rogers Smith, Lisa Sullivan, and Sylvia Tesh for their readings and criticisms. We also owe a great deal to many people we met as participants in the first Daniels campaign. Our assessment of the Daniels administration was informed by interviews with Douglas Rae, Daniels's first chief administrative officer, and Paul Bass, a local journalist, who was one of the administration's more outspoken progressive critics.

1. For a general statement of the deracialization debate, see Huey L. Perry's introduction in this volume. More specific statements are provided by Joseph P. McCormick II, "The November Election and the Politics of Deracialization," *New Directions* 17 (1990): 23–27; Joseph P. McCormick II and Charles E. Jones, "The Conceptualization of Deracialization Revisited: Thinking through the Dilemma," in *Dilemmas in Black Politics: Issues of Leadership and Strategy,* edited by Georgia A. Persons (New York: HarperCollins, 1993), 66–84; Saundra C. Ardrey and William E. Nelson, "The Maturation of Black Political Power: The Case of Cleveland," *PS: Political Science and Politics* 23 (June 1990): 148–51; Alvin J. Schexnider, "The Politics of Pragmatism: An Analysis of the 1989 Gubernatorial Election in Virginia," *PS: Political Science and Politics* 23 (June 1990): 154–56.
2. Schexnider, "Politics of Pragmatism," 154–56.
3. Robert C. Smith, "Recent Elections and Black Politics: The Maturation or Death of Black Politics?" *PS: Political Science and Politics* 23 (June 1990): 160–63.
4. Ardrey and Nelson, "Maturation of Black Political Power," 17.
5. Adolph L. Reed, Jr., *The Jesse Jackson Phenomenon* (New Haven, Conn.: Yale University Press, 1986), 61–67.
6. Charles V. Hamilton, "Deracialization: Examination of a Political Strategy," *First World* 1 (Mar./Apr. 1977): 3–5.
7. Smith, "Recent Elections," 161.
8. The 1990 census puts New Haven's black population at 35 percent, Hispanics at 13.2 percent, and whites at 49 percent.
9. "Daniels Ahead," *New Haven Register,* Sept. 3, 1989, A1.
10. There were no exit polls to provide any more precise estimates of racial voting patterns.
11. After DiLieto withdrew from the race, most prominent African Americans endorsed Daniels, with the notable exception of two ministers who had recently received contracts and appointments from DiLieto's administration.
12. Polling data indicate the success of Daniels's efforts to communicate position on crime and other issues. At the end of the campaign, 48 percent of poll respondents who were aware of Daniels named crime and drugs as issues he had discussed, while only 34 percent were able to say the same for DeStefano. Forty-

two percent of those aware of DeStefano were unable to name an issue he had discussed, but only 26 percent of those aware of Daniels were unable to name an issue he had discussed ("Daniels Ahead").

13. J. Phillip Thompson, "David Dinkins' Victory in New York City: The Decline of the Democratic Party Organization and the Strengthening of Black Politics," *PS: Political Science and Politics* 23 (June 1990): 147; Anna Ponder, "Commitments, Constraints, and Coalitions: A Study of Mayor John C. Daniels, 1969–91," unpublished paper, 1992, 14–15.

14. See Ponder, "Commitments, Constraints, and Coalitions," 16.

15. Data obtained from the New Haven City Clerk's office show that as of August 30, 1989 (one week before the primary), Daniels had raised $291,079 to DeStefano's $184,609.

16. For positive accounts of Lee's administration, see Robert Dahl, *Who Governs?: Democracy and Power in an American City* (New Haven, Conn.: Yale University Press, 1961); Nelson Polsby, *Community Power and Political Theory* (New Haven, Conn.: Yale University Press, 1963); Raymond Wolfinger, *The Politics of Progress* (Englewood Cliffs, N.J.: Prentice-Hall, 1974); Paul E. Peterson, *City Limits* (Chicago: University of Chicago Press, 1981). For critiques suggesting that Lee's urban renewal programs served major developers and businesses at the expense of New Haven's poor and minority citizens, see William Domhoff, *Who Really Rules?: New Haven and Community Power Reexamined* (Santa Monica, Calif.: Goodyear, 1978); Fred Powledge, *Model City* (New York: Simon and Schuster, 1970); Norman Fainstein and Susan Fainstein, "New Haven: The Limits of the Local State," in *Restructuring the City,* edited by Susan Fainstein et al. (New York: Longman, 1983), 27–79; Clarence Stone and Heywood Sanders, "Reexamining a Classic Case of Development Politics: New Haven, Connecticut," in *The Politics of Urban Development,* edited by Clarence Stone and Heywood Sanders (Lawrence: University Press of Kansas, 1987), 159–81.

17. Peterson, *City Limits.*

18. Fainstein and Fainstein point out that city planning documents show that 7,850 units of low-income housing were destroyed between 1956 and 1972 as a result of urban renewal and highway construction, while only 2,214 units were constructed in the same period. As much as one-fifth of the entire city population was uprooted ("New Haven," 47–49).

19. Smith, "Recent Elections," 161.

20. Paul Bass, "Retirement and Warning from New Haven Mayor," *New York Times,* May 30, 1993, B9.

21. Ponder, "Commitments, Constraints, and Coalitions," 22–25.

22. The *New Haven Register* described Daniels's choice of Nicholas Pastore as police chief as "brilliant" (Feb. 18, 1990). Pastore, who had been second in command under DiLieto, resigned from the force after testifying that he had helped to carry out DiLieto's orders to tap the phones of student radicals and community activists in the 1960s. He then spent ten years working in real estate, while continuing to develop an outspoken perspective on law enforcement issues.

23. Douglas Rae, interview, New Haven, Conn., June 19, 1990.

24. Clifton Graves, "Police Chief Deserves Chance to Earn Community's Respect," *New Haven Register,* Mar. 1, 1990, 11.

25. Rae, interview, New Haven, Conn., Nov. 19, 1990; Ponder, "Commitments, Constraints, and Coalitions," 19–20.

26. Martine C. Costello, "Cops Rip Chief over Morale," New Haven Register, Apr. 19, 1991, 1.

27. Andi Rierden, "In the Fight against Urban Despair, a Fresh Face and a Firm Grip," New York Times, July 27, 1990, B1.

28. Daniels's liberal critics saw Rowe as the person in the administration who best represented a politics of mobilization and empowerment among the city's poorest citizens. They believe that her departure after less than two years in New Haven to become commissioner of the state's Income Maintenance Department for Governor Lowell Weicker reflected her frustration not only with the city's budget crisis but also with her own marginalization within the Daniels administration and its more general lack of leadership (Paul Bass, interview, New Haven, Conn., Dec. 6, 1990). The programs she implemented, however, remained in effect.

29. Bass, interview, New Haven, Conn., June 19, 1990.

30. Costello, "Cops Rip Chief."

31. There was a statewide drop in infant mortality rates from 1989 to 1990 from 8.9 deaths per 1,000 births to 7.9, but neither Hartford nor Bridgeport showed anything like New Haven's decreases. The infant mortality rate among black infants in Hartford in 1990, for example, was 26.1 deaths per 1,000 births, more than double New Haven's rate. This discussion of the drop in New Haven's infant mortality rate is drawn from Jackie Fitzpatrick, "Taking Prenatal Care to Those in Need," New York Times, Jan. 2, 1994, B1; Abram Katz, "Prenatal Effort Cuts Baby Deaths," New Haven Register, Dec. 3, 1993, 3; Adrienne C. Hedgspeth, "Infant Death Rate Drops," New Haven Register, Dec. 2, 1993, 1; Gene Trainor, "Infant Deaths Fall 45%," Connecticut Post, Dec. 2, 1993, A1; Rae, interview, New Haven, Conn., Aug. 29, 1994.

32. Laura Johannes, "New Study Backs Needle-Exchange Program in City," New Haven Register, July 22, 1992, 3–4.

33. Connecticut ranks second among the states in its dependence on property taxes, which represent 57 percent of local government revenue. See Connecticut Conference of Municipalities Public Policy Reports, "Connecticut's Overdependence on the Property Tax" (Dec. 21, 1993, no. 93–20r), "Comparison of Property Taxes in Connecticut" (Jan. 3, 1994, no. 94-01), and "Indicators of Need in Connecticut Municipalities: Measures of Municipal Distress," vols. 1 (Nov. 1991) and 2 (July 1992).

34. Hedgspeth, "Pro-School Group Gives Daniels Bad Grades," New Haven Register, Dec. 15, 1990, 3; Bass, "Retirement and Warning from New Haven Mayor," New York Times, May 30, 1993, B9.

35. Josh Kovner, "Ideas on Crime Split Candidates," New Haven Register, Nov. 3, 1991, B1.

36. "Einhorn's Showing Best for GOP since 1975," New Haven Register, Nov. 6, 1991, 18.

37. Hedgspeth, "Justice Drops Out of the Race," New Haven Register, Aug. 21, 1993, 3.

38. Mark Zaretsky and Martine Costello, "DeStefano Routs Yopp in New Haven,"

New Haven Register, Sept. 15, 1993, 1; "Skiest Says It's Not Over Yet," *New Haven Register,* Sept. 16, 1993, 3.

39. Other sources confirm this view of the Daniels transition period (Bass, interview, New Haven, Conn., Dec. 6, 1990).

40. William Julius Wilson, "Race-Neutral Policies and the Democratic Coalition," in *The American Negro Reference Book* (Englewood Cliffs, N.J.: Prentice-Hall, 1990); Wilson, "Race-Neutral Policies and the Democratic Coalition," *American Prospect* 1 (Jan. 1990): 74–81.

41. Thomas Edsall, *The New Politics of Inequality* (New York: Norton, 1984), 23–66.

9

The Deracialization Strategy and African American Candidates in Memphis Mayoral Elections

Sharon D. Wright

On October 4, 1991, Willie W. Herenton defeated nine-year incumbent Richard C. "Dick" Hackett by 172 votes to become the first elected African American mayor of Memphis, Tennessee.[1] This landmark election occurred in a city that was best-known for the exploitative boss politics of Edward H. Crump, the segregationist atrocities of Mayor Henry Loeb, and the assassination of Martin Luther King, Jr. This chapter examines Herenton's and other mayoral elections in Memphis in 1975, 1979, and 1982 in the context of the deracialization hypothesis. I contend that the deracialization concept does not apply to African American participation in Memphis mayoral elections. This chapter will show a racially polarized voting pattern in the 1975, 1979, and 1982 mayoral runoff elections and the 1991 general election.

In many cities, black candidates have attracted substantial support from white voters by using a deracialization strategy, deemphasizing racial issues, such as affirmative action and racial preference schemes, racial polarization, and the problems of the inner-city, and highlighting issues that would not alienate the white electorate.[2] Before Willie Herenton's 1991 victory, the experiences of African American candidates in Memphis differed greatly from those of African American candidates in other large urban settings: black candidates in Memphis were unable to garner significant white crossover support regardless of their use of deracialized strategies. In 1975 and 1979, black mayoral candidate W. Otis Higgs, Jr., focused on encouraging white crossover support by emphasizing race-neutral issues but was defeated and gained limited crossover support.[3] In 1982, black mayoral candidate J. O. Patterson, Jr., at first used deracialization but later abandoned it when he did not receive white crossover support. In 1991, Willie Herenton did not pursue the path of deracialization. Perceiving it as a waste of time, he made few attempts to win white votes, believing that race was an inevitable issue in Memphis politics. The Herenton campaign was almost entirely geared toward mobilization of the African American voting majority.

The data used for this analysis are election returns from all Memphis precincts in the 1975, 1979, and 1982 runoff elections and the 1991 general election. Data show that white voters in Memphis did not provide substantial crossover support to black candidates regardless of whether campaigns were deracialized. Moreover, with the exception of the 1967 election, black voters also did not provide major crossover support to white candidates.

The 1975 and 1979 Mayoral Elections

In 1975 and 1979, Otis Higgs emerged as the first serious African American contender for the mayoral office in Memphis.[4] His campaigns can best be described as employing dual strategies that emphasized one set of issues in the black community and an entirely different set to whites.[5] As part of his efforts, Higgs made personal appearances and campaigned through white-owned print and television media outlets. When addressing whites, he projected a nonthreatening image and emphasized race-neutral issues such as cutting property taxes, improving the quality of public schools, reducing crime, and improving city hall leadership. Higgs also spoke before black audiences, made appeals through media outlets geared toward African Americans, and conducted a grassroots effort to mobilize the black electorate. Since he realized that most of his support would come from black voters, he worked more actively in the predominantly black areas of Memphis. His visibility in the black community was designed to emphasize that, unlike white politicians, he cared about them and would not ignore their interests if elected.[6]

Scholars have pointed out that black candidates who conduct deracialized campaigns do not have to completely abandon racial themes. Charles V. Hamilton states, "Maintaining a 'deracialized image' does not mean that a black mayor or candidate cannot adopt strong positions on racial justice."[7]

Jesse Raphael Borges cites two components of racialized campaign messages: racial conciliation and symbolic significance themes.[8] Otis Higgs used both in his two mayoral campaigns. Concerning racial conciliation, he stressed that as mayor he could more effectively lessen racial strife than his white opponent, Wyeth Chandler. Higgs also explained the symbolic implications of electing a black mayor. For African Americans, his election would exemplify black unity and racial pride. By electing Higgs, white voters would send a message to the nation that they were progressive and would support a black contender if assured of fair treatment.

Despite these appeals, Higgs's deracialized 1975 mayoral campaign was unsuccessful. Voting patterns split along racial lines in both the general and runoff elections. In the runoff, the incumbent, Wyeth Chandler, defeated Higgs by a wide margin (approximately 31,055 votes), receiving 89.9 percent of the white vote and 3.2 percent of the black vote.[9] Higgs received approximately 14,800 white votes (10.1 percent) and 68,400 black votes (96.8 percent).

In the 1979 runoff election, Higgs again faced two-term incumbent Chandler in what was described as "the most colorless campaign in the history of [Memphis]."[10] Again using a dual strategy, Higgs focused on the issues of economic development, crime, property taxes, budget deficits, unemployment, and strikes by firefighters, police, and school teachers. However, he was a victim of blatant racial animosity from fearful whites. First, shortly after the results of the general election were announced, Mayor Chandler requested a listing of registered white voters who failed to participate in the general election from the Shelby County Election Commission so that he could encourage both their turnout and support. Moreover, on the night before the runoff election, a cross was burned in front of Higgs's home by an unknown person. In this polarized runoff election, Chandler, with 52.9 percent of the total vote (91 percent of which were from white voters), defeated Higgs, who received 47.1 percent of the total vote (98 percent of which were from black voters).[11]

The 1982 Mayoral Runoff Election

Initially, it appeared that the 1982 runoff election would be racially neutral.[12] The candidates, J. O. Patterson, Jr., and Dick Hackett, adopted the term "love-in" as a campaign theme. During the 1982 election, both pledged to focus on key issues, such as cutting property and payroll taxes, increasing the number of police patrols, improving schools and furthering economic development, rather than personal attacks. Patterson, who received 40.6 percent of the total vote in the primary election as opposed to 30 percent for Hackett, originally planned to use a deracialized campaign because he felt it was unnecessary to heighten race as an issue. Other campaigns of black mayoral candidates had demonstrated that highlighting race would only alienate white liberals whose support Patterson greatly needed to win the election.[13]

Approximately two weeks before the runoff, a shift occurred in Patterson's campaign strategy. First, Bishop J. O. Patterson, Sr., the presiding bishop of the Church of God in Christ and Patterson's father, equated financial support for his son's campaign with religious duty. At the annual convocation of the Church of God in Christ, Patterson, Sr. urged approximately thirty to forty thousand members of his church to "cooperate with God, think less of material wealth and lend a hand to [Patterson, Jr.'s] campaign. . . . The conscience of Memphis should honor a black man with the office of mayor."[14]

Approximately one week before the runoff, frustrated with Hackett's lead in the polls, Patterson publicly ended the "love-in" and made stronger racial appeals. He also realized that the needed white crossover support was not forthcoming. The only result of the "love-in" was that black voters lacked enthusiasm for a lackluster campaign. Charles V. Hamilton has found that black candidates who completely avoid the issue of race may alienate black voters. This alienation usually translates into lower levels of black turnout and support.[15]

Beginning what would become his usual strategy in subsequent campaigns against African American challengers, Dick Hackett refused to respond to charges of discrimination stemming from his performance as city court clerk. Hackett's campaign had several advantages. In addition to abundant funds, the white population in 1982 continued to outnumber that of blacks by approximately 5 percent. Hackett also realized that Patterson was scaring away the little support he had from white liberals. In addition, Hackett did not want to risk alienating black voters with racial appeals as had other white candidates when faced with the threat of a credible black contender.[16] Hackett later won the runoff with 54.2 percent of the overall vote (94 percent from white voters) as opposed to 45.8 percent for Patterson (98 percent from black voters).[17]

The 1991 Mayoral Election

The 1991 mayoral race was not as racially explosive as previous elections had been but was definitely more controversial. Willie Herenton chose not to employ the strategy of deracialization in his bid for mayor. Although Herenton and Dick Hackett claimed their respective platforms would mitigate racial divisions, both also sought to maintain cohesive blocs. Early in the campaign, Herenton claimed "[that he did not want] to get elected because he [was] black, but rather because [he was] eminently qualified and also [happened] to be black."[18] Contrary to this statement, Herenton's entire campaign, ranging from his selection as a consensus candidate to the final get-out-the-vote campaign, was directed toward African American voters. Herenton believed that black candidates can only successfully seek white crossover votes after they have organized the black electorate.[19] Since only four months remained before the October election and past Memphis mayoral elections showed the refusal of black and white citizens to cross racial lines, Herenton aimed most of his appeals at black voters. His campaign conducted a four-month mobilization effort in the black community. The strategy included an emphasis on Herenton as a consensus candidate, massive voter registration drives, the encouragement of black voter turnout, and an attempt to attract white crossover votes. A federal ruling that banned runoffs in city elections was an intervening factor for Herenton's victory.

The Choice of a Consensus Candidate

Research on mayoral elections that included African American contenders has found a positive correlation between the entrance of an appealing black candidate and increased black voter registration and turnout percentages.[20] Realizing that one of the major dilemmas for previous black mayoral contenders had been the splitting of the black vote, Memphis's black leadership decided to select and support one consensus candidate in the 1991 race.[21] The dilemma for black Memphians, as it had been in previous elections, was in selecting one black citizen to run for mayor.

The problems faced by black Memphians bore remarkable similarity to those confronted by Chicago blacks prior to the 1983 election of Harold Washington as that city's first black mayor. In both cities, African American citizens faced difficulty in selecting one black contender for entry in the mayoral race. Under the direction of the Chicago Black United Communities organization, Harold Washington was chosen as the consensus candidate by approximately thirty thousand African Americans who responded to surveys. As in Chicago, black Memphians in 1991 also decided to choose one representative. Several black leaders considered entry, including Benjamin L. Hooks, executive director of the NAACP, three-time mayoral candidate and lawyer Otis Higgs, former school superintendent Willie Herenton, U.S. Representative Harold Ford (D-Memphis), City Councilman Shep Wilbun, Jr., City Councilman and Baptist minister Kenneth T. Whalum, and Dr. Talib-Karim Muhammad, head of the Islamic Center of Memphis.

There was not only a conflict as to whom the consensus candidate would be, but also a dispute between Congressman Harold Ford and Memphis City Councilman Shep Wilbun, Jr., as to how the contender would be chosen. Whereas Ford believed that African American community leaders should select the candidate in a leadership summit, Wilbun favored convening a less elitist African American people's convention. In April 1991, approximately two thousand black Memphians attended Wilbun's convention. This number was far short of the expected number of participants. The convention overwhelmingly selected Herenton as the consensus candidate. Two months later in June 1991, Herenton was again selected as the consensus candidate at Ford's summit meeting of approximately five to six hundred black religious, political, and community leaders.

After the black community chose Herenton as the consensus candidate, other serious black contenders withdrew from the race. This was the first year in which both black leaders and citizens had collectively chosen and pledged to support one candidate for mayor of Memphis. In addition, black voter registration slightly outnumbered that of whites. In the end, the 1991 mayoral race consisted of two principal candidates: Dick Hackett and Willie Herenton.[22]

Voter Registration Drives and Turnout Rates

Herenton's campaign organizers embarked on a huge voter registration effort. Past African American candidates were defeated because white voter registration surpassed that of blacks. Thus, white majorities usually produced victories for white candidates. In spite of a chronic shortage of funds, Herenton conducted a vigorous grassroots campaign. Although he could not persuade the white business community to furnish much-needed funds or white citizens to provide crossover support, he possessed the power of persuasion in the black community. He conducted the type of open, public campaign that easily attracted media coverage and that has typically proven beneficial to black mayoral candidates for ensuring a large black voter turnout.[23] His campaign included visiting streets, churches, restaurants, stores, and other public places, giving speeches, leading marches, and distributing campaign literature.

In the final ten days before the 1991 election, Herenton held a "get-out-the-vote campaign." During this time, he increased attempts to encourage a high black turnout. This final preelection day effort included an increased number of speeches, marches, community meetings, and other events. Moreover, Herenton received a major boost when civil rights leaders Martin Luther King III, Jesse Jackson, and Congressman Harold Ford made several appearances both with him and on his behalf. They hoped Herenton's election as the first black mayor would diminish the image of Memphis as the assassination site of Martin Luther King, Jr.

On October 3, the day before the election, 182,761 blacks were registered in contrast to 168,790 whites and 29,161 who were classified as "others."[24] The 1991 mayoral election was significant in that both black voter registration and turnout rates surpassed levels of white participation in these two categories for the first time in Memphis history. The black voter registration level outnumbered that of whites by approximately fourteen thousand.

In addition, the black turnout rate of 48 percent was approximately 4 percent higher than white turnout.

Studies of black and white voting behavior have found that both groups usually vote along racial lines, seldom casting crossover votes.[25] The city of Memphis was similar to other large urban areas where black and white voting patterns tended to be racially polarized. For this reason, both Herenton and Hackett primarily targeted voters in black and white communities, respectively, while making limited attempts to attract crossover support.

Attracting racial crossover support in a racially polarized election sometimes provokes the wrath of oppositional individuals and groups. Notwithstanding the backlash faced by those who did provide racial crossover support, Hackett received some endorsements from prominent African Americans. In contrast, Herenton failed to gain public support from white leaders.

During his 1991 mayoral campaign, Dick Hackett made more attempts to attract the black vote than did Herenton for white support. Moreover, Hackett campaigned more actively for the black vote in 1991 than in his previous campaigns. Prior to this mayoral campaign, his usual practice included paid television and radio advertisements and avoidance of open confrontations with his black rivals. During 1991, Hackett had to change his strategy; he was in dire need of black votes. Therefore, he made several "handshaking stops" at shopping areas in black neighborhoods, distributing campaign leaflets and encouraging black citizens to support him. Hackett also held backyard receptions before small racially mixed groups at the homes of black middle-class Memphians.

Despite these efforts, Hackett and Herenton received the same percentage of racial crossover votes (Table 9–1). In fifty-nine precincts with predominantly black voters, Herenton received 95 percent of the votes, Hackett 4 percent, and Robert "Prince Mongo" Hodges less than 1 percent.[26] In thirty-one precincts with predominantly white voters, Hackett received 95

TABLE 9–1

Citywide Estimate of Racial Voting Behavior in
Memphis Mayoral Election, 1991

	Blacks %	Whites %
Hackett	1.5	98.5
Herenton	98.5	1.5
Hodges	0.5	0.5
Total	100.0	100.0

Source: Board of Election, Shelby County, Tennessee.

percent of votes, Herenton 4 percent, and Hodges less than 1 percent.[27] Based on the overall precinct totals shown in Table 9–1, Hackett and Herenton received over 95 percent of votes from whites and blacks citywide.

Since its enactment in 1965, the Voting Rights Act has been applied either to improve or eradicate at-large systems that work to the detriment of black voters. The runoff procedure, one feature of these systems, usually results in black majorities being unable to elect black candidates especially when both blacks and whites vote in a polarized manner. Runoff procedures require that if the candidates fail to receive a designated majority of the total vote (usually 50 percent), the two with the highest vote percentages have to compete in a runoff election. Various scholars have researched the negative effects that majority vote requirements have had on black candidates. While some have found that black candidates were not placed at a disadvantage in runoffs,[28] others have stated that the lower black participation rate in runoffs was detrimental to the candidacies of black contenders.[29]

In November 1988, Dr. Talib-Karim Muhammad filed a class-action suit challenging at-large elections for mayor and city council. Muhammad argued that these elections diluted black votes by giving African Americans less of an opportunity than white citizens to participate in the political process and to elect their desired candidates. To demonstrate this contention, Muhammad's suit pointed out that a history of discrimination against blacks in the city of Memphis and the state of Tennessee resulted in racially polarized voting patterns. Tables 9–2 and 9–3 support Muhammad's argument that black mayoral candidates who competed against white contenders and qualified for the runoff were later defeated primarily because of higher white bloc voting and turnout.

In February 1991, the U.S. Justice Department filed a lawsuit against the city of Memphis, alleging that at-large election systems discriminated against blacks. The lawsuit was later consolidated with Muhammad's earlier suit, specifically targeting runoff elections, at-large elections, and the city's annexation policy. In July 1991, U.S. District Judge Jerome Turner banned runoffs in city elections. He reasoned that a provision requiring runoff elections in races where candidates failed to receive a majority of 50 percent or more was designed to dilute black voting so that whites would win elections.[30] As a result, Herenton, with 172 votes more than Hackett, did not have to face Hackett in a runoff election (Table 9–4). Because black voter turnout in past runoffs had been substantially lower than in general elections, a high probability existed that Herenton would have lost a runoff election mainly because of racially polarized voting.

TABLE 9–2

Racial Voting Patterns in Memphis Mayoral Elections that Resulted in Runoffs

	Candidate	General Election			Runoff Election		
		Black %	White %	Total %	Black %	White %	Total %
1975	Higgs	80.0	10.0	35.1	96.8	10.1	42.0
	Chandler	3.0	70.0	46.5	3.2	89.9	58.0
	Turner	16.0	19.0	16.4			
	Others	1.0	1.0	2.0			
1979	Higgs	94.0	8.0	45.2	98.3	8.7	47.1
	Chandler	3.0	82.0	46.8	1.7	91.3	52.9
	Halloran	2.0	8.0	7.0			
	Others	1.0	2.0	1.0			
1982	Patterson	94.0	1.0	40.7	98.5	6.0	45.8
	Hackett	3.0	90.0	29.8	1.5	94.0	54.2
	Cody	2.0	7.0	26.2			
	Others	1.0	2.0	3.3			

Source: Board of Election, Shelby County, Tennessee.

TABLE 9–3

Racial Turnout in Memphis Mayoral Elections
that Resulted in Runoffs

	General Election			Runoff Election		
	Black %	White %	Total %	Black %	White %	Total %
1975	36.0	64.0	55.0	56.5	59.1	57.96
1979	42.0	58.0	49.5	42.4	57.6	59.1
1982	55.0	65.0	55.0	60.0	68.0	55.0

Source: Board of Election, Shelby County, Tennessee.

TABLE 9–4

General Election Results, 1991

Candidate	Total Votes	Percent
Hackett	122,413	49.4
Herenton	122,585	49.4
Hodges	2,921	1.2
Total	247,919	100.0

Source: Board of Election, Shelby County, Tennessee.

Conclusion

Willie Herenton's razor-thin margin of victory was the culmination of years of black frustration over conservative white administrations that stymied black political and economic inclusion.[31] Before the slim 172-vote victory can be fully understood, it is necessary to address some of the factors in the severe racial polarization that caused the deracialization strategy to fail so miserably for African American candidates in Memphis mayoral races.

One factor in the low levels of white crossover support was the image projected by the candidates. Higgs and Patterson simply lacked charisma and both had severely disorganized campaigns compounded by a shortage of funds. Moreover, Higgs was politically inexperienced. Neither campaign had a credible theme. Higgs's "Yes, We Can" and Patterson's "love-in" themes focused on racial harmony but not solid issues. Moreover, both lacked public endorsements from white leaders that might have convinced white voters of their competence.

Second, Higgs and Patterson were disadvantaged by opposition from strong white contenders. In 1975 and 1979, white incumbent Wyeth Chandler benefited from his strong administrative record and conservative background. He also was the son of three-term mayoral incumbent Walter Chandler. Patterson's opponent, Dick Hackett, headed Mayor Chandler's Action Center for six years.

Third, Higgs and Patterson actively sought to maintain their racial voting bloc but neglected vigorous racial crossover attempts. They bused black voters to the polls but, with the exception of a few appearances, did not actively pursue white crossover votes.

Finally and most importantly, Higgs and Patterson did not attract white crossover support because of the racially polarized nature of the city of Memphis. This is shown in population shifts accelerated by white flight, racially segregated residential patterns, black and white employment and income gaps, and racially segregated social lives.[32]

The narrow vote margin prompts the question of whether the Herenton victory was merely a fluke. Studies have found that black political mobilization efforts organized around one charismatic individual are usually short-lived.[33] Various studies also have discovered that the degree of racial polarization worsens and white flight accelerates after the election of a black mayor.[34] This results in an even larger black voting majority that almost ensures future elections of black mayors.

While seeking reelection, black incumbent mayors often are forced again to address racial issues. One issue concerns competition from white candidates whose campaign platforms emphasize both overt and covert racial subject matter. White candidates' attempts are often operationalized by an overexaggeration of the strained relationships between the predominantly black political establishment and the predominantly white business community. After the election of black mayors, whites have often left the cities and taken their largely middle-class tax base with them. Ironically, the declining economic state of predominantly black cities provides an issue for white mayoral candidates to capitalize upon during mayoral reelection campaigns.

In the 1995 general election, Mayor Herenton was not challenged by an African American contender. He received over 95 percent of the black vote and endorsements from the majority of black leaders and organizations. He was reelected by an overwhelming margin, receiving approximately 75 percent of the total vote (40 percent of which came from white voters).

In some cities, whites who initially refused to support African American candidates later became more receptive after blacks' elections and successful first terms.[35] It remains to be seen whether Memphis voters will manifest this trend beyond the 1995 election, or whether they will resume the practice of voting primarily on the basis of racial identity.

Notes

1. A final audit later narrowed this margin of victory to 136 votes.
2. Joseph McCormick II, "The November Elections and the Politics of Deracialization," *New Directions* 17 (1990): 22.
3. Higgs garnered approximately 10 percent in 1975 and 8 percent in 1979 runoff elections, the highest percentages of the white vote ever received by a black mayoral candidate.
4. In 1967, A. W. Willis, Jr., was the first African American to run for mayor of Memphis under the new mayor-council form of government. He ran against six white candidates including former mayor Henry Loeb and incumbent William B. Ingram. Backed by a solid white vote (90 percent of the total vote), Loeb eventually defeated Ingram in the runoff election. Willis received approximately 39 percent of the black vote and virtually no white crossover votes. This was 12.5 percent of the total, or approximately 18,000 votes.
5. Jesse Rafael Borges, "Beyond Deracialization: Towards a Comprehensive Theory of Black Electoral Success," paper presented at the annual meeting of the American Political Science Association, 1993.
6. Ibid.
7. Charles V. Hamilton, "Blacks and Electoral Politics," *Social Policy* 9 (May/June 1978): 26.
8. Jesse Raphael Borges, "Beyond Deracialization."
9. Sharon D. Wright, "Aftermath of the Voting Rights Act of 1965: Racial Voting Patterns in Memphis Mayoral Elections, 1967–1991," Ph.D. dissertation, University of Tennessee at Knoxville, 1993.
10. Terry Keeter, "Colorless Campaign Should Have Been the Reason Higgs Lost," *Memphis Commercial Appeal,* Nov. 1979, A1.
11. Ibid.

12. In 1982, Patterson served as the first black appointed mayor of Memphis after the incumbent Wyeth Chandler resigned to accept a circuit court judicial appointment. Governor Lamar Alexander appointed Patterson to serve as interim mayor. This 1982 special election was ordered to choose a successor to serve the remaining twelve months of Chandler's term. Had it not been for a majority vote requirement, J. O. Patterson, Jr., would have been the first black elected mayor of Memphis because of his 40.6 percent total in the primary election as compared to 30 percent for candidate Dick Hackett.

13. William E. Nelson, Jr., and Philip J. Meranto, *Electing Black Mayors: Political Action in the Black Community* (Columbus: Ohio State University Press, 1977); Richard A. Keiser, "The Rise of a Biracial Coalition in Philadelphia," in *Racial Politics in American Cities,* edited by Rufus P. Browning, Dale R. Marshall, and David H. Tabb (New York: Longman, 1990); Raphael Sonenshein, *Politics in Black and White: Race and Power in Los Angeles* (Princeton, N.J.: Princeton University Press, 1993).

14. Barbara Burch, "Patterson Campaign Gets Push in Father's Sermon," *Memphis Commercial Appeal,* Nov. 1982, A1.

15. Hamilton, "Blacks and Electoral Politics," 26.

16. Paul Kleppner, *Chicago Divided: The Making of a Black Mayor* (DeKalb: Northern Illinois University Press, 1985).

17. Wright, "Aftermath," 80.

18. "Mayoral Candidates and the Issues Where They Stand," *Memphis Commercial Appeal,* Aug. 1991, B1.

19. Hamilton, "Blacks and Electoral Politics," 25.

20. Michael B. Preston, "The Election of Harold Washington: An Examination of the SES Model in the 1983 Chicago Mayoral Election," in *The New Black Politics: The Search for Political Power,* edited by Michael B. Preston, Lenneal J. Henderson, Jr., and Paul L. Puryear (New York: Longman, 1987); Saundra C. Ardrey, "Cleveland and the Politics of Resurgence: The Search for Effective Political Control," in *Dilemmas of Black Politics: Issues of Leadership and Strategy,* edited by Georgia A. Persons (New York: HarperCollins, 1993).

21. In both 1983 and 1987, incumbent Dick Hackett coasted to victory in general elections as a result of fragmented black votes. In 1983, seven African American candidates challenged him for the mayoralty. These included three serious black contenders: attorney D'Army Bailey, Tennessee State Senator John Ford, and Otis Higgs. The other four candidates were virtual unknowns: singer/songwriter Timothy "El Espada" Matthews, hairstylist Peggy Robinson, salvage company owner Lilliard Anthony (L. A.) "Tony" Watts, and grocer Lugene Williams. Benefiting from their entrance, Hackett received 57.2 percent of the total vote, 4 percent of which was from black voters. John Ford, a member of the politically influential Harold Ford organization, received a higher total vote percentage than the other black candidates with approximately 23 percent; Higgs received 16 percent; and Bailey garnered 3.1 percent. All seven of the black candidates split approximately 4 percent of the white vote.

In 1987, the black vote split in three ways as a result of the candidacies of

City Councilwoman Minerva Johnican, former Tennessee Representative Dedrick "Teddy" Withers, and postal worker Walter Franklin. Hackett again breezed to victory, receiving approximately 58 percent of the total vote (15 percent of which was cast by black voters). Another white contender, Bill Gibbons, received approximately 25 percent of the black vote. Johnican received 52 percent of the black vote, less than 1 percent of the white vote, and approximately 23 percent of the total vote. Withers and Franklin both had approximately 1 percent of the total vote.

22. Robert "Prince Mongo" Hodges, a successful restaurant owner who claims to be an alien from another planet, was a third candidate in the 1991 race.

23. Nelson and Meranto, *Electing Black Mayors,* 60.

24. Shelby County, Tennessee, Board of Election returns.

25. Thomas F. Pettigrew, "Black Mayoralty Campaigns," in *Urban Governance and Minorities,* edited by Herrington Bryce (New York: Praeger, 1976), 14–28; Richard Murray and Arnold Vedlitz, "Racial Voting Patterns in the South: An Analysis of Mayoral Elections from 1960 to 1977 in Five Cities," *Annals* 39 (Sept. 1978): 29; Charles S. Bullock III, "Racial Crossover Voting and the Election of Black Officials," *Journal of Politics* 46 (1984): 238.

26. Wright, "Aftermath," 170.

27. Ibid.

28. Bullock, "Aftermath of the Voting Rights Act: Racial Voting Patterns in Atlanta-Area Elections," in *The Voting Rights Act: Consequences and Implications,* edited by Lorn S. Foster (New York: Praeger, 1985), 185–208. See also Bullock and Loch K. Johnson, *Runoffs in the United States* (Chapel Hill: University of North Carolina, 1992).

29. Stephen G. Wright, "Voter Turnout in Runoff Elections," *Journal of Politics* 51 (1989): 385.

30. Chris Conley, "U.S. Judge Bans Runoffs in At-Large Contests," *Memphis Commercial Appeal,* July 1990, A1.

31. Neither the Hackett nor the Chandler administrations made more than token black appointments during their years as mayor. Also, a worsening problem for black Memphians was unemployment. During the three Hackett administrations, the unemployment rate for blacks was double that of whites. During the eighties, blacks were three times more likely than whites to be unemployed.

   In addition to a massive unemployment problem, the Hackett administration was accused of a lack of commitment to Memphis public schools. Herenton, who retired in June 1991 as Memphis city schools superintendent, often complained about the lack of support from the Hackett administration for the school system which, because of white flight, was approximately 80 percent black. Because of its financial depletion, the school system had to use some of its cash reserves to offset a $6 million deficit in the 1990–91 school year. School officials also had to ask the Shelby County Commission to raise property tax rates in order to offset an anticipated $35 million deficit in the 1991–92 school year.

   While gaps between black and white unemployment levels continued to widen and problems of poverty, crime, drugs, inadequate housing, and racial polarization continued to plague the city, the Hackett administration focused on attracting tourists to the city. Approximately $22 million in taxes and private monies were contributed toward tourist projects. Although some were moderately successful, such as the Catherine the Great exhibit of eighteenth-century Russian art and the redevelopment of the Beale Street historic district, others were severe money losers such as the 52-acre Mud Island river park, which opened in 1982 before Hackett became mayor but continued to lose profits during his terms as mayor.

32. Sandra Vaughn, "Memphis: The Heart of the Mid-South," in *In Search of the New South: The Black Urban Experience in the 1970s and 1980s* (Tuscaloosa: University of Alabama Press, 1989), 105–15.

33. Ardrey, "Cleveland," 114–15.

34. Charles H. Levine, *Racial Politics and the American Mayor: Power, Polarization, and Performance* (Lexington, Mass.: Lexington Books, 1974).

35. Sharon Watson, "The Second Time Around: A Profile of Black Mayoral Reelection Campaigns," *Phylon* 45 (Fall 1984): 166.

10

The Governance of Kurt Schmoke as Mayor of Baltimore

Lenneal J. Henderson, Jr.

In his book *Citistates: How Urban America Can Prosper in a Competitive World,* Neal Pierce observes that "the social disability of America's citistates is rooted in historic antiurbanism, overlain in our time by ethnic and racial prejudices."[1] The paradox of antiurbanism is that nearly 80 percent of America's 258 million people live in "urban places," including suburbs. More than 60 percent of the population resides in older, inner cities. Consequently, the differences in the human and physical infrastructure of both inner cities and suburbs are a major issue for the civic infrastructure of the modern metropolis. The glaring decay, decline, and distress that currently besiege many inner-city populations and an increasing number of suburban areas are likely to continue without the civic culture being able to abate or reverse this development.

The city of Baltimore and its greater metropolitan area have struggled through more than three decades of inner-city decline, suburban ascendancy, class and racial conflict, central business district upturns and downturns, fiscal stress, and soaring crime. On the surface, the relationship between the city of Baltimore and its suburban neighbors is similar to that existing between many U.S. inner cities and their suburbs: the central city continues to descend into a socioeconomic, racial, fiscal, business, educational, and criminal justice abyss, while concomitantly ever-expanding suburbs become more immersed in their own identity, growth, and economic and social issues to the virtual exclusion of concern for the plight of their inner-city neighbors.

While Baltimore city has declined in population from nearly 950,000 in 1950 to 736,000 in 1990,[2] the proportion of African Americans has increased from 23.7 percent in 1950 to 59.2 percent in 1990. Moreover, there are striking differences between the median family income in Baltimore city and the surrounding suburbs. Median family income in Baltimore city was $28,217 in 1989. In the same year, Harford County to the east of the city had a median family income of $45,923, and Howard County's median family income of $61,088 was the highest in the state.

Associated with these differences in income rates is the decline in the city's industrial, commercial, and fiscal base. For example, the city's residential property tax rate is nearly $6 per hundred dollars of assessed valuation. No Baltimore suburb has yet reached $3 per hundred. Large employers, particularly Bethlehem Steel, Westinghouse Corporation, McCormick Company, and the Maryland Port Authority have either sharply reduced investment, jobs, and operations in Baltimore city or located new facilities outside of the city.[3] The most striking symbol of Baltimore's industrial and commercial transformation is the emergence of Johns Hopkins University as the city's largest employer, with more than sixteen thousand employees. Hopkins replaced Bethlehem Steel in this distinction some years ago.

Crime, particularly drug-related homicides by African American males, represents a severe challenge to the city. Record levels of drug use, HIV infection, teenage pregnancy, homelessness, morbidity, infant mortality, and child abuse beset many Baltimore neighborhoods. Connected to these trends are major challenges faced by the city's public schools. Schools are often asked to be the surrogates of many community institutions that are damaged or dysfunctional, including families, places of worship, and professional organizations.

Much of this deterioration of Baltimore and other U.S. cities is the result of national and international macroeconomic trends. The decline of manufacturing in the United States, poor balance of trade and balance of payment postures, and federal and state fiscal woes are among the constellation of issues besetting Baltimore city. Another part of the context is the position of both the Baltimore and Washington suburbs. The suburbs have grown at the expense of Baltimore city. While Baltimore city was once 40 percent of the population of Maryland, it is now just 15 percent, and the Washington, D.C., suburban counties of Prince George's and Montgomery each have populations exceeding the Baltimore city population.[4] As Neal Pierce has suggested, not only must Baltimore city make a deal with the counties in its own metropolitan statistical area (MSA) but also with the entire Baltimore-Washington Consolidated Metropolitan Statistical Area (CMSA).

In addition to the macroeconomic and metropolitan factors, a fundamental component of the context is the varied condition of Baltimore's neighborhoods. Some relatively affluent neighborhoods seek either city-financed or neighborhood-financed security to protect their citizens from what they perceive as the ogre of encroaching violent crime. Other neighborhoods struggle to survive poor housing, beleaguered public schools, expanding health care problems, continued decline of community commercial infrastructure, and epidemic rates of crime, particularly violent crime and particularly in African American neighborhoods.

In the face of this grim constellation of difficult challenges, Baltimore struggles to abate and reverse its deterioration. The city is also attempting to revitalize its economic, human, physical, institutional, and civic infrastructure through the development of projects and programs orchestrated through the civic, public, business, and nonprofit sectors.[5]

Civic capacity is built through citizens' heightened consciousness of what needs to be done to improve their city. Civic capacity is initially aided by a transformation in the spirit and psychology of the city as it mobilizes to face its challenges. The transformation proceeds through the stages of mobilization, institution building, and inclusion in the governmental decision-making process, with the process resulting in physical evidence of improvement: new housing, revitalized schools, new businesses, committed churches, and a lively civitas. It is not likely that all of the actors, resources, and processes of this transformation will be located within the city. Outside investors, venture capitalists, federal and state funds, nonprofit organizations, and even overseas investment may be involved.

Redevelopment in Baltimore

Despite severe demographic, social, economic, and fiscal challenges, Baltimore is experiencing redevelopment. Over the past two decades, the city has experienced continuous revitalization through a combination of the redevelopment of its central business district and harbor area and through determined efforts to revitalize some neighborhoods as well as develop new neighborhoods. As Baltimore indicated in its successful 1991 application for the All-American City competition, the Inner Harbor is now a major tourist attraction, consisting of new high-rise office/apartment complexes and hotels. In addition, Camden Yards, a new professional baseball stadium for the Baltimore Orioles, is an unqualified commercial and symbolic success and, as an extension to the subway system, twenty miles of light rail opened in 1992. Moreover, the Maryland Biotechnology Institute and state economic development officials are on the verge of undertaking a $54 million economic development project for the state. In the fall of 1993, the Christopher Columbus Center, an Inner Harbor showcase for Maryland's biotechnology development effort, received the federal government's final installment of $10.3 million to help pay for the $148 million marine biotechnology laboratory and exhibition hall.[6]

The city has labored diligently to extend the success of the Inner Harbor and the Camden Yards baseball stadium to its neighborhoods. Neighborhoods continue to be a major tradition, foundation, and resource for the city's civic infrastructure. More than seven hundred neighborhood associations are registered with the city's Department of Planning. In addition, there are over thirty citywide or umbrella organizations in Baltimore to combine, coordinate, and reinforce the efforts of smaller groups. Citywide organizations, such as the Citizens' Planning and Housing Association (CPHA) and Baltimoreans United in Leadership Development (BUILD), focus specifically on neighborhood housing, education, and civic development. With over half of the city's population either over the age of fifty or under the age of eighteen, with high rates of high school dropouts, teenage pregnancies, HIV infection, and homicide, these civic and community-based organizations are vital resources for both maintenance and development of Baltimore neighborhoods.

The creative leadership of Baltimore's Mayor Kurt Schmoke and city council leaders has contributed substantially to the city's ongoing renewal. They both lead and follow the lead of neighborhood institutions and business organizations, such as the Greater Baltimore Committee (GBC), the Investing in Baltimore Committee (IBC), and the Baltimore Chamber of Commerce. In addition, the mayor has advocated the decriminalization of some drugs, needle exchanges to curb HIV and hepatitis infections, and a strong community policing philosophy. He recruited a dynamic new superintendent of public schools in 1991 who has sought to improve both the quality of education and reputation of the public schools through school restructuring and the placing of nine schools under contract to the Tessaract Corporation to improve achievement levels.

Moreover, Project RAISE (Raising Ambition Instills Self-Esteem) is a public-private partnership designed to dramatically decrease the high school dropout rate and improve the life chances of very low-income, inner-city public school students. Project RAISE is a seven-year commitment to provide groups of approximately sixty children, selected from the poorest performing schools in the city, with paid school-based program coordinators and volunteer one-on-one mentors recruited by community-based sponsoring organizations such as churches and businesses.

RAISE began in May 1988 with children entering the sixth grade and will continue to monitor them through high school. Each RAISE student graduating from high school is guaranteed the opportunity to attend college or career school or to obtain employment.[7] The project is a vibrant symbol of both the renewal and community empowerment occurring in Baltimore.

Two Case Studies

It is useful to examine two exemplary cases of renewal, both of which have received national, indeed international, attention. The first is the community of Sandtown-Winchester. This neighborhood had descended into the deepest recesses of urban blight, decay, violence, and destruction. However, the residents of Sandtown-Winchester, with outstanding support from the Enterprise Foundation[8] and Mayor Kurt Schmoke, committed themselves to transforming the conditions facing their neighborhood. They began with a spiritual and psychological commitment and converted it into a mobilization, institution building, and coalition initiative.

Under the name "Community Building in Partnership" (CBIP), residents of the city, the Enterprise Foundation, and other supporters are working together to set goals and develop programs to make all housing fit and affordable, to improve schools so that all students graduate ready to work or go to college, to make health care, including substance abuse treatment, available to all residents, to provide job training and placement services in the neighborhood along with small business assistance for resident entrepreneurs, to better integrate the human services network to support the needs of all family members, to work with the police on new approaches to community policing, and much more.[9]

Almost 50 percent of Sandtown-Winchester's residents live in poverty; nearly 40 percent have no income. Nearly 90 percent of the women giving birth to children are unmarried. This seventy-two-square-block stretch of West Baltimore now shows every sign of becoming one of the most astounding recovery stories in urban America. Projects valued at more than $60 million have been planned, begun, or completed, ranging from the Healthy Start initiative to reduce infant mortality to the $18 million Nehemiah Housing project that will build 227 townhouse-style homes on the site of a decrepit bakery building. Residents have organized and managed a food and clothing cooperative, and thirty community gardens have been planted.

As Neal Pierce has pointed out, there is no comprehensive evidence that these combined efforts have been transformative. But every visitor to Sandtown-Winchester—anyone aware of the convergence of these efforts or the diverse coalition developed to pursue these efforts—will see that a spiritual and psychological transformation has occurred and is catalyzing change and revitalization in this courageous neighborhood.[10]

As both CBIP and the Enterprise Foundation have made clear, community building, grassroots organizing, leadership development, and resident-led activities are central to the transformation process. CBIP works closely with existing community organizations, such as the Fulton Community

Association and the Committee United to Save Sandtown. CBIP provides support to several groups, including Sandtown-Winchester Improvement Association and BUILD, to organize their constituencies around pressing issues such as public safety and education and to participate in CBIP activities. There are over forty churches in the neighborhood, many with activist agendas, that sponsor antidrug rallies, offer day care and after-school programs, and provide assistance to needy families. CBIP has implemented over fifty new projects to address immediate needs in the neighborhood and to lay the foundation for long-term change. These projects include the development of over a thousand new housing units as well as prenatal, maternal, and early childhood programs.[11]

Five key elements of the concept of redevelopment are evident in the Sandtown-Winchester story. First, residents mobilized themselves. They provided the initial spiritual and psychological boost. Second, redevelopment is inclusive. Residents of all backgrounds and needs are recruited and invited to participate in projects and coalitions of public, private, and nonprofit institutions. Third, project activities focus both on arresting further decline and on community development. Fourth, a comprehensive approach to community issues is evident: housing, employment, drugs, health care, maternal care, children, seniors, employment, green space, and policing are all integrated into the redevelopment initiatives. Fifth, an active and dynamic civic consciousness is emerging, not only internally directed toward neighborhood needs and projects but externally directed to other neighborhoods, institutions, and networks.[12]

Neighborhoods facilitate renewal by not only mobilizing their residents but others in the city as well. Sandtown-Winchester has become a national model of neighborhood redevelopment. As Harold McDougal points out, neighborhoods must pursue development of their physical and human infrastructure as well as seek to restore the concept of a "base community" of peer groups of people who evaluate developments in the community.[13] While Sandtown-Winchester represents one heralded turn-around story, several more are in progress in the city. With the urging of community-based organizations and the support of the Johns Hopkins Hospital/Medical School complex, other distressed communities in East Baltimore are making positive changes.

The Contract

The key to the Baltimore redevelopment experience lies in the nature of the informal contract between itself and its citizens. Based in a rich civic culture, the contract includes:

1. A balance of downtown and neighborhood development;
2. Close working relationships between citywide civic organizations (like CPHA and BUILD) and local communities and
   neighborhoods;
3. Active involvement of the city government both as broker and
   catalyst as well as leader and advocate;
4. Inclusiveness of persons of diverse racial, ethnic, religious, geographic, and class, income, and other backgrounds, even at
   the expense of occasional conflict and stalemate;
5. Tenacity, determination, innovation, and drive even in the face
   of the most ominous combination of urban problems; and
6. Intercommunity development among neighborhoods, levels of
   government, city and suburbs, and various types of business,
   religious, cultural, and public institutions.

Mayor Schmoke and the Theory of Deracialization

Given both the complexity of the Baltimore context and the efforts of Kurt
Schmoke and the city's political leadership to "turn around" the social, economic, and fiscal condition of the city, we must carefully revisit the theory of
deracialization. As Joseph McCormick and Charles E. Jones aptly indicate,
the concept of deracialization can be employed to refer both to agenda-setting
strategy and to electoral strategies of political aspirants and elected incumbents. The agenda-setting component is a policy dynamic that is frequently
connected to the electoral dynamic. Conversely, the electoral strategic component implies a policy posture and approach. Consequently, the agenda-
setting and electoral strategic elements are largely inseparable. Schmoke's approach to race as an agenda-setting strategy is connected not only to his
policy and administrative strategies as mayor but also to the furthering of his
electoral ambitions and aspirations.

Given both Schmoke's agenda-setting and electoral approaches, further theoretical refinement of the concept of deracialization is essential. A key
conceptual distinction between deracialization and transracialization is derived from the experience of Mayor Schmoke. McCormick and Jones define
deracialization as an electoral strategy as a process of "conducting a campaign
in a stylistic fashion that defuses the polarizing effects of race by avoiding explicit reference to race-specific issues, while at the same time emphasizing
those issues that are perceived as racially transcendent, thus mobilizing a
broad segment of the electorate for purposes of capturing or maintaining
public office."[14] They apply this definition particularly to African American
candidates in predominantly white districts and jurisdictions. They identify

three key components of deracialization: political style, mobilization tactics, and issues.

Deracialization, Hyperracialization, and Transracialization

First, Baltimore is 60 percent African American. Paradoxically, race is such a conspicuous part of the political context that neither white nor black politicians in Baltimore need to refer to it in explicit terms. Second, although Schmoke's political style is perceived as relatively low key on racial issues, his efforts "to defuse the polarizing effects of race" are considered by the mayor and his supporters as a transracial strategy, not a deracial strategy. The essential distinction between *trans*racial and *de*racial strategies is the extent to which race remains as an operating symbol and tenet of the campaign strategy. Schmoke continually includes issues of racial and ethnic identity in both his electoral and policy strategies. He does not attempt to defuse racial issues by either excluding them from campaign rhetoric or minimizing their significance in policy agenda-setting. But Schmoke is adamant about the need for various racial and ethnic groups to both maintain their self-identities while transcending issues of race and focus on both common agendas and ultimate social, economic, and fiscal needs.

Third, outside of electoral strategy, concepts of deracialization and transracialization require a more explicit linkage with policy dynamics. Georgia A. Persons's compelling analysis of big city black mayoralties, while primarily electoral in orientation, also provides a helpful framework for the examination of racial policy dynamics. Persons distinguishes three "developmental paths" of African American mayors: (1) insurgency characterized by racial appeals, social reform, and challenges to established politics, (2) racial reconciliation designed to woo nonblack voters, and (3) institutionalization of black mayoralties into the fabric of American political life.[15] These patterns are manifest in both electoral strategies and policy strategies. The social reform agenda in policy agenda setting and formulation embraces a Lowian use of distributive, redistributive, and regulatory policies[16] designed both to achieve racially inclusive social reform and to institutionalize the mayoral regime in order to successfully contest the next election.

In addition, policy implementation strategies pursued by Mayor Schmoke include assiduous efforts to mobilize coalitions to comprehensively improve the Sandtown-Winchester community, continue the development of the central business district, reduce drug use and distribution, and improve public schools.[17] These strategies reinforce the racial identity of predominantly African American Sandtown-Winchester while encouraging a multiracial, multijurisdictional, and intergovernmental coalition to accelerate its development. Site-based management of selected Baltimore public schools includes the concept of reinforcing the ethnic identity of specific schools while allowing for multiracial and multi-institutional involvement in raising the level of student achievement. Indeed, policy evaluation criteria, whether embodied in formal program evaluations or public perceptions, often balance the needs for racial identity of African Americans and other groups with the need for transracial coalitions.

Consequently, theories of deracialization could reflect a continuum (Figure 10–1) ranging from hyperracial politics, including race-baiting, to race-neutral politics where no or minimal reference is made to race by any candidate. This continuum distinguishes several conceptual elements:

1. Electoral and policy strategies are distinguished;
2. At the electoral level, elections with two or more African American candidates are distinguished from those with one or more African American and other candidates;
3. At the policy level, racial strategies are associated with various phases, or cycles of the policy process: agenda setting, policy formulation, policy adoption, policy implementation, and policy evaluation;[18]
4. Politics internal to the jurisdiction associated with African American officials and politics external to such jurisdictions are distinguished from each other.[19]

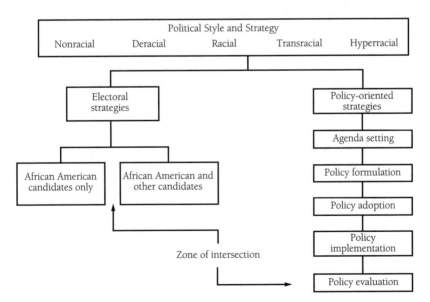

Figure 10–1. The Electoral and Policy Racial Continuum.

Fundamentally, this conceptualization of racial strategies is analytically inductive rather than deductive. Instead of developing a general characterization of the political style and strategy of Schmoke from an overarching conceptual frame, it infers from a sample of the mayor's decisions his political style, mobilization strategy, and policy management strategy. The advantage of this approach is its appreciation of variations in strategy dependent upon the policy issues, contexts, and players with whom the mayor interacts. These issues may transcend explicit racial categories or be strongly associated with race. They may involve neighborhood, interneighborhood, citywide, or city-suburban contexts and may define roles for a variety of interest groups, elected officials, and intergovernmental players at all levels of and beyond the city.

Mayor Schmoke's decisions generally reflect a transracial decision-making style on most policy issues, in most contexts, and with most policy players. However, his decisions have spanned a broad range of substantive and symbolic matters, both deracial and nonracial. His political and governing styles are not easy to classify using either the traditional model of black politics or the more recent one suggested by the deracialization concept. The concept of transracial politics captures more of Mayor Schmoke's style than does deracialization, but even here the fit is not complete; this is understandable, given the changing nature of black politics in the United States. When established social relations undergo changes, conceptual and theoretical developments usually lag behind. Additional scholarly work on Mayor Schmoke and other emerging black politicians like him is needed to produce a conceptual classification that fully explicates the new realities of African American political life.

Notes

1. Neal Pierce, *Citistates: How Urban America Can Prosper in a Competitive World* (Washington, D.C.: Seven Locks Press, 1993), 17.
2. *Census News,* Baltimore City Department of Planning, Mar. 1991, 1.
3. Neal Pierce, Curtis Johnson, Carol Steinbach, and Lenneal J. Henderson, Jr., "Baltimore and Beyond," *Baltimore Sun,* May 5, 1991, A3.
4. Pierce, *Citistates,* 123–56.
5. See Lenneal J. Henderson, Jr., "Empowerment through Enterprise in the African-American Community," in *The State of Black America, 1993,* edited by Billy Tidwell (New York: National Urban League, 1993), 91–108.
6. Bill McConnell, "Columbus Center: Some Dare Call It Pork," *Warfield Business Record,* July 30-Aug. 5, 1993, 1.
7. Baltimore Office of Promotions, Application for the All-American City Award, 3.
8. The Enterprise Foundation was established by the developer and humanitarian

James Rouse. Although headquartered in Columbia, Maryland, the Foundation is a major partner in the Sandtown-Winchester development.

9. Patrick M. Costigan, "Tackling Crime through Community Building," *Baltimore Sun,* Jan. 13, 1993, A15.

10. Pierce, "Taking It All Together," *Baltimore Sun,* July 12, 1993, A7.

11. Community Building in Partnership (CBIP), Neighborhood Transformation Demonstration, Sandtown-Winchester, Progress Report, August 1993, 1–2.

12. Ibid.

13. Harold McDougal, *Black Baltimore: Towards a Theory of Community* (Philadelphia, Pa.: Temple University Press, 1993).

14. Joseph P. McCormick II and Charles E. Jones, "The Conceptualization of Deracialization: Thinking through the Dilemma," in *Dilemmas of Black Politics: Issues of Leadership and Strategy,* edited by Georgia A. Persons (New York: Harper-Collins, 1993), 66–84, 76.

15. Georgia A. Persons, "Black Mayoralties and the New Black Politics: From Insurgency to Racial Reconciliation," in *Dilemmas of Black Politics,* edited by Persons, 40.

16. Theodore J. Lowi, *The End of Liberalism: Ideology, Policy, and the Crisis of Public Authority* (New York: Norton, 1989).

17. Henderson, "Baltimore: Managing the Civics of a Turn Around City," *National Civic Review* 82 (Winter 1993). See also Harold McDougal, *Black Baltimore,* 145–77.

18. See Dennis Palumbo, *Public Policy in America: Government in Action* (New York: Harcourt, Brace, Jovanovich, 1988), 19.

19. See David Rusk, *Cities without Suburbs* (Washington, D.C.: Woodrow Wilson Center Press, 1993), 37.

IV

**Deracialization:
A Comprehensive Perspective**

11

Deracialization and the New Black Politics

Robert B. Albritton, George Amedee, Keenan Grenell, and Don-Terry Veal

The Voting Rights Act of 1965 began a new era of empowerment for African Americans in the arena of American politics.
The demise of formal constraints on political participation, a result of this legislation, produced not only large increases in African American registration
and voting in the states of the deep South but also huge proportionate increases in the number of black elected officials (Figure 11–1). Most importantly, these changes transformed the political context in those states in ways
that included "black agendas" as significant components of politics at national, state, and local levels.

Accompanying these political gains have been important shifts in the
arenas of black politics. The most important of these shifts has been the
change from an emphasis on national politics, which characterized the civil
rights movement, to the politics of state and local government. Withdrawal of
support for black agendas during the conservative shift in national politics,
beginning in 1969, was offset by advancement of these agendas through election of black mayors, state legislators, law enforcement officials, and even a
black governor in one of the states of the Old Confederacy. Tenuous successes
in northern cities, such as Chicago, Cleveland, New York, and Philadelphia,
have been matched by emerging dominance of black political figures in Atlanta, Birmingham, New Orleans, and a host of smaller municipalities in the
southern United States. (Detroit is the one northern city with a permanent
black majority.)

In addition to its symbolic qualities, the emergence of significant black
political leadership makes possible the advancement of a black political
agenda representing collective interests of minorities at all governmental

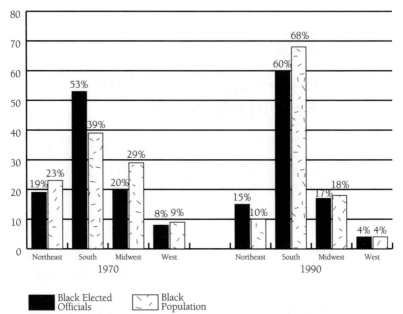

Figure 11–1. Regional Distribution of Black Elected Officials and Black Population, 1970 and 1990. *Source:* Joint Center for Political and Economic Studies, Black Elected Officials (Washington D.C., 1990)

levels. Although components of this agenda do not differ markedly from traditional agendas of industrial democracies (e.g., urban development, equal opportunity, educational access, employment, access to medical care, etc.), African Americans, as the largest minority group, are most mobilized in support of these agendas even though the reforms benefit a much larger group of Americans.

The distinction between symbolic representation and advancement of black political agendas offers two strategies that are pursued by African American politicians. The first is a "race-neutral" politics that deemphasizes black political agendas in order to accommodate white supporters, relying instead on race as a cue to mobilize support among African American voters. The second is a "race-specific" politics in the sense that race is interpreted as the cue for representation of black political agendas. When race is not a cue to voting, however, these agendas are sometimes sublimated or even co-opted in favor of other agendas.

One of the most significant shifts in the "New Black Politics" is the movement away from traditional sources of political recruitment—churches and the civil rights movement. A new generation of professional, highly educated political aspirants has arisen to seek political office as a career path, but this generation has had little or no direct involvement with civil rights organizations and its youth places it beyond direct contact with the historic advances of the 1950s and 1960s. These generational cleavages have significant implications for political alignments within national, state, and local political arenas.

Because political gains by African Americans have come about as a result of increased voter participation, the impact of political mobilization becomes increasingly crucial for continuing progress toward representational equality. Perhaps even more important, from an analytical perspective, are patterns of political participation and mobilization when race is not a cue to voting. Implications of cleavages within black political majorities are clearly one of the most significant new developments within a new black politics.

This chapter identifies two perspectives on the new black politics. The first considers implications of strategies designated as race-neutral or race-specific for what some consider a progressive black political agenda. The second perspective examines some trends in political participation in major urban areas and their implications for the future of black politics.

Race-Neutral Strategies

Race-neutral political strategies build upon the notion of a deracialized politics that deemphasizes the issue of race in voting decisions. Such an electoral strategy may be aimed at broadening the appeal of African American candidates to white voters by projecting either a neutral position on issues perceived to have appeal to African American voters as a group or by advancing inclusive social strategies without regard to race as a primary focus.[1] Charles V. Hamilton sees potential for such strategies as a means to achieve greater representational parity for African Americans while, at the same time, achieving progress toward what might be called progressive black political agendas.[2]

More recent approaches to deracialization strategies point to the liabilities of a strictly race-neutral politics. William E. Nelson argues that electoral successes in Cleveland failed to advance progressive agendas and, instead, were marked by "co-optation" politics that benefited primarily "white agendas" in return for aggrandizement of African American political elites.[3] Charles E. Jones suggests significant problems with the "race-neutral" strategies pursued by Virginia Governor L. Douglas Wilder, including (1) the abandonment of significant efforts to mobilize black voters as a constituency of popular support, (2) advocating fiscal conservatism and centrist social politics, (3) emphasizing tough stands on crime, and (4) ingratiating himself with traditional, conservative political leaders—and in other ways abandoning progressive policy agendas beneficial to African Americans.[4]

The critical issue in contemplating strategies of "race-neutral" politics is whether they imply abandonment of the so-called progressive black agenda. Election successes of prominent African American politicians, such as Wilder, Mayor David Dinkins (New York), and Mayor Norm White (Cleveland), suggest support for strategies of race-neutral politics that position candidates as moderate to conservative with regard to the needs of African American constituencies.

Some scholars argue that deracialized politics forces politicians to engage in programs that advance the interests of constituents without involving racial implications.[5] Others suggest that political strategies that do not specifically aim at mobilization of African American voters are likely to sacrifice progressive black agendas in order to gain support from white elites.[6] Jones argues that Wilder's campaign strategy emphasizing positions favored by conservative white voters had the effect of distancing him from positions that would benefit African American constituencies.[7] Moreover, Ron Daniels argues that moves toward a race-neutral politics have become a major obstacle in implementing a progressive black agenda.[8]

Both sides of the debate seem to agree that the concept of race-neutral political strategies has to do with the extent to which racial cues are used in elections. As these strategies become increasingly common and are associated with increases in representational parity, they need to be evaluated on two dimensions. First, what effect do racial cues have on the dynamics of elections—voter participation, crossover voting, and election successes? Second, to what extent do race-neutral strategies employed by African American politicians contribute toward implementing policies of interest to black constituencies or toward a positive black agenda?

Political Strategies in a Deracialized Politics

Table 11–1 offers a conceptualization of the range of electoral strategies defined as "race-neutral" politics. These strategies follow a continuum based on three key dimensions: (1) emphasis on race as a voting cue, (2) scope of voter appeal, (3) representation of a pro-black agenda. Race as a voting cue relies upon high levels of mobilization and participation of African American voters for electoral success. The scope of voter appeal is characterized by the degree to which appeals are made to other racial groups and by development of biracial coalitions. Third, the typology includes a stance either advocating or distancing the candidate from pro-black issues. In theory, combinations of these

TABLE 11-1
Typology of Race-Neutral Strategies in Selected Political Campaigns, 1983–1991

Typology	Race-Specific (1)	Modified Race-Specific (2)	Race-Neutral (Absence of Racial Cues) (3)	Extremely Race-Neutral (4)
Selected Campaigns	Harold Washington party campaigns, Chicago, 1991	Harold Washington for mayor of Chicago, 1983 and 1987	Sidney Barthelemy for mayor of New Orleans, 1986	L. Douglas Wilder for governor of Virginia, 1989
Saliency of Race	*High use of racial cues	*Some use of racial cues	*Absence of racial cues	*Absence of racial cues
Status of Pro-black Agenda	*High identification with pro-black agenda	*Selected issues of pro-black agenda	*Symbolic representation of pro-black agenda	*Distance campaign from pro-black issues
Broadness of Voter Appeal	*All-black independent party strategies	*Biracial coalition building strategy	*Appeal to white voters as the decisive factor	*Minimize direct appeal to blacks; conservative appeal to whites

strategies are related to specific election outcomes in the form of voter participation and electoral success.

Four campaigns have been chosen to represent the continuum of race-
neutral political strategies. At one end is the strategy pursued by the Harold
Washington Party in the Chicago and Cook County elections of 1991. The
concerted effort to mobilize African American voters by the use of race as a
voting cue clearly establishes this strategy as an example of race-specific politics. A strong effort was made to portray these campaigns as an independent
political strategy representing a progressive agenda that would more seriously
address the needs and interests of African American constituencies in Cook
County. Although there were belated efforts to incorporate symbolic representation of other racial groups, the campaigns appealed primarily to African
American voters as a distinct interest outside structures of the Democratic
party. Despite these appeals, voter participation among African Americans
was low and the campaigns resulted in little support at the polls.

The Chicago mayoral campaigns of Harold Washington, in 1983 and
1987, represent strategies somewhat distanced from those of the Harold
Washington Party. Although Washington's symbolic representation of black
interests was combined with a clear identification with a progressive black
agenda (e.g., increased participation of minorities in business), his appeal ex-
tended to issues of interest to other races as well.[9] During Washington's first
term in office, his negotiation of bond ratings for Chicago won him approval
among white elites, and he was seen as representing both African American
and public interests. These broad appeals across racial lines resulted in high
levels of support from Latino voters and white liberals, although race still
proved to be an important cue for voting, in terms of both mobilizing high
levels of turnout among African American voters and the high levels of white
opposition.

The 1986 election for mayor of New Orleans offers an intriguing
variant on race-neutral strategies when race is *not* a cue to voting. The contest
between two black candidates, Sidney Barthelemy and William Jefferson,
meant that racial cues should not be a significant factor.[10] Under these conditions, identification with a pro-black agenda became the deciding issue in a
race in which white voters determined the outcome. Although both candidates attempted to appeal to both white and black voters, Barthelemy appeared as more "moderate," while Jefferson was portrayed in endorsements
by former Mayor Ernest Morial and many African American political organizations as more sympathetic to a pro-black agenda.

The absence of race as a cue to voting resulted in significant turnout
declines in predominantly black precincts and a heightened role for white
voters in determining the outcome. The result was the election of Barthelemy,
who had less identification with the pro-black agenda.

The most extreme example of race-neutral politics is African American candidates' total abandonment of agendas that represent perceived interests of black voters. L. Douglas Wilder's campaign for governor of Virginia in 1989 (as well as his brief campaign for president in 1992) represents a strategy that appeals to centrist and conservative elements of white voters, while establishing some distance between the candidate and the black political agenda. Taking black support for granted and relying only on symbolic appeals to African American voters, Wilder established positions that sought support among the conservative white elements of his state. The result was the election of an African American candidate in a predominantly white, conservative state. Jones argues that this strategy of race-neutral politics implies forsaking effective progress for African Americans for the sake of symbolic gains.[11]

The Detroit Mayoral Elections, 1973 and 1977

A baseline for understanding trends in declining African American voter participation is offered by the Detroit mayoral campaigns. After an intensive effort to mobilize African American voting support, Detroit elected its first African American mayor in 1973. Mayor Coleman Young remained the incumbent for nearly two decades, a period in which African American voter participation suffered significant declines. Although districts represented in Table 11–2 are not strictly comparable due to boundary changes, they do represent the overall course of political participation in predominantly African American election districts in Detroit in overall turnout.

Why did African American political participation decline in Detroit? One of the most important factors may be an absence of race as a voting cue. Without a specific black-white contest (and absence of political party cues), voters have difficulty distinguishing candidates on the basis of the few, subtle cues that remain. In addition, there has been little significant contestation of Young's leadership.

A second possible factor in the decline may be a disillusionment with politics as an effective means of social change. Despite the election of an African American mayor, this time period (1973–85) is associated with rising poverty, unemployment, and crime in Detroit. Those who anticipated significant positive changes in their lives because of the election of an African American mayor found little to reinforce political mobilization as an effective agent to improve their lives. Cynicism associated with disappointing life experiences of this type is an important factor in the decline of African American voter participation in American inner cities.

These two factors are replicated in the experience of voters in other geographic areas and account for the phenomenon of declining voter turnout

TABLE 11–2

Turnout in Predominantly Black Electoral
Districts in Detroit Mayoral Elections, 1973
and 1985

District	1973 %	1985 %
8	53.6	30.1
9	48.0	33.5
10	49.1	27.3
11	36.7	23.9
12	48.9	27.9
15	36.7	40.8
22	52.8	33.0
23	43.3	32.7
24	47.3	25.8
Average Turnout	46.7	31.4

Source: Wilbur C. Rich, "Coleman Young and Detroit Politics," in *New Black Politics,* edited by Preston
et al., 1982.

among African Americans. Absence of voting cues has a significant impact on
voter turnout in virtually all populations. In the absence of racial cues, voters
find themselves without a significant basis for choosing among candidates
and resolve cross-pressure in the voting decision by not voting at all. Unful-
filled hopes for amelioration of social ills, however unrealistic, produce negative evaluations of the efficacy of the ballot. The importance of these factors in
the future of African American voter participation is a topic amenable to examination through longitudinal analysis, as suggested here.

The Chicago Mayoral Elections, 1979–89

Although in 1983 race provided an important cue in mobilizing African
American voters in Chicago to elect the first African American mayor of the
city, a more complex analysis of the saliency of race as a variable determining
voter turnout can be made for this election. Even with race as a voting cue,
African American voter turnout was predictably low (Table 11–3) in Harold
Washington's first mayoral campaign. Only four years later, he received the
nomination in a Democratic party primary, an election contest in which the
level of African American voter turnout doubled (Table 11–3).

TABLE 11–3

Turnout in Selected Chicago Mayoral Primaries and
General Elections, 1979–89

Primary	White Turnout %	Black Turnout %
1979	48.9	34.5
1983	64.6	64.2
1987	82.7	74.8
1989	54.7	36.8
General Election		
1983	67.2	73.0
1987	80.4	76.6
1989	62.6	43.7

Source: Robert T. Starks and Michael B. Preston, "Harold
Washington and the Reform in Chicago, 1983–87," in *Racial
Politics in American Cities,* ed. Browning et al.; Paul Kleppner
and Garth Taylor, "The Erosion of Washington's Voting Coalition," unpublished paper, n.d.

Evidently, the important difference was not simply the existence of
racial cues to voting but also a perception that Washington represented an
agenda incorporating substantive gains for African Americans through the
use of politics as an instrument of social change. A second motivation for
voters was a perception that election of the first African American mayor was
a genuine possibility. Having won the primary, Washington supporters
carried these incentives into the general election of 1983, a highly charged
contest that essentially followed racial lines.[12] For the first time in Chicago
history, African American voter participation surpassed that of whites
(Table 11–3).

The conviction that Washington's first four years as mayor provided
substantive advances in the fortunes of African Americans in their access to
government, parity of government services, and benefits of city employment
and contracts increased the saliency of race as a voting cue in the 1987 election. Although African American voter turnout increased above the record
levels of 1983, *white* voter turnout also increased by an even larger percentage
(Table 11–3). Washington's efforts to gain support among Spanish-speaking
voters of the city proved successful, as they, along with increases in support
from more liberal whites, provided the margin of victory.[13] Yet Washington's
second mayoral win demonstrated his political vulnerability in a racially divided city and reinforced a political strategy that required coalition building
along race-neutral lines.

Following Washington's death, these laboriously constructed voter
coalitions disintegrated. Defeat of Acting Mayor Eugene Sawyer in the

Democratic primary of 1989 and the overwhelming defeat of an African American independent candidate in the general election was associated with large declines in African American voter turnout (Table 11–3). Clearly, racial cues lost their saliency for African American voters, as Richard M. Daley, a white candidate, defeated Timothy Lewis, an African American Independent candidate, even in some predominantly African American election districts.

These election patterns among African American voters in Chicago during the Harold Washington years raise important theoretical issues for understanding the new black politics. Most important are the conditions in which race becomes a salient factor in mobilizing voter turnout. Under some circumstances race becomes a critical cue to voting by African Americans; in others, such as the elections of 1979 and 1989, race is relatively benign in its influence on the voting behavior of African American voters.

The distinguishing characteristic of the 1983 and 1987 campaigns was a perception of Washington as a representative of a progressive black agenda. Combined with this agenda, race became an important cue for voters to choose among candidates. Absence of a clear racial agenda in 1979 and 1989 was insufficient to activate race as a mobilizing factor among African American voters. The resulting decline in African American voting, combined with the fact that race was a salient factor among white voters, allowed a white candidate to win the mayoral election of 1989.

The Mayoral Elections in New Orleans, 1977–86

Mayoral elections in New Orleans during the 1980s suggest a different dynamic when race is not a cue to voting. In 1977, Ernest Dutch Morial became the first African American mayor of New Orleans as a result of an historically high turnout by African American voters (Table 11–4). That turnout declined slightly in 1982 when the incumbent Morial was opposed by a white candidate. By 1986, however, white politicians conceded dominance of African American voters and did not seriously contest election of an African American mayor. Under these conditions, internal rivalries divided the African American vote, producing a runoff between Sidney Barthelemy, a powerful member of the city council, and State Senator William Jefferson in 1986.

Two features of this election invite comparisons with those of Detroit and Chicago. As in the Detroit mayoral election, absence of racial voting cues is associated with large declines in African American voter participation. As in Chicago, these declines are associated with enhanced influence of white voters on election outcomes. In Chicago, where race still operated as a voting cue, it meant election of a white mayor in 1989. In New Orleans, it meant that white voters held the balance of power in deciding the outcome in 1986.

TABLE 11–4

Turnout in New Orleans Mayoral Elections,
1977–86

Year	Type of District	Turnout %
1977	Predominantly black	75.0
	Racially mixed	75.3
	Predominantly white	74.0
1982	Predominantly black	72.5
	Mixed/black majority	78.8
	Mixed/white majority	77.0
	Predominantly white	75.0
1986	Predominantly black	55.4
	Mixed/black majority	61.7
	Mixed/white majority	60.1
	Predominantly white	60.1

Source: Huey L. Perry and Alfred Stokes, "Politics
and Power in the Sun Belt: Mayor Morial of New Orleans," in New Black Politics, ed. Preston et al., 1987.

These features of the 1986 election had implications for what were
perceived as black political agendas. In the predominantly African American
wards, Jefferson received a substantial majority of the vote (62.3 percent). In
areas of the city with higher proportions of white voters, the vote went to
Barthelemy by significantly larger margins. The overall margin of victory by
Barthelemy does not reflect relative support within the African American
community, implying that white voters were able to determine the choice between these two candidates in favor of the one who was perceived as less
identifiable with a black agenda (i.e., more representative of white agendas for
the city).

This inference is supported by comparing the vote in both the primary
and general elections. In the primary, which was contested by white as well as
African American candidates, Jefferson's strong support within predominantly African American voting areas enabled him to lead the field. In the
runoff, white areas of the city provided overwhelming support for
Barthelemy, who received 58 percent of the citywide vote.

As Table 11–4 shows, voter turnout was significantly lower in predominantly African American election areas in the 1986 election. The fact
that voter turnout declined for both African Americans and whites indicates,
once again, the important role of racial cues for both white and black voters
in determining how they will cast their ballots. The more obvious decline in

predominantly African American areas, however, simply enhanced the role of white voters in determining the city's future agendas.

The Role of Racial Cues and Black Political Agendas

Shifts in voter participation levels represented by longitudinal perspectives on mayoral elections in Detroit, Chicago, and New Orleans are common to other American cities. Although socioeconomic status is highly significant in explaining election turnout, race as a voting cue appears second only to party identification as an overriding factor in voting decisions. In the absence of racial cues, many African Americans appear to resolve the ensuing cross-pressure by not voting at all.

The data also imply that racial cues are less significant for African Americans than for white voters. In Chicago elections, for example, race is not a highly salient factor unless it is combined with support for an identifiable black agenda. Where race cues are absent (as in New Orleans) and candidate identification with black agendas is ambiguous, socioeconomic determinants become more salient in the voting decision—represented by the pivotal role of white voters in election outcomes.

More generally, racial cues appear to be necessary conditions for mobilizing African American voter participation. They are not, however, sufficient factors in obtaining African American voter turnout in the absence of significant commitments to agendas that have specific relevance for blacks. Thus, the presence of African American candidates in an election is not a sufficient factor to mobilize black voter support. In the case of elections between white candidates, the necessary conditions are absent to encourage voters in the belief that electoral outcomes will have significant implications for their lives. Whether or not this is an accurate assessment, such a conclusion has important implications for new forms of politics at national, state, and local levels.

Conclusion

This chapter has attempted to suggest new agendas for research on the African American political experience that have taken shape as a result of what some scholars have called the deracialization movement.[14] Although these agendas have profound implications for strategies of a new black politics, they focus less on older themes—ideology, advocacy, and insurgency—and more on experiences that seem to represent discontinuities with the past.

One example is the rapid growth in electoral successes. Increasing

control of government institutions by African American elected officials focuses attention not only on conditions that represent sweeping changes in the
political landscape but also on the impact of these advances on conditions of
African American empowerment. Is political control associated with im-
provements in quality of living, or are there other factors that render politics
peripheral to African Americans' interests? This is an issue of continuing interest for both theory and practice in political science.

Other issues arise in analyzing the relationships between African
American political leaders and their constituents. The content of African
American political agendas and their relationships to the symbols and substance of black politics is a topic that needs substantive analysis. Race as a
cue to voting is not enough to enlist loyal voter support. When race is not
a cue, questions arise over competition for political support, especially in
areas where whites represent the balance of power.

One characteristic of these agendas is that they are based upon political achievements of African Americans. It is successful electoral competition
by African Americans that has transformed the arena of the new black politics. These successes pose both divisive and unifying consequences for
African American political communities. In an earlier era, the goals of activists
and political leaders were the same. Today, the concept of a black political
agenda often pits African American politicians who prefer a deracialized or
race-neutral politics against those who prefer a politics of advocacy. These
two models of African American politics are fertile fields for continuing
analysis.

Notes

1. William Julius Wilson, "Race-Neutral Programs and the Democratic Coalition,"
   American Prospect 1 (Jan. 1990): 74–81.
2. Charles V. Hamilton, "Deracialization: Examination of a Political Strategy," *First
   World* 1 (Mar./Apr. 1977): 3–5.
3. William E. Nelson, Jr., "Cleveland: The Rise and Fall of the New Black Politics,"
   in *The New Black Politics: The Search for Political Power,* edited by Michael B. Preston, Lenneal J. Henderson, Jr., and Paul L. Puryear (New York: Longman, 1982),
   187–208.
4. Charles E. Jones, "The Election of L. Douglas Wilder: The First Black Governor
   of Virginia," *Western Journal of Black Studies* 15 (1991): 103–13.
5. Hamilton, "Deracialization," 3.
6. Nelson, "Cleveland," 188; Manning Marable, *Black American Politics: From the
   Washington Marches to Jesse Jackson* (London: Verso, 1985); Ron Daniels, "Intensifying the Struggles for Human Rights," *Black Collegian*, Sept./Oct. 1990, 44–46.
7. Jones, "Election of L. Douglas Wilder," 132–33.

8. Daniels, "Intensifying the Struggle," 44.
9. Paul Kleppner and Garth Taylor, "The Erosion of Washington's Voting Coalition," unpublished paper.
10. Huey L. Perry and Alfred Stokes, "Politics and Power in the Sun Belt: Mayor Morial of New Orleans," in *New Black Politics*, Preston et al., 1987, 222–55.
11. Jones, "Election of L. Douglas Wilder," 141.
12. Paul Kleppner, *Chicago Divided: The Making of a Black Mayor* (DeKalb: Northern Illinois University Press, 1985), 187.
13. Ibid.
14. Georgia A. Persons, ed., *Dilemmas of Black Politics: Issues of Leadership and Strategy* (New York: HarperCollins, 1993).

Conclusion: The Value of Deracialization as an Analytical Construct in American Politics

Huey L. Perry

As Thomas S. Kuhn has observed, disciplines grow by the introduction of new ideas, concepts, theories, and paradigms.[1] These new paradigms must be evaluated by scholars for their theoretical soundness and for their ability to explain empirical phenomena before they can be accepted in a discipline or subfield. Since its introduction into the black politics subfield of political science in 1989, the concept of deracialization has undergone substantial scrutiny to determine its theoretical and empirical value. The purpose of this book has been to provide a comprehensive, systematic assessment of deracialization from a theoretical and empirical perspective. The chapters have dispassionately examined deracialization, with some authors concluding that the concept offers some analytic insight into explaining black political phenomena and others concluding with a more critical assessment of the concept. Moreover, these chapters have examined deracialization at all levels of the political system.

The purpose of this concluding chapter is not simply to rehash the findings of the individual chapters. Rather, I wish to reflect on the volume as a whole to see if it provides lessons that will improve our common understanding of the deracialization concept. In other words, I wish to craft a synthetic assessment of the deracialization concept. Deracialization has been an elusive concept. But because it has been examined in a substantial number of elections over its recent scholarly history, the concept has begun to take on form and substance.

Deracialization is useful for explaining black politics in the United States in the period since the presidential administration of Ronald Reagan. The civil rights movement, the federal government's response to it by enacting the pioneering civil rights legislation of the 1960s, and the Reagan administration's negative response to the civil rights revolution of the 1960s produced the conservative national political environment that gave birth to deracialization. It is not so much that President Reagan caused the national mood to become conservative initially as that he reflected the conservatism of the national political mood. However, once in office, Reagan used the enormous symbols and persuasiveness of the presidency to strengthen conservative leanings in national politics.

Reagan's brand of conservatism included an unstated desire that African Americans should soften their emphatic push for full incorporation into the mainstream of American politics, society, and economy, which had been unleashed by the civil rights revolution. While the country's conservative mood was growing increasingly wary of African American advances in society produced by their participation in the political process, blacks had exhausted their electability in majority black districts and jurisdictions but not their desire to increase their representation in the political system. African Americans sought to increase that representation by running for election in majority white districts and jurisdictions. As a means of easing some whites' concerns about supporting black candidates, some black candidates sought election in majority white districts and jurisdictions in a way that departed from traditional black politics. The belief was that this strategy would result in black candidacies that would not alienate white voters and would thus increase African American chances of getting elected.

The experience of Governor L. Douglas Wilder in Virginia, Senator Carol Moseley-Braun in Illinois, Mayor David Dinkins in New York, Mayor Norman Rice in Seattle, and Louisiana State Representative Troy Carter in the 102d District in New Orleans point to the possibilities of the deracialization concept. All of these elections convey important messages about the possibilities of deracialization for furthering black politics. The Wilder and Moseley-Braun elections demonstrate that blacks can win elective office to important statewide political offices. The Moseley-Braun election carries additional significance because of her gender. In 1987, there were only five African Americans who held influential statewide political offices.[2] Dinkins's election is important because it demonstrates that blacks can be elected in the nation's largest metropolises. Wilder's and Carter's elections are important because they demonstrate that blacks can successfully utilize the deracialization strategy in the South. This is very crucial because deracialization is predicated on a significant number of whites being fair-minded enough to respond positively to universal appeals by black candidates. It is logical to assume that such white voters are in shorter supply in the South, given that the most severe oppression of blacks by whites in the United States occurred in the South.

On the other hand, the failure of Harvey Gantt and Andrew Young to successfully deploy the deracialization strategy, in statewide races in North Carolina and Georgia respectively, points out important limitations to the concept. Gantt's defeat in the U.S. Senate race in North Carolina demonstrates the difficulty of black candidates using the deracialization strategy to defeat an incumbent white candidate. His inability is dramatically reinforced by the realization that only one black candidate in contemporary American politics has successfully used deracialization to defeat an incumbent white candidate: conservative Republican Gary Franks defeated liberal Democratic Congressman Tony Moffitt in the Fifth Congressional District in Connecticut in 1990. This clearly indicates that the deracialization concept has formidable limitations.

Young's defeat in his bid for the governorship in Georgia suggests that black candidates must perform a delicate balancing act in order for deracialization to be effective. Young's failure was in part due to the fact that not enough whites responded to his nonracial appeal and in part due to the fact that Young was overzealous in his pursuit of white voters to the extent that he ignored and alienated a significant number of black voters. His unsuccessful use of deracialization indicates the enormous burden placed on African American candidates in trying to adhere to a fine line between a successful nonracial appeal to white voters while at the same time not ignoring and alienating black voters.

The elections of John Daniels in New Haven and Kurt Schmoke in Baltimore suggest a different limitation of the deracialization concept. Both of these candidates won their election, but deracialization was not especially relevant to their victory. Daniels's election demonstrates that black candidates running on a progressive set of issues (including racially progressive issues) can win elections to public office in majority white districts and jurisdictions. Schmoke's victory provides the same basic lesson, although the applicability is somewhat lessened by the fact that Baltimore was about 50 percent black and 50 percent white at the time of Schmoke's first election as mayor.

Finally, although deracialization is likely to be an important and enduring part of the political landscape in American politics, it will supplement but not replace traditional black politics—at least not in the foreseeable future. African Americans elected to public office in majority black districts and jurisdictions will continue to embrace racial themes and issues in their campaign and governing styles. In doing so they will richly contribute to the future of American political life. Traditional black politics will constitute the mainstay of black political life in the United States. Deracialization will continue to exist in politics but it will be episodic and uneven. There is the outside chance that the successful application of traditional black politics and deracialized black politics will help create a level of consciousness among the American public so that neither style of black politics in its pure form will be necessary. If that is the case, both traditional black politics and deracialized black politics would be positive contributions to the advancement of American politics.

Notes

1. Thomas S. Kuhn, *The Structure of Scientific Revolutions* (Chicago: University of Chicago Press, 1970).
2. Linda Williams, "Black Political Progress in the 1980s: The Electoral Arena," in *The New Black Politics: The Search for Political Power,* edited by Michael B. Preston, Lenneal J. Henderson, Jr., and Paul L. Puryear (New York: Longman, 1987), 115.

Contributors

ROBERT B. ALBRITTON is associate professor of political science at Northern Illinois University, DeKalb.

GEORGE AMEDEE is director of the Office of Grants at Southern University, New Orleans.

KEENAN GRENELL is assistant professor of political science and coordinator of the African-American Entrepreneurship Project at Auburn University.

LENNEAL J. HENDERSON, JR., is distinguished professor in the department of government and public administration and senior fellow at the William Donald Schafer Center for Public Policy at the University of Baltimore.

JOHN D. HUTCHESON is professor of urban studies at Georgia State University, Atlanta.

PHILIP A. KLINKNER is assistant professor of political science at Hamilton College, Clinton, New York.

JAMES L. LLORENS is associate professor of political science and chair of the department at Southern University, Baton Rouge.

ROGER K. ODEN is professor of political science and dean of the College of Arts and Sciences at Governors State University, University Park, Illinois.

ERROL G. PALMER is chief executive officer of Palmer Research and Associates, a human resource management and marketing research and training firm, and an adjunct professor in the human resource management program at Chapman University, Orange, California.

SHARON K. PARSONS is assistant professor of public administration at Southern University, Baton Rouge.

HUEY L. PERRY is professor of political science and coordinator of research and services for the School of Public Policy and Urban Affairs at Southern University, Baton Rouge.

CAROL A. PIERANNUNZI is assistant professor of political science at Kennesaw State College, Marietta, Georgia.

CHARLES L. PRYSBY is professor of political science and chair of the department at the University of North Carolina, Greensboro.

ALVIN J. SCHEXNIDER is professor of political science and chancellor of Winston-Salem State University, Winston-Salem, North Carolina.

MARY SUMMERS is a doctoral candidate in the Department of Political Science at Yale University.

J. PHILLIP THOMPSON is assistant professor of political science at Barnard College.

DON-TERRY VEAL is a doctoral candidate in the department of political science at Northern Illinois University, DeKalb.

MYLON WINN is associate professor in the Institute of Public Science at Seattle University.

SHARON D. WRIGHT is assistant professor of political science at the University of Missouri, Columbia.

Selected Bibliography

Abney, Glenn, and Thomas R. Lauth. "The Line Item Veto in the United States: An Instrument for Fiscal Restraint or an Instrument for Partnership?" *Public Administration Review* 45 (1985): 372–77.

Abramowitz, Alan I. "Explaining Senate Election Outcomes." *American Political Science Review* 82 (1988): 385–403.

Ardrey, Saundra C. "Cleveland and the Politics of Resurgence: The Search for Effective Political Control." In *Dilemmas of Black Politics,* edited by Persons, 109–28.

Ardrey, Saundra C., and William E. Nelson. "The Maturation of Black Political Power: The Case of Cleveland." *PS: Political Science and Politics* 23 (June 1990): 148–51.

Arian, Asher, Arthur Goldberg, John Mollenkopf, and Ed Rogowsky. *Changing New York City Politics.* New York: Routledge, 1991.

Baker, Donald P. *Wilder: Hold Fast to Dreams.* Introduction by Rev. Jesse L. Jackson. Washington, D.C.: Seven Locks Press, 1989.

Barnes, James A. "Into the Mainstream." *National Journal,* Feb. 1960, 263.

Bell, Derrick. *Faces at the Bottom of the Well: The Permanence of Racism.* New York: Basic, 1992.

Browning, Rufus, and Dale R. Marshall, eds. "Black and Hispanic Power in City Politics: A Forum." *PS: Political Science and Politics* 18 (Summer 1986): 573–640.

Browning, Rufus P., Dale R. Marshall, and David H. Tabb. *Protest Is Not Enough: The Struggle of Blacks and Hispanics for Equality in Urban Politics.* Berkeley: University of California Press, 1984.

———, eds. *Racial Politics in American Cities.* New York: Longman, 1990.

Bullock, Charles S., III. "Aftermath of the Voting Rights Act: Racial Voting Patterns in Atlanta-Area Elections." In *The Voting Rights Act: Consequences and Implications,* edited by Lorn S. Foster, 185–208. New York: Praeger, 1985.

————. "Racial Crossover Voting and the Election of Black Officials." *Journal of Politics* 46 (1984): 238–51.

Bullock, Charles S., III, and Loch K. Johnson. *Runoffs in the United States*. Chapel Hill: University of North Carolina Press, 1992.

Button, James W. *Blacks and Social Change: Impact of the Civil Rights Movement in Southern Communities*. Princeton, N.J.: Princeton University Press, 1989.

Campbell, Angus, Phillip E. Converse, Warren E. Miller, and Donald E. Stokes. *The American Voter*. New York: John Wiley and Sons, 1960.

Cavanaugh, Thomas, and Denise Stockton. *Black Elected Officials and Their Constituencies*. Washington, D.C.: Joint Center for Political Studies, 1983.

Citrin, Jack, Donald Phillip Green, and David O. Sears. "White Reaction to Black Candidates: When Does Race Matter." *Public Opinion Quarterly* 54 (1990): 74–96.

Cleveland, Harlan. *The Future Executive*. New York: Harper and Row, 1972.

Coleman, Mary D., and Leslie B. McLemore. "Continuity and Change: The Power of Traditionalism in Biracial Politics in Mississippi's Second Congressional District." In *New Black Politics,* edited by Preston et al., 1987, 45–58.

Dahl, Robert. *Who Governs?: Democracy and Power in an American City*. New Haven, Conn.: Yale University Press, 1961.

Domhoff, William. *Who Really Rules?: New Haven and Community Power Reexamined*. Santa Monica, Calif.: Goodyear, 1978.

Drake, St. Clair, and Horace R. Cayton. *Black Metropolis: A Study of Negro Life in a Northern City*. New York: Harper and Row, 1945.

Drake, W. Avon, and Robert D. Holsworth. "Richmond and the Politics of Calculated Cooperation." In *Dilemmas of Black Politics,* edited by Persons, 87–108.

DuBos, Clancy. "Enthusiastic Amateurs: Troy Carter." *Louisiana Political Review* 2 (Nov./Dec. 1991): 30–31.

Edds, Margaret. *Free at Last: What Really Happened When Civil Rights Came to Southern Politics*. Bethesda, Md.: Adler and Adler, 1987.

Edsall, Thomas. *The New Politics of Inequality*. New York: Norton, 1984.

Eichenthal, David R. "Changing Styles and Strategies." In *Urban Politics: New York Style,* edited by Jewel Bellush and Dick Netzer. Armonk, N.Y.: M. E. Sharpe, 1990.

Eisinger, Paul K. "Black Employment in Municipal Jobs: The Impact of Black Political Power." *American Political Science Review* 76 (1982): 380–92.

Ellison, Christopher G., and David A. Gay. "Black Political Participation Revisited: A Test of Compensatory, Ethnic Community and Public Arena Models." *Social Science Quarterly* 70 (Mar. 1989): 101–19.

Engstrom, Peter, and Michael McDonald. "The Election of Blacks to City Councils." *American Political Science Review* 75 (1981): 344–55.

Fainstein, Norman, and Susan Fainstein. "New Haven: The Limits of the Local State." In *Restructuring the City,* edited by Susan Fainstein, Norman Fainstein, Richard C. Hill, Michael P. Smith, P. Jefferson Armstead, and Marlene Keller, 27–79. New York: Longman, 1983.

Fleer, Jack D., Roger C. Lowery, and Charles L. Prysby. "Political Change in North Carolina." In *The South's New Politics,* edited by Robert H. Swansbrough and David M. Brodsky, 107–23. Columbia: University of South Carolina Press, 1988.

Fuchs, Ester R. *Mayors and Money: Fiscal Policy in New York and Chicago.* Chicago: University of Chicago Press, 1992.

Glazer, Nathan, and Daniel P. Moynihan. *Beyond the Melting Pot.* Cambridge: MIT Press, 1963.

Gosnell, Harold. *Negro Politicians.* Chicago: University of Chicago Press, 1935.

Gottdiemer, Mark. *The Decline of Urban Politics: Political Theory and the Crisis of the Local State.* Beverly Hills, Calif.: Sage, 1987.

Green, Charles, and Basil Wilson. *The Struggle for Black Empowerment in New York City: Beyond the Politics of Pigmentation.* New York: Praeger, 1989.

Groffman, Bernard, and Chandler Davidson. *The Impact of the 1965 Voting Rights Act.* Princeton, N.J.: Princeton University Press, 1994.

Hamilton, Charles V. "Blacks and Electoral Politics." *Social Policy* 9 (May/June 1978): 21–27.

———. "Blacks and the Crisis in Political Participation." *Public Interest* 34 (1974): 188–210.

———. "Deracialization: Examination of a Political Strategy." *First World* 1 (Mar./Apr. 1977): 3–5.

———. Foreword. In *New Black Politics,* edited by Preston et al., 1982, xvii–xx.

———. "Social Policy and the Welfare of Black Americans: From Rights to Resources." *Political Science Quarterly* 101 (1986): 239–55.

Henderson, Lenneal J., Jr. "Baltimore: Managing the Civics of a Turn Around City." *National Civic Review* 82 (Fall 1993): 329–39.

———. "Black Politics and the American Presidential Elections." In *New Black Politics,* edited by Preston et al., 1982, 3–27.

———. "Empowerment through Enterprise in the African-American Community." In *The State of Black America, 1993,* edited by Billy Tidwell, 91–108. New York: National Urban League, 1993.

Holden, Matthew, Jr. "The Rewards of Daring and the Ambiguity of Power: Perspectives on the Wilder Election of 1989." In *The State of Black America, 1990,* edited by Billy Tidwell, 49–73. New York: National Urban League, 1990.

Jones, Charles E. "The Election of L. Douglas Wilder: The First Black Governor of Virginia." *Western Journal of Black Studies* 15 (1991): 103–13.

Jones, Charles E., and Michael Clemons. "A Model of Racial Crossover Voting: An Assessment of the Wilder Victory." In *Dilemmas of Black Politics,* edited by Persons, 128–46.

Jones, Mack H.. "Black Office Holders in Local Governments of the South: An Overview." *Politics 1971: Problems of Political Participation* 1 (1971): 49–72.

Karnig, Albert K., and Susan Welch. *Black Representation and Urban Policy.* Chicago: University of Chicago Press, 1980.

———. "Electoral Structure and Black Representation on City Councils." *Social Science Quarterly* 63 (Mar. 1982): 99–114.

Keech, William R. *The Impact of Negro Voting: The Role of the Vote in the Quest for Equality.* Chicago: Rand McNally, 1968.

Keiser, Richard A. "The Rise of a Biracial Coalition in Philadelphia." In *Racial Politics in American Cities,* edited by Browning et al., 49–74.

Key, V. O., Jr. *Southern Politics in State and Nation.* New York: Vintage, 1949.

Killian, Lewis, and Charles Grigg. *Racial Crisis in America: Leaders in Conflict.* Englewood Hills, N.J.: Prentice-Hall, 1964.

Kilson, Martin. "Problems of Black Politics: Some Progress, Many Difficulties." *Dissent* 36 (1989): 526–34.

Kleppner, Paul. *Chicago Divided: The Making of a Black Mayor.* DeKalb: Northern Illinois University Press, 1985.

Kleppner, Paul, and Garth Taylor. "The Erosion of Washington's Voting Coalition." Unpublished paper.

Kramer, G. H. "The Effects of Precinct-Level Canvassing on Voting Behavior." *Public Opinion Quarterly* 34 (1971): 560–72.

Kuhn, Thomas S. *The Structure of Scientific Revolutions.* Chicago: University of Chicago Press, 1970.

Lawson, Steven F. "The New Black Politicians: From Protest to Empowerment." In *Running for Freedom: Civil Rights and Black Politics in America since 1941,* 146–82. Philadelphia, Pa.: Temple University Press, 1991.

Levine, Charles H. *Racial Politics and the American Mayor: Power, Polarization, and Performance.* Lexington, Mass.: Lexington Books, 1974.

Long, Norton. "Politicians for Hire." *Public Administration Review* 24–25 (1965): 115–20.

Lowi, Theodore J. *The End of Liberalism: Ideology, Policy, and the Crisis of Public Authority.* New York: Norton, 1989.

Luebke, Paul. *Tar Heel Politics: Myths and Realities.* Chapel Hill: University of North Carolina Press, 1990.

Mack, Ally, Mary Coleman, and Leslie B. McLemore. "Current Trends in Black Politics: Prospects and Problems." In *Contemporary Southern Politics,* edited by James F. Lea, 107–23. Baton Rouge: Louisiana State University Press, 1988.

Makielski, Stan J., Jr. "The New Orleans Mayoral Election." *Urban Politics and Urban Policy Section Newsletter* 4 (1990): 11–13.

Marable, Manning. *Black American Politics: From the Washington Marches to Jesse Jackson.* London: Verso, 1985.

———. "A New Black Politics." *The Progressive* 54 (Aug. 1990): 18–21.

———. *Race, Reform, and Rebellion.* Jackson: University Press of Mississippi, 1991.

Matthews, Donald, and James W. Prothro. *Negroes and the New Southern Politics.* New York: Harcourt, Brace, and World, 1966.

McCormick, Joseph P., II, and Charles E. Jones. "Deracialization Revisited: Thinking through the Dilemma." In *Dilemmas of Black Politics,* edited by Persons, 66–84.

McDougal, Harold. *Black Baltimore: Towards a Theory of Community.* Philadelphia, Pa.: Temple University Press, 1993.

Mladenka, Kenneth R. "Blacks and Hispanics in Urban Politics." *American Political Science Review* 83 (1989): 165–91.

Mollenkopf, John Hull. *A Phoenix in the Ashes: The Rise and Fall of the Koch Coalition in New York City Politics.* Princeton, N.J.: Princeton University Press, 1992.

Morrison, Minion K. C. *Black Political Mobilization: Leadership, Power, and Mass Behavior.* Albany: State University of New York Press, 1987.

Murray, Richard, and Arnold Vedlitz. "Racial Voting Patterns in the South: An Analysis of Mayoral Elections from 1960 to 1977 in Five Cities." *Annals* (Spring 1978): 29–39.

Neilson, Melany. *Even Mississippi.* Tuscaloosa: University of Alabama Press, 1989.

Nelson, William E., Jr. "Cleveland: The Rise and Fall of the New Black Politics." In *New Black Politics,* edited by Preston et al., 1982, 187–208.

Nelson, William E., Jr., and Philip J. Meranto. *Electing Black Mayors: Political Action in the Black Community.* Columbus: Ohio State University Press, 1977.

Oden, Roger K. "Black Political Power in Gary, Indiana: A Theoretical and Structural Analysis." Ph.D. dissertation, University of Chicago, 1977.

Orfield, Gary, and Carole Ashkinaze. *The Closing Door: Conservative Policy and Black Opportunity.* Chicago: University of Chicago Press, 1991.

O'Toole, Lawrence J., Jr. "Harry F. Byrd, Sr. and the New York Bureau of Municipal Research: Lessons from the Ironic Alliance." *Public Administration Review* 46 (1986): 113–23.

Palumbo, Dennis. *Public Policy in America: Government in Action.* New York: Harcourt, Brace, Jovanovich, 1988.

Parker, Frank R. *Black Votes Count: Political Empowerment in Mississippi after 1965.* Chapel Hill: University of North Carolina Press, 1990.

Perry, Huey L. "Black Politics and Mayoral Leadership in Birmingham and New Orleans." *National Political Science Review* 2 (Apr. 1990): 154–60.

———. "Deracialization as an Analytical Construct in American Urban Politics." *Urban Affairs Quarterly* 27 (Dec. 1991): 181–91.

———. "Recent Advances in Black Electoral Politics." *PS: Political Science and Politics* 23 (June 1990): 141–42.

———. "The Evolution and Impact of Biracial Coalitions and Black Mayors in Birmingham and New Orleans." In *Racial Politics in American Cities,* edited by Browning et al., 140–52.

Perry, Huey L., and Alfred Stokes. "Politics and Power in the Sunbelt: Mayor Morial of New Orleans." In *New Black Politics,* edited by Preston et al., 1987, 222–55. Reprinted in Harry A. Bailey, Jr., and Jay M. Shafritz, eds. *State and Local Government and Politics: Essential Readings,* 129–66. Itasca, Ill.: F. E. Research Publishers, 1993.

Persons, Georgia A. "Black Mayoralties and the New Black Politics: From Insurgency to Racial Reconciliation." In *Dilemmas of Black Politics,* edited by Persons, 38–65.

———. "The Election of Gary Franks and the Ascendancy of the New Black Conservatives." In *Dilemmas of Black Politics,* edited by Persons, 194–208.

———, ed. *Dilemmas of Black Politics: Leadership, Strategy, and Issues.* New York: HarperCollins, 1993.

Peterson, Paul E. *City Limits.* Chicago: University of Chicago Press, 1981.

Pettigrew, Thomas F. "Black Mayoralty Campaigns." In *Urban Governance and Minorities,* edited by Herrington Bryce, 14–28. New York: Praeger, 1976.

Pierannunzi, Carol, and John D. Hutcheson Jr. "Electoral Change and Regime Maintenance: Maynard Jackson's Second Time Around." *PS: Political Science and Politics* 23 (June 1990): 151–53.

Pierce, Neal. *Citistates: How Urban America Can Prosper in a Competitive World.* Washington, D.C.: Seven Locks Press, 1993.

Piliawsky, Monte. "The Impact of Black Mayors on the Black Community: The Case of New Orleans' Ernest Morial." *Review of Black Political Economy* 13 (Spring 1985): 5–24.

Pinderhughes, Dianne. "Political Choices: A Realignment in Partisanship among Black Voters." In *The State of Black America,* edited by J. D. Williams. New York: National Urban League, 1986.

Polsby, Nelson. *Community Power and Political Theory.* New Haven, Conn.: Yale University Press, 1963.

Powledge, Fred. *Model City.* New York: Simon and Schuster, 1970.

Preston, Michael B. "Black Politics and Public Policy in Chicago: Self-Interest versus Constituent Representation." In *New Black Politics,* edited by Preston et al., 1982, 159–86.

———. "The Election of Harold Washington: An Examination of the SES Model in the 1983 Chicago Mayoral Election." In *New Black Politics,* edited by Preston et al., 1987, 139–71.

Preston, Michael B., Lenneal J. Henderson Jr., and Paul L. Puryear, eds. *The New Black Politics: The Search for Political Power.* 1982. 2d ed. New York: Longman, 1987.

Prysby, Charles L. "Attitudes of Southern Democratic Party Activists toward Jesse Jackson: The Effects of the Local Context." *Journal of Politics* 51 (1989): 305–18.

Putnam, Robert. "Investing in Social Capital." *National Civic Review* 82 (Spring 1993): 101–7.

Ransom, Bruce. "Black Independent Electoral Politics In Philadelphia: The Election of Mayor W. Wilson Goode." In *New Black Politics,* edited by Preston et al., 1987, 256–90.

Reed, Adolph. "A Critique of Neo-Progressivism in Theorizing about Local Development Policy: A Case Study from Atlanta." In *The Politics of Urban Development,* edited by Clarence N. Stone and Heywood Sanders. Lawrence: University of Kansas Press, 1987.

Rich, Wilbur C. *Coleman Young and Detroit Politics.* Detroit, Mich.: Wayne State University Press, 1989.

Robinson, Theodore, and Thomas Dye. "Reformism and Representation on City Councils." *Social Science Quarterly* 59 (June 1978): 131–41.

Rosenthal, Alan. *Governors and Legislatures: Contending Powers.* Washington, D.C.: Congressional Quarterly Press, 1990.

Rusk, David. *Cities without Suburbs*. Washington, D.C.: Woodrow Wilson Center Press, 1993.

Sabato, Larry J. *Virginia Votes, 1987–1990*. Charlottesville: Center for Public Service, University of Virginia, 1991.

Salamon, Lester M. "Leadership and Modernization: The Emerging Black Political Elite in the American South." *Journal of Politics* 35 (1973): 615–46.

Schexnider, Alvin J. "Political Mobilization in the South: The Election of a Black Mayor in New Orleans." In *New Black Politics,* edited by Preston et al., 1982, 221–38.

———. "The Politics of Pragmatism: An Analysis of the 1989 Gubernatorial Election in Virginia." *PS: Political Science and Politics* 23 (June 1990): 154–56.

Shefter, Martin. *Political Crisis/Fiscal Crisis: The Collapse and Revival of New York City*. New York: Basic, 1985.

Smith, Robert C. "Black Power and the Transformation from Protest to Politics." *Political Science Quarterly* 96 (Fall 1981): 1–43.

———. "Recent Elections and Black Politics: The Maturation or Death of Black Politics?" *PS: Political Science and Politics* 23 (June 1990): 160–63.

Snider, William O. *Helms and Hunt: The North Carolina Senate Race, 1984*. Chapel Hill: University of North Carolina Press, 1985.

Sonenshein, Raphael J. "Biracial Coalition Politics in Los Angeles." In *Racial Politics in American Cities,* edited by Browning et al., 33–48.

———. "The Dynamics of Biracial Coalitions: Crossover Politics in Los Angeles." *Western Political Quarterly* 42 (1989): 342–43.

———. *Politics in Black and White: Race and Power in Los Angeles*. Princeton, N.J.: Princeton University Press, 1993.

Stillman, Richard J., II. *The Rise of the City Manager*. Albuquerque: University of New Mexico Press, 1974.

Stone, Clarence. *Regime Politics: Governing Atlanta, 1946–1988*. Lawrence: University of Kansas Press, 1989.

Stone, Clarence, and Heywood Sanders. "Reexamining a Classic Case of Development Politics: New Haven, Connecticut." In *The Politics of Urban Development,* edited by Clarence Stone and Heywood Sanders, 159–81. Lawrence: University Press of Kansas, 1987.

Summers, Mary, and Philip Klinkner. "The Daniels Election in New Haven and the Failure of the Deracialization Hypothesis." *Urban Affairs Quarterly* 27 (Dec. 1991): 202–15.

Taueber, Karl F., and Alma F. Taueber. *The Negro in the Cities*. Chicago: Aldine, 1965.

Thernstron, Abigail M. *Whose Votes Count? Affirmative Action and Minority Voting Rights*. Cambridge, Mass.: Harvard University Press, 1987.

Thompson, J. Phillip. "David Dinkins' Victory in New York City: The Decline of the Democratic Party Organization and the Strengthening of Black Politics." *PS: Political Science and Politics* 23 (June 1990): 145–47.

Vaughn, Sandra. "Memphis: The Heart of the Mid-South." In *In Search of the New South: The Black Urban Experience in the 1970s and 1980s,* 105–15. Tuscaloosa: University of Alabama Press, 1989.

Walter, John C. *The Harlem Fox: J. Raymond Jones and Tammany, 1920–1970.* Albany: State University of New York Press, 1989.

Walters, Ronald W. *Black Presidential Politics.* Albany: State University of New York Press, 1988.

Walton, Hanes. *Invisible Politics: Black Political Behavior.* Albany: State University of New York Press, 1985.

Watson, Sharon. "The Second Time Around: A Profile of Black Mayoral Reelection Campaigns." *Phylon* 45 (Fall 1984): 166–78.

Weaver, Robert C. *The Negro Ghetto.* New York: Oxford University Press, 1943.

Welch, Susan. "The Impact of At-Large Elections on the Representation of Blacks and Hispanics." *Journal of Politics* 52 (1990): 1050–76.

Wilder, L. Douglas. Keynote address. In *1990 Symposium on the State of the States: Women, Black and Hispanic Elected Leaders.* Charlottesville: Center for Public Service, University of Virginia/Eagleton Institute of Politics, Rutgers University, 1991.

Williams, Linda. "Black Political Progress in the 1980s: The Electoral Arena." In *New Black Politics,* edited by Preston et al., 1987, 97–135.

———. "White/Black Perceptions of the Electability of Black Political Candidates." In *Black Electoral Politics,* edited by Lucius J. Barker, 45–64. New Brunswick, N.J.: Transaction Books, 1990.

Wilson, James Q. "The Negro in American Politics: The Present." In *The American Negro Reference Book,* edited by John Preston Davis. Englewood Cliffs, N.J.: Prentice-Hall, 1966.

———. *Negro Politics: The Search for Leadership.* New York: Free Press, 1960.

Wilson, William Julius. "Race-Neutral Policies and the Democratic Coalition." *American Prospect* 1 (Jan. 1990): 74–81.

Wolfinger, Raymond. *The Politics of Progress.* Englewood Cliffs, N.J.: Prentice-Hall, 1974.

Wright, Gerald C., Jr. "Contextual Models of Electoral Behavior: The Southern Wallace Vote." *American Political Science Review* 71 (1977): 497–508.

Wright, Sharon D. "Aftermath of the Voting Rights Act of 1965: Racial Voting Patterns in Memphis Mayoral Elections, 1967–1991." Ph.D. dissertation, University of Tennessee, Knoxville, 1993.

Wright, Stephen G. "Voter Turnout in Runoff Elections." *Journal of Politics* 51 (1989): 385–96.

Yancey, Dwayne. *When Hell Froze Over.* Roanoke, Va.: Taylor Publishing, 1988.

Index